STAFF DEVELOPMEN
IN PRIMARY SCHOOI

Ken Jones
Janet Clark
Stephen Howarth
Gillian Figg
Ken Reid

Blackwell Education

First published 1989
Published by
Basil Blackwell Ltd
108 Cowley Road
Oxford OX4 1JF
England

British Library Cataloguing in Publication Data
Staff development in primary schools.
1. Schools. Teachers. In-service training
I. Jones, Ken, *1950–*
371.1′46

ISBN 0–631–16898–2
ISBN 0–631–16899–0 pbk

Typeset in 10 on 12 point Melior by
Wearside Tradespools, Fulwell, Sunderland
Printed in Great Britain by
T. J. Press (Padstow) Ltd., Cornwall

Contents

Acknowledgements

This book is a distillation of experiences gained from in-service work in primary schools and with primary teachers. The authors are grateful for the support of primary colleagues and acknowledge the two-way benefits which have accrued from their contact with fellow professionals in the field of primary education.

We would particularly like to thank the following for making our consultancy work possible and for contributing to sections in this book: John Roberts for his work on small primary schools; Sheena Ball for her contribution to our thinking about teacher self-evaluation; David Tyler for the suggestions on management; Helen Collins for the section on special needs; Paul Roper and Sue James for providing the opportunity for us to work with teams of teachers in their schools; John O'Brien for sharing his thoughts when the idea for a book was first suggested; Jim Watkins for his continuing energy in providing opportunities for consultancy work through GRIDS; Charlie; Bob Bullock for his contribution on primary science; Diane O'Sullivan and Peter Williams for sharing their wide experience of consultancy work in language; Jill Long for her ideas on primary mathematics; James Nash for his support in publication of the book.

PART ONE

THE PROCESS OF STAFF DEVELOPMENT

1 Setting the scene

1.1 The need for staff development

Primary schools have been subjected to a variety of demands for change in recent years. Traditionally, change which emanated from within could be planned for and so gradually permeate existing school structures in a private, or at least non-public, way. Many of the most recent changes, by contrast, have had three things in common:

1. They are, in the most part, externally imposed.
2. They have to be met within well defined, often extremely short, time-scales.
3. They carry with them increased educational, political or economic accountability.

Consider, for instance, the influence on schools and primary teachers of the National Curriculum and its related assessment requirements, the Local Education Authority Training Grants Scheme (LEATGS – previously known as GRIST or grant-related in-service training), the curricular, contractual and management implications of the Education Reform Act of 1988, new conditions of service for teachers, the changing influence and responsibilities of governing bodies, the allocation of curriculum and leadership responsibilities within schools, and local financial management schemes – to name but a few. The phrase 'the status quo is not an option' became the cliché of the 1980s. Somewhere among these changes, and in the everyday lives of schools, lies the formal responsiblity for the development of staff.

The status quo is not an option.

Heads and teachers in primary schools have been forced to come to terms with these changes. Many have done so successfully. Some have been *proactive* (anticipating or generating change) rather than *reactive* (acting in response to the initiatives of others). Conversely, others have struggled to keep HMI, LEA officers and advisers, governors and parents in a positive state of mind in the face of diverse and often conflicting messages about the ways in which pupils should be educated. One of the challenges of the 1990s is how to manage the changes without losing sight of the reason why schools exist, namely as institutions to promote learning in the children who are obliged to attend them.

The need for the continuing professional development of heads and teachers is an indispensable part of any strategy to meet the consequences and the challenge of change. Before the 1980s, the professional development of teachers tended to be a hit and miss, *ad hoc* affair, with apparently no coherent individual or institutional plan. By the late 1980s, it had become contractual and structured. The acronym INSET had become part of every teacher's vocabulary. 'Staff development', too, has become a function of the head's managerial role. The 1987 Conditions of Service state that heads have a responsibility for:

> Ensuring that all staff in the school have access to advice and training appropriate to their needs in accordance with the policies of the maintaining authority for the development of staff.
>
> (para 8b)

While this requirement is easy to record, the deeper issues may not be fully understood by all heads and teachers. Many of the staff development systems and policies were drawn up hurriedly in response to the LEATGS proposals of 1986. During 1987 and 1988, the management of staff development in many primary schools became synonymous with the need to spend an INSET budget and the fulfilment of the 'directed time' regulation of the revised teachers' contracts.

For many heads, therefore, through no fault of their own, the building of staff development structures in schools was hurried and pragmatic rather than reflective and ideal. A considerable number found themselves well into the practice of staff development before the underlying principles had been understood. Inevitably, some schools already have better and more clearly defined staff development policies than others. In fact, it is probably fair to say that in some schools little more than lip service is currently being given to staff development programmes, with ensuing disadvantage to teachers and pupils alike.

1.2 What is staff development?

Education is a process, not a one-off occurrence. Teachers are 'in service' from their first day on contract to the time they retire. During this period they will experience a variety of forces which will produce change in knowledge, understanding, skills and, probably, attitude. Without this change, 'schooling', as opposed to education, will stagnate. The most radical changes in the last decade have been imposed by central government, but to be effective there must be some impact on pupil learning and change has therefore to be assimilated by the school.

It is the responsibility of the primary headteacher to manage resources (including staff) so as to provide a suitable education for the pupils attending the school. This cannot be done effectively without a team of teachers (the 'staff') working together to the benefit of the pupils in their care. Just as pupils are *entitled* to a broad, balanced and relevant curriculum, so teachers have the same entitlement to professional development support within the context of their current employment. There are no longer any quiet oases within the schools where teachers can recline and watch the world go by. Professionally, we need to heed William Blake's warning: 'Expect poison from the standing water'. INSET provides the necessary oxygen for teachers to survive as educated and trained professionals. Staff development programmes provide the means for teachers to experience continuing education as part of a team of professionals.

'expect poison from the standing water'

1.3 Purpose of the book

The purpose of this book is to unravel the confused recent history of the growth of staff and teacher professional development in primary schools. In doing so, we explore some of the basic concepts associated with the management of staff development and provide some practical guidelines on the ways in which staff development programmes can be approached and managed in schools. We do not intend to write at length about the recent history of staff development. We have done this elsewhere (Jones, O'Sullivan and Reid, 1987; O'Sullivan, Jones and Reid, 1988). Rather, we wish to concentrate on making staff development programmes happen and work.

This is a difficult task. There is no one model of a staff development programme which has utility for every kind of primary school. Primary schools vary so much in size, region and organisation (Reid, Bullock and Howarth, 1988) that it would be impossible to meet every situation in a given amount of space. Principles of good practice, however, are transferable. To assist with the practical focus of the book, we will use examples of schools in action to illustrate the ways in which a support structure for staff development can be initiated.

While no one model can represent all primary schools (the context of the small rural primary school, for example, has little in common with that of the inner city or large suburban primary school), case studies do help to bring home the point that staff development concerns real teachers and pupils in real situations. In the final analysis, policies require action if they are not to be discredited. Staff development is a practical activity.

At the end of Chapters 3 to 9 we raise 'issues for consideration'. We deliberately do not provide answers to the questions that are posed as issues. Readers will have their own preferred strategies for each part of the staff development process. The model school and the related issues have been used successfully in management training courses and heads/advisers may find the model useful for setting up their own INSET activities on staff development.

The book is written in clearly defined sections so that busy heads, teachers, advisers and governors can 'dip in' at chosen points. Part One examines the staff development process itself and begins to trace the progress of the head of Greenbank School in his search for a suitable support structure for staff development. Part Two illustrates ways in which school-focused INSET might be implemented. Part Three looks at curriculum issues from a staff development perspective. Part Four considers the issues underlying staff and professional development in more depth.

2 INSET and staff development: the relationship

In the next two chapters, we introduce some ideas about the way in which a support structure for staff development may be initiated. We have chosen to present these ideas through the eyes of Mr Jackson, recently appointed to the headship of the fictional Greenbank County Primary School, a fairly large suburban school. He faces a number of challenges: falling rolls; the need to 'market' his school in a competitive way; dealing with a newly-constituted governing body; responsibility for the management of his school's budget; meeting the requirements of the National Curriculum and, not least, ensuring that pupils are happy in their learning environment. He finds that there are varying attitudes in his staff – some are enthusiastic, some not so. This is the reality of many primary schools.

2.1 Facing change

Mr Jackson places staff development high on his list of priorities for his new school and is keen to learn about how staff development programmes can be managed most effectively. In a conference for local headteachers on managing staff development he was pleased to discover that he was not alone in his struggle to come to terms with meeting the demands of LEATGS. He could identify with the concerns of the other heads as common problems and issues gradually emerged.

Participants at the conference were asked to list and then prioritise their areas of concern with regard to staff development. Their responses were:

- how to overcome staff reluctance to take part in INSET;
- how to identify the particular needs of the staff and the school;
- how to balance individual and whole-school needs;
- how to balance school needs and LEA/nationally determined directives;
- how to divide and allocate resources fairly;
- how to cover all National Curriculum areas with only a small staff;
- how to meet the new assessment requirements;
- how to maintain a stable curriculum when staff were continually changing (redeployment, promotion, etc);
- how to share and extend teacher expertise;
- how to motivate teachers who have been teaching for a long time;
- how to involve nursery, infant and junior staff;
- how to cope with lack of supply cover for INSET;
- how to add staff development to an already high workload without it becoming a 'teachers' detention';
- how to identify appropriate expertise for delivering school-based INSET;
- how to ensure efficient and *effective* staff development;
- how to ensure that INSET is meaningful, appropriate and relevant;
- how to evaluate INSET.

During the day, questions were raised regarding the identification and analysis of teachers' INSET needs, the management of coherent staff development programmes and the evaluation of INSET (in particular the likely benefits accruing to *pupils* of teachers attending INSET activities). It became apparent to Mr Jackson that the concept of staff development was deeper and more complex than he had imagined. It also confirmed his view that a well organised staff development programme for his teachers could motivate and stimulate them and pay dividends for his school and pupils in the longer term.

2.2 Turning theory into practice

The concept of school-focused INSET as outlined at the training day was obviously not new, but the link between this and the professional development of individual teachers was more complex. In 1972, the James Report had drawn attention to the three 'cycles' of teacher education (initial, induction and in-service) and had recommended that a professional tutor be designated to co-ordinate programmes for the latter two.

However, although the need for structured in-service programmes had been recognised, creative thinking in the development of teacher INSET was lacking. INSET was seen as 'going on a course'. Teachers left school for a day or attended courses at colleges or teachers' centres. On return to school they found it difficult to communicate to their colleagues new ideas which they had gained from attending the course. It was even worse for those who had been seconded for a term or a year. The problems of 're-entry' were often insurmountable and the benefits of the INSET experience were rarely passed on to other teachers in the school. 'Course-goers' were often treated with cynicism and suspicion as INSET was seen by many as career enhancement rather than professional development. Some teachers became 'professional course-goers', others proudly boasted that they had avoided INSET for fifteen years with no detriment to their teaching. Those who attended courses frequently had little to report since the relationship between theory and practice was often difficult to ascertain.

The characteristics of the 'traditional' INSET practices were outlined by Cooper (1986) (Figure 2.1, column 1). It took a central government

Figure 2.1 INSET past and future

The old INSET	*Aims of INSET post LEATGS*
Fragmented – no LEA strategy	LEAs to have a co-ordinated INSET strategy
Top-down needs identification	Bottom-up needs identification process – teachers to articulate needs within institutional LEA and national priorities
INSET courses menu-led	INSET activities to be curriculum-led
Participants mainly enthusiastic volunteers often pursuing personal career development (B.Ed., M.Ed. etc)	Whole teaching force to participate. Confluence of interest between career development and institutional (pupil) needs
Little institutional involvement	Schools to be at the centre of the INSET process – identifying needs, providing follow-up and evaluation
Little or no evaluation. No consideration of cost-effectiveness or effect of training on pupils' education	Evaluation to be built in
'Muddling along' rather than proactive planning	Explicit management mechanisms
Wide variation in funding between LEAs	LEAs to have an even provision

initiative (one of many in the 1980s) to begin to systematise the haphazard provision of INSET in England and Wales. In 1983, the Technical and Vocational Education Initiative (TVEI) had been launched in secondary schools and further education colleges with a massive injection of funding. Most of the funds were spent on technical equipment to support this scheme. The speed at which TVEI was introduced cruelly exposed the lack of expertise of secondary school teachers to meet the demands of the new initiative. The TRIST (TVEI-Related In-Service Training) programme was therefore introduced in 1985 to remedy this deficiency.

As part of the TRIST programme, additional funds were provided for secondary teachers and further education lecturers to attend and run INSET activities which were focused on classroom issues. An important indicator of success was the extent to which *pupils* benefited from the INSET activity attended by their teachers. Since most of the TRIST funding was devolved to schools, heads were forced to set up management structures to enable staff development to take place efficiently. For most schools this was achieved by designating a senior member of staff to act as a staff development co-ordinator, who was then trained in management skills. Many co-ordinators were able to collaborate with co-ordinators from other schools to provide sophisticated staff development support for teachers in their schools.

Primary schools, however, were not part of the TRIST scheme and consequently most missed out on a crucial stage in the development of awareness and skills to meet the demands of the 'new INSET' which was to follow.

The success of TRIST paved the way for the introduction of the GRIST (Grant-Related In-service Training) regulations heralded in *Better Schools* (DES, 1985) and introduced through DES circular 6/86 (*Local Education Authority Training Grants Scheme*). The main purposes of GRIST (later known as LEATGS) were:

> . . . to promote more systematic and purposeful planning of in-service training; . . . to promote the professional development of teachers; . . . to encourage more effective management of the teaching force; and to encourage training in selected areas which are to be accorded national priority.

The element of accountability within this was not disguised. Para 23 of the circular stated:

> All training . . . should be monitored and evaluated by the authority to assess how far it has contributed to more effective and

> efficient delivery of the education service.

and that (para 38)

> it is for authorities . . . to ensure that they obtain value for money.

The LEATGS regulations effectively came on line in 1987 at a time when schools were also faced with coming to terms with the 1986 Education Act, the revised teachers' contracts requiring teachers to be available to work under the direction of the head for up to 1265 hours per year and the introduction of 'INSET days' for school- or LEA-determined INSET. The National Curriculum requirements and other components of the 1988 Education Reform Act necessitated further changes to the style and philosophy of school management.

The nature of INSET support required to enable teachers to meet these developments was also changing. Cooper's summary of the new developments is given in Figure 2.1, column 2. *Funding* has changed (schools now have their own INSET budgets); *participation* has changed (larger numbers now attend; activities for whole staff are common); *providers* – those who run INSET activities for teachers – have changed (no longer is INSET provided exclusively by higher education lecturers and LEA advisers, teachers now attend activities provided by colleagues, teams of 'trainers' and management consultants, often from outside education); *venues* have changed (much more INSET is school based; the number of residential, hotel-based activities is increasing); *methods* of delivery have changed (the emphasis is now on participatory learning styles and application of 'training' skills).

2.3 Defining key terms

It is not surprising that many primary heads found themselves at a disadvantage when, in a very short period of time, they had to come to terms with the staff development philosophy and practice which secondary schools and advisers had been more gradually involved in over the two years of the TRIST programme. For Mr Jackson, the first step was to untangle some of the jargon that had mushroomed in the vocabulary of secondary staff development co-ordinators. Since few staff development books were addressed to primary heads and teachers, he spent time reading some of the publications and handbooks that emanated from the TRIST experience. (A selection is given in the bibliography at the end of this book.) He passed one or two of these on to his deputy to seek her comments and advice. He also arranged a brief meeting with the staff development co-ordinator of his local secondary school to make contact and to find out what local progress had been made.

Mr Jackson then felt he had begun to come to terms with providing working definitions for some of the new vocabulary. His definitions of key terms to his staff included the following:

- *INSET* – originally taken to mean in-service education and training. Now increasingly defined as in-service training. (The significance of this distinction is brought out in Chapter 16 of this book.)
- *professional development* – the *individual* requirements of teachers in a broad professional capacity. May extend outside their current responsibilities and beyond the context of their present school.
- *staff development* – the requirements of teachers as members of *staff* in their present school. The requirements may be weighted more towards the needs of the school rather than of the individual teacher.
- *school-based INSET* – activities held on school premises.
- *school-focused INSET* – activities related to issues of current concern to the school but not necessarily held on school premises.

Figure 2.2 The staff development cycle

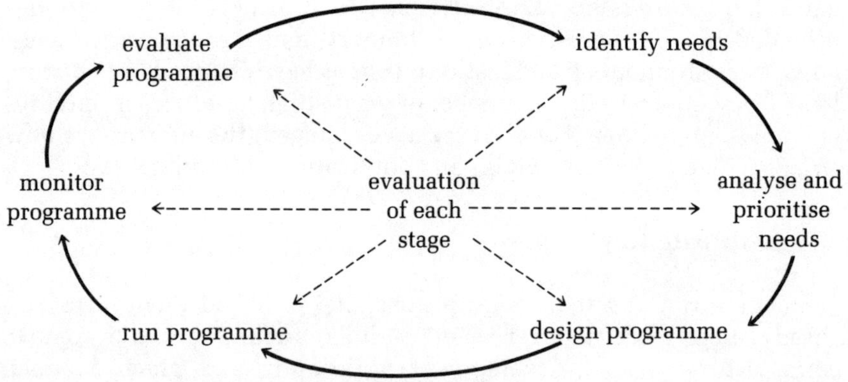

Mr Jackson found the idea of the 'staff development cycle' helpful in structuring his thoughts on how to proceed. The cycle diagram appears in many forms and at differing levels of complexity. At this early stage of development he found the simplest version (Figure 2.2) to be the most effective. Put even more crudely, it could be summarised as:

- Where are we?
- Where do we want to be?

- How do we get there?
- How will we know when we've got there?
- Where do we go next?

2.4 Meeting national requirements

Mr Jackson listed the main initiatives coming to him from local and national levels and begin to consider the implications for himself and his staff. They included:

- National Curriculum programmes of study (those which were available either as interim or final reports);
- National Curriculum attainment targets and assessment requirements;
- Records of Achievement;
- appraisal;
- mixed-age class groupings;
- local management of schools;
- policy formulation;
- 'cascading' skills;
- teaching styles;
- regulations regarding out-of-school activities;
- teacher shortage;
- lack of expertise in particular curriculum areas;
- governing bodies;
- teacher morale.

There were many more initiatives whose implications he could not foresee. They included:

- licensed teachers;
- National Curriculum areas (those whose working parties had not yet reported);
- job-sharing;
- the effects of reporting at ages 7 and 11;
- mixed-age pupil groupings based on assessment;
- the involvement of the reformed governing body.

Mr Jackson's next task was to reflect on the nature of his school and its staff. We consider his reflection further in Chapter 3.

3 Greenbank: one school's experience

3.1 The school

The fictional Greenbank County Primary School is situated on the fringes of a large industrial conurbation. Its catchment area comprises mixed local authority and private housing. It stands in a quiet cul-de-sac off the main road joining two suburban towns.

The school was built in 1969 to serve an increase in private housing provision. Projected roll numbers for the late 1970s were over 300, but this figure has never been achieved. Over recent years roll numbers have begun to decline, because of the increasingly high cost of private housing in the area and a static, gradually ageing population in the local authority housing. The school, therefore, has always had a more-than-adequate amount of space.

The pupils are generally well cared for and parents are, for the most part, co-operative and very willing to assist in aspects of the work of the school. There was no shortage of parents willing to serve on the governing body and the election of parent governors was keenly fought.

3.2 The staff

Mr Jackson (Headteacher)

Mr Jackson began teaching 12 years ago after obtaining a B.Ed. Hons degree at the local Institute of Higher Education. His main subject area was art and craft. His first post was some distance away in an urban comprehensive school as a member of the art department but he returned to teach in a local primary school after three years. He became deputy head in another large local primary school where he gained a reputation as an energetic innovator. He was respected as a good leader and sound organiser as well as being an imaginative classroom teacher.

He moved to Greenbank almost one year ago. He had thought of studying for an M.Ed. degree but deferred this decision because of the promotion to his present position. Most of his teaching experience has been with older junior children and he secretly wishes he knew more about infants. He has inherited some fairly detailed schemes of work in mathematics and language from the previous head but these do not appear to influence the work of staff to any noticeable extent. He is fairly optimistic about the effects of the National Curriculum on his school and feels that he can use the opportunity to review the curriculum in a positive way. He has attempted to see all the staff individually for an informal interview since his appointment to assess their personal strengths and interests. No written job descriptions are to be found.

He looks upon this appointment as something of a challenge, feeling that the school has never achieved its full potential. A first step seems to be to encourage the staff to share ideas. He is unsure how to begin the process.

Mrs Thomas (Deputy head)

Has taught at the school for 15 years, the last ten as deputy. She had previously taught in a nearby junior school. Mrs Thomas is something of a local personality, well respected by parents and colleagues alike. She firmly believes that top juniors are the ideal class for a deputy head teacher, whose role it is 'to prepare these children for the comprehensive school'. She operates a 'skills and frills' timetable. Her room is formal with not much evidence of children's work from direct experience. She welcomed Mr Jackson's appointment as head, seeing her main role as deputy as that of assisting and supporting him – although more from a sense of duty than from conviction.

Miss Grove (Class teacher – new entrant)

Graduate PGCE English. Was highly regarded and recommended to Mr Jackson by her PGCE course tutors. Very talented in both art and sport. Very enthusiastic. Believes in actively involving the children in their own learning and follows a topic-based approach. The children in her class are benefiting from her imaginative teaching. Mr Jackson enjoys visiting her class. At this early stage in her career he is reluctant to give her too much responsibility, but encourages her to assist other staff in extra-curricular activities. He regards her as a young teacher of great potential, a view shared by the primary adviser attached to the school.

Mrs Lever (Class teacher responsible for infant department)

Has taught at the school for six years. The previous headteacher had given her responsiblities for the infant department. No clear definition of duties had ever been negotiated with her.

Mrs Lever is aware of the problem and raised it with the head during her initial interview with him. Mr Jackson has resolved to solve this dilemma by a redefinition of responsibilities in the near future.

Miss Morris (Class teacher responsible for science)

B.Ed., with her main subject area for her teaching qualification environmental studies. Has taught for six years. Very willing but lacks dynamism. She sees her role in curriculum leadership as ordering equipment and keeping it in reasonable working order. No scheme of work exists in the area of science. She has attended a number of county-organised science in-service courses but they do not seem to have affected her own practice or her contribution to science in the school. Mr Jackson has asked for a parents' evening to explain the changes in teaching science in primary schools and its part in the National Curriculum but, although she readily agreed when asked, nothing has been done to set it in motion. Mr Jackson has the feeling that some of her topic work is repetitive and unstructured. Her record-keeping leaves much to be desired.

Mr Callaghan (Class teacher responsible for mathematics)

A gentle, calm teacher. Mathematics graduate (2:1). Mr Jackson realises that it is unusual to have such a highly-qualified mathematics graduate in a primary school and he expects great things. However, no clear definition of duties exists at present. Mr Jackson thinks Mr Callaghan needs his support and that good mathematics practice can best permeate the school by allowing Mr Callaghan to work on an individual basis with his teaching colleagues. Mr Jackson feels that a higher profile would be difficult for Mr Callaghan until he gains in confidence. He is responding to this approach and a number of interesting mathematical displays have begun to appear on the display boards in the corridors outside his room.

Mrs Scott (Class teacher responsible for language)

Has been teaching for many years. Holds very firm views about the teaching of reading and favours a scheme which many would regard as outdated even if they valued such schemes in the first place. She is a strong personality who regards teaching quality as being directly related to length of service. The children in her class appear to be well disciplined while she is with them.

Mrs Barratt (Class teacher)

Originally trained as a junior teacher but has taught infants since being appointed to the school. She has therefore had to 'retrain'. Some of this new experience has been gained on the job by trial and error, but she has actively sought advice from the adviser, has attended INSET courses and read widely. She is very well respected by parents.

Miss Pugh (Class teacher)

Qualified in 1970 (B.Ed. main subject Humanities). She studied part time for three years at the local Institute of Higher Education and obtained her M.Ed. in 1983. Her dissertation addressed the conceptual development of young children through an investigation of their drawing. Her classroom reflects a thoughtful, careful approach. To Mr Jackson everything seems almost too purposeful. He finds it very difficult to judge the effect of Miss Pugh's M.Ed. on the rest of the school, even at the level of promoting interest in the children's artwork. She is a quiet, retiring person and he wishes he could find a way to allow her undoubted intelligence and clear thinking to permeate beyond the walls of her classroom.

Mrs Broadbent (Class teacher)

A late entrant to the profession having worked for some time in a variety of clerical and secretarial posts. She became interested in teaching as her own family grew up and has recently completed a four-year B.Ed. degree in primary education. Her main subject areas have concerned English literature and drama but she has a specific interest in children's reading. She has discovered that her outlook is similar to that of Miss Grove, and Mr Jackson has noted that they appear to be working very well together. She respects Mrs Scott's experience and length of service but considers her approach to reading somewhat outmoded. Unlike Miss Grove, Mrs Broadbent has sufficient confidence to express her views on this matter and this has led to some overt differences of opinion in staff meetings.

3.3 Plan of school

A plan of the school is reproduced in Figure 3.1, with current room allocation shown in Figure 3.2.

Figure 3.1 Plan of Greenbank County Primary School

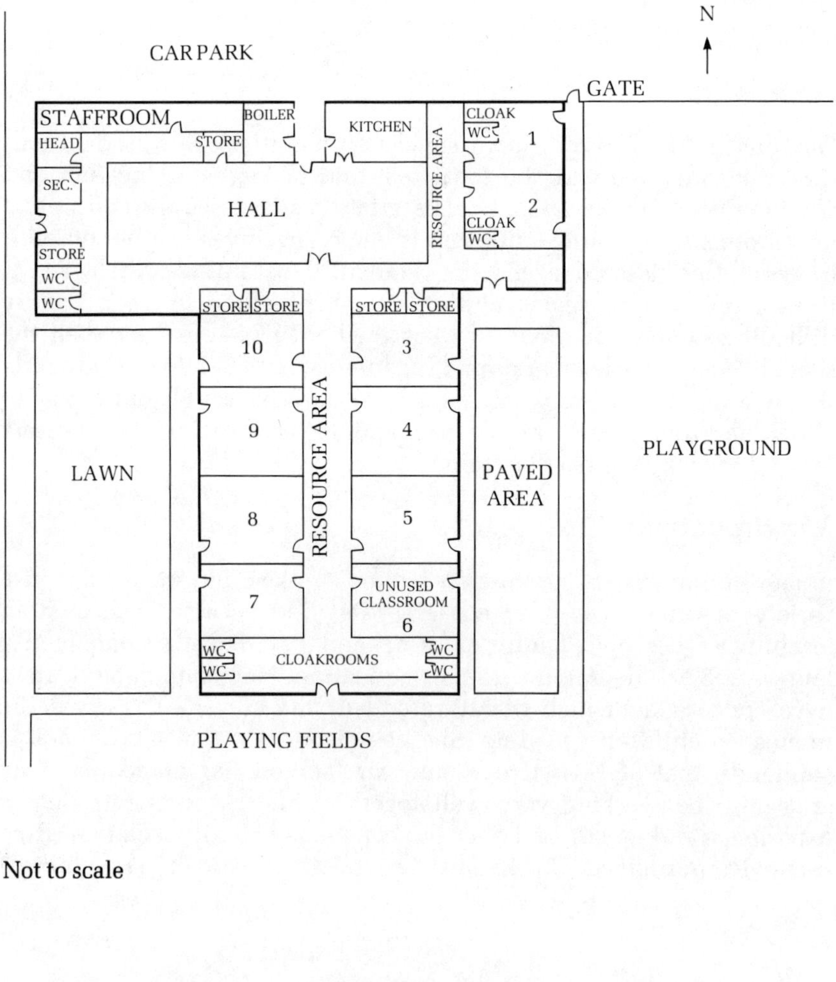

Not to scale

Figure 3.2 Room allocation at Greenbank County Primary School

Room	*Class no.*	*Class size and age range*	*Teacher*
1	9	28 5+/R5s	Miss Pugh
2	8	26 6+/5+	Mrs Lever
3	7	27 7+/6+	Mrs Barratt
4	6	29 7+	Mrs Scott
5	5	30 8+	Miss Morris
6	Unused	(miscellaneous storage/practical activities)	
7	4	28 9+/8+	Miss Grove
8	3	30 9+	Mrs Broadbent
9	2	26 10+	Mr Callaghan
10	1	29 10+	Mrs Thomas (DH)

3.4 Aims of the school

Mr Jackson has been left a set of school aims by the previous head, about which he feels dissatisfied. One of the first tasks he has set himself is to achieve a new set of goals for the school. He is aware that the National Curriculum will provide a framework, but that it is for schools themselves to decide upon their own approaches. He is hoping that he will be able to achieve these goals by working in co-operation with his staff and as part of the staff development programme.

1 The school aims to provide a happy, disciplined environment in which all children can achieve their full intellectual, social and physical potential.
2 At the end of the primary stage the child should:
   - be able to read with fluency and understanding;
   - be able to apply the four rules of number;
   - have a knowledge of both local and world wide history and geography;
   - have developed motor control and co-ordination;
   - have developed respect for others;
   - be able to make reasoned moral judgements;
   - be able to use basic research skills such as following an index or list of contents;
   - know simple facts of science;
   - be able to speak clearly;
   - be able to listen attentively;
   - be able to apply the basic rules of grammar;
   - be able to write in legible handwriting.

On close enquiry, Mr Jackson soon discovers that the staff has not been consulted about these 'aims'. In fact, only Mrs Thomas, the deputy head, seems to know of their existence. No one can recall having seen them. The National Curriculum proposals and final documents, together with related INSET, seem to provide an opportunity to re-appraise not only content but approaches to learning and teaching.

3.5 Where does Mr Jackson go next?

At first sight, Mr Jackson's task seems daunting, to say the least.

- Where does he start?
- How does he start?

In a situation of falling rolls, a long-term task will inevitably include changing the pedagogical approaches of some staff to accommodate new class groupings. Some staff are over reliant on published schemes. Science is a significantly neglected area and a core subject in the National Curriculum. Staff need to address the issues of attainment targets, assessment and record-keeping. Standards of display are patchy. Greenbank has not developed a coherent or united sense of purpose.

Mr Jackson faces three dilemmas. First, making the curriculum and management of the school successful. Second, introducing change into the school. Third, carrying the parents, staff and governors with him. For all these reasons, Mr Jackson believes that the formulation and implementation of a coherent staff development policy is a vital ingredient in his long-term plans.

In the next chapter, we consider some of the alternative strategies available to primary headteachers in setting up their own staff development programmes.

Issues for consideration

a) Where do the strengths and weaknesses of Mr Jackson's staff lie?
b) How should he begin to introduce a professional, evaluative approach to needs identification?
c) Do individual members of his staff stand out as possible leaders who will support him in his task?
d) Should he begin by reconstituting the aims of the school in the light of the requirements of the National Curriculum?

e) Whom should he involve at this stage: governors? advisers? consultants?
f) Should his approach to staff be formal (with written documentation and policies, or perhaps a four-stage plan) or informal (increasing individual confidence through discussion and encouragement)?
g How would each member of staff react to formal and informal approaches?
h) How can (should?) he make his staff aware that he intends to follow a process similar to that summarised in the staff development cycle model (Figure 2.2)?

PART TWO

FORMALISING THE PROCESS

4 Initiating the process

4.1 Introduction

In the first part of this book, we considered the reality of starting staff development schemes from the perspective of Mr Jackson, Head of Greenbank School. In Part Two we will suggest how schools formalise their staff development processes. But first let us once again reflect on Mr Jackson's position.

Where does Mr Jackson begin? His situation is no different from that of most other primary heads. Firmly fixed in his mind is the model of the staff development cycle (see Figure 2.2) which appears eminently logical and sensible. Nevertheless, he is still not absolutely clear what it implies in terms of practical activities. He has also spent some time puzzling about the meaning of the questions 'Where are we now?' and 'Where do we want to be?' and has come to the conclusion that he is not completely sure how they should be interpreted. Does the 'we' refer to the pupils, to individual teachers, or to the staff as a whole? Following on from this, 'whose' needs are being identified?

In thinking about his own school, Mr Jackson reflects that many of his staff might not be too ready to admit to having 'needs', or, alternatively, that they might be unwilling to express their real concerns in case this implied some sort of 'failure' on their part. As he pondered these issues, Mr Jackson came to realise that his own uncertainties and lack of confidence meant that his thoughts had remained at the level of ideas and were purely abstract. In reality, no real progress had been made in putting these ideas into action. He decided, therefore, to approach a lecturer at his local college with the purpose of clarifying his thinking in order to find ways of implementing and initiating the staff development process in his own school.

The discussion which ensued ranged far more widely than Mr Jackson had anticipated. It uncovered and explained the layers within the staff development process. It helped to provide answers to some of his searching and fundamental questions. It became clear to Mr Jackson that the purpose of staff development was to increase the effectiveness of staff both as individuals and as team members to the ultimate benefit of pupils, teachers and the whole school. This was, he determined, an agreeable aim. The discussion then moved on to consider the most likely way of achieving such individual and team effectiveness.

As the talk progressed, it became increasingly clear to Mr Jackson that a number of issues had to be given very careful consideration before initiating and implementing a programme of staff development. Of these, an understanding of the nature of change in any institution emerged as being of primary importance. This meant looking carefully at the central and vital role that individual teachers must play if a staff development programme is to be more than a superficial 'consulting' exercise. It is to these two interrelated issues, therefore, that Mr Jackson now turned his attention. But he decided that, first, he needed to delve further into theory. From his reading, he ascertained a number of points which we will discuss in the ensuing sections.

4.2 Teachers and change

A school that is adapting and developing in response to changing situations is one which is constantly assessing and modifying its practice. But schools are not abstractions, they are communities of individuals; when we talk of schools modifying their practice, we are really referring to the contribution that each teacher makes in this process. In thinking about the 'developing' school, we are in the same breath referring to the 'developing' teacher. So, it is at the level of the teacher that an understanding of the staff development process must begin.

It has become commonplace to state that people cannot be changed but can only change themselves. This is certainly the case with teachers. They cannot be developed through the force of imposed changes. They can only 'develop' and realise their professional potential as a result of their personal understanding of the change and their recognition of its relevance and importance. Such understanding can only be internally derived and is usually acquired when the change 'makes sense' in terms of teachers' personal experiences and thinking.

It follows, therefore, that a climate conducive to staff development is one which is teacher-centred in that it maximises the opportunities for individual growth and development to occur. Conversely, a climate which acts either wittingly or unwittingly as a constraint on teachers' learning is not one in which staff development can thrive.

For many schools, the introduction and implementation of a staff development programme constitutes a significant change to the way in which the school has traditionally been organised and run. In such schools it was not uncommon for staff to expect headteachers to take responsibility for making most decisions and for in-service training to be confined to a core of motivated (and often upwardly mobile!) teachers. The introduction of programmes of school-based INSET, which followed the changes in INSET funding, witnessed the beginning of change in that staff became more involved in curriculum decisions. Too often, however, the process has been *ad hoc*, confined to extra hours and has not really had an effect on classroom practice. In this context, staff development programmes which arise out of the involvement of all staff in both decision-making and classroom implementation represent a substantial change of direction. The experiences of schools which are already embarked on staff development programmes of this kind suggest that these programmes are most likely to be successful in situations where the staff:

- accept that change and development are an integral, normal and essential feature of the life of the school;
- are aware of their professional responsibility in contributing to decision-making;
- are willing to question their own practice and that of their colleagues from a range of perspectives;
- recognise that better teaching and learning are created by evaluation of classroom practice;
- are able and willing to share their own experiences and learn from those of colleagues.

As already indicated, for many primary schools, the introduction of staff development programmes based on the features outlined above represent important changes in themselves. Critically, it places the emphasis on the seminal role of teachers in the process of school improvement.

Previous attempts at introducing changes into school have undoubtedly influenced teachers' attitudes. Too often, teachers have been at the receiving end of externally imposed changes which have not taken into account teachers' real problems, perspectives or interests and have made extensive, often unrealistic, demands on time. If teachers are to be committed to staff development, then, as a first priority, it is important that it is a meaningful process which addresses areas identified by *teachers* as beneficial.

The question of how teachers are to be encouraged to participate meaningfully in this process brings us back to Mr Jackson's problem. From his reflections he began to recognise the kind of change and development that would need to take place in his school. The climate or school ethos that exists in every school – either positively or negatively – assumed paramount importance. At the same time, it was necessary to focus on two kinds of change – personal and interpersonal. Personal change occurs as teachers develop the qualities and skills required to examine, gain insights into and make decisions about their own practice. Interpersonal change results from teachers' capacity to communicate effectively and honestly with colleagues (Easen, 1985).

Both kinds of change are more easily achieved in schools where teachers have high self-esteem, and are confident, open, willing to share their understandings with others, prepared to voice their own views and be tolerant of diverse opinions. It is unlikely that these personal qualities, along with the necessary evaluative and interpersonal skills, will develop in a climate where relationships are not based on respect, trust, openness and honesty.

Mr Jackson determined to develop Greenbank along these lines. But how could he establish a suitable, viable climate?

4.3 Difficulties in establishing a suitable climate

What, then, are the difficulties in establishing this climate? These will, of course, vary from one school to another, but one or a combination of the following factors are likely to be present in many institutions.

4.3.1 Previous history of attempts at change

The effect on teachers' attitudes of previous attempts at introducing change into the school has already been touched on but should not be underestimated. Teachers are busy people and if they have previously invested time and energy in changes which they have not identified, may not have been in sympathy with, and which have had few positive classroom outcomes, then they will not readily wish to repeat the experience. Teacher involvement in the identification of issues for staff development is, therefore, vitally important.

4.3.2 *External pressures*

With the National Curriculum and accompanying assessment requirements, many teachers feel that the autonomy they once had in making individual decisions about the curriculum is disappearing and that, in this new context, their own views will have diminished relevance.

4.3.3 *Passiveness*

Some teachers prefer to be told what to do rather than being consulted about the change process. In an age when there is so much controversy and debate about the purpose and place of education in our society, this is not surprising. The accountability pressures that are currently becoming more prominent can only exacerbate these feelings of insecurity.

4.3.4 *Psychological barriers*

The majority of people feel greater security and confidence in their work when they are using well tried and tested methods which they have developed skill and confidence in using. Change spells uncertainty and insecurity. As such, change clearly has the potential to erode rather than build confidence – initially, at least.

4.3.5 *Social barriers*

The necessity for teachers to share experiences with colleagues and to use them in discussions about the school's curriculum can pose a number of difficulties which can be subsumed under the word 'social'. First, we have the fact that in many schools, headteachers are traditionally expected by staff to accept responsibility for taking decisions. In a situation where the needs of schools are often discussed between the headteacher and LEA advisers with little or no consultation with teachers, this expectation can be seen to be justified. Second, we have to take into account the feeling that prevails in many staffrooms that good working relationships are created by harmonious and unproblematic staff discussions. Unfortunately, this stress on harmonious relationships is often achieved at the expense of the expression of considered but possibly contentious views and feelings. The capacity to listen to, understand and, if appropriate, accommodate diverse approaches often lies undeveloped in schools where it has become routine to agree with and follow the suggestions of a dominant few. But for the staff development process to be effective there is a need for feelings, beliefs and values to be 'above water' and thus open to confrontation and negotiation. The very 'niceness' of staff to each other can therefore act as a constraint on development.

Finally, we need to highlight two more general factors that are widely considered to frustrate teachers in their efforts to obtain the job satisfaction that helps to sustain motivation and commitment in many professions. First, there is the structure of the teaching profession itself. The observation is frequently made that the task facing the new entrant to the profession is the same as that assigned to a teacher who has been twenty years in the job; some cynics would go further and say that a teacher with 20 years' experience has really had one year 20 times over. While this is clearly a gross misrepresentation, it does have a grain of truth in that most professions are characterised by explicit career progress rather than by increasingly competent practice being displayed within a static position, as in the case of teaching. As the impact of falling rolls has been to create an ageing profession with fewer career opportunities, this has become a vitally important issue. We have to think carefully about how teachers with limited opportunities for career change or promotion can be motivated.

> Has a teacher with 20 years' experience really had one year's experience 20 times over?

Second, difficulties are created by the nature of the task of educating. If job satisfaction and motivation are created by continual positive results and feedback, it is not obvious how this can be achieved in teaching, where outcomes are complex, ambiguous, indeterminate and long-run. Achievement scores are not, on their own, seen as adequate measures of outcome, with most teachers believing that 'teachers are hired to educate children, to produce important lasting changes in behaviour not short-term changes in test-scores' (Medley, 1979). The consequence of this is that teachers must rely on the reflection and feedback of others to gauge their effectiveness, and to be credible this must come from those whom teachers believe can make authoritative and meaningful comments about the teaching process. This becomes a role that headteachers and fellow professionals must perform.

4.4 Role of the head in creating a school's climate

Armed with a better understanding of the kind of climate conducive to staff development, Mr Jackson now sets about considering how he can best create a facilitating environment in his own school. How can he provide the conditions which will encourage staff to become more confident; open; willing to share their concerns, understanding and insights; critical of their own practice and able to use failure positively; aware of the relationship between external pressures and internal development; able to deal confidently with parents, governors, advisers – and, as well as this, ensure that they are highly motivated and deeply committed?

Mr Jackson decides to start from the basic principles that people are motivated and committed in situations where they have:

- a sense of belonging;
- a sense of achievement;
- a sense of appreciation;
- a sense of influence;
- a sense of ownership.

Mr Jackson decides that this climate can best be created by paying attention to classroom practice, relationships, interactions, values, hopes and feelings. But he also concludes that 'paying attention to' will not be enough. To begin with, he realises, he will have to use his position to organise the school in such a way that opportunities for staff to engage in climate-setting activities are not optional but essential; to achieve this, his leadership must be exercised positively. At the same time, he does not want to assume the role of, or be perceived as, simply the 'manager' of the process – he wants to be part of it. The role of 'facilitator' or 'gatekeeper' will not be sufficient if his teachers are to appreciate the principles underlying the process and to see that his intentions are genuine. Also, if he is to be viewed as a credible provider of support and inspiration, then it is imperative that he becomes an active participant in the whole process. With these ideas in mind, Mr Jackson sets about applying these general principles in his own school setting.

4.4.1 Building self-esteem and confidence

As head, he sees a need to:

1 Recognise and appreciate all achievements.
2 Give teachers opportunities to demonstrate their strengths by:
   - holding meetings in classrooms where teachers can display work and demonstrate interests to colleagues;
   - providing opportunities for younger teachers to work with more

experienced staff (very important in building the self-esteem of older teachers).

3 Always separate the personal from the professional, eg stress that problems lie in the limitations of the approach not the capacity of the teacher.

4 Provide plenty of positive reinforcement by:
- continually praising efforts;
- talking in teachers' language when discussing practice (ie moving beyond global statements 'keep up the good work' to precise discussion of selected issues);
- seeing mistakes as inevitable and something to learn from rather than indications of failure;
- expressing appreciation not only verbally but sometimes through written communication (eg memos, letters);
- providing support in the face of criticism (eg from parents, governors);
- giving teachers opportunity to interact directly with LEA advisers and other professionals.

4.4.2 Encouraging openness and sharing

1 Visit classrooms frequently in order to understand teacher's situation and share concerns.
2 Discuss teaching regularly, reflecting with teachers on their classroom experiences.
3 Make efforts to ensure that the language that the teacher uses to describe the teaching process is shared.
4 Encourage teachers to embrace new ideas and take risks by setting an example.
5 Rotate chairmanship of meetings.
6 Give careful consideration to seating arrangements at meetings.
7 Invite teachers to help in setting the agenda for meetings.
8 Use meetings to discuss values as well as more practical aspects of teaching.
9 Develop systems for improving channels and methods of communication.
10 Encourage team work by setting up working parties to look at specific issues – keep these flexible and rotate the membership.

4.4.3 Developing trust

1 Delegate responsibilities in a clear way – along with the authority to carry these out.

2 Draw up the head's job description in negotiation with staff.
3 Abide by decisions made by staff.
4 Listen actively to what teachers are saying.

Clearly, all of these activities – listening, observing, discussing, reflecting, planning and organising – are extremely time consuming if they are to be properly accomplished. Where is a busy headteacher to find this time?

Priorities
If school improvement is dependent on staff development programmes of the kind described, then sufficient time must be allocated to ensure the effectiveness of component parts of the process. This means establishing priorities and thus making choices – never easy when commitments appear to have equal importance. For example, do I talk to a parent for half an hour or do I share a lesson with a teacher? Do I leave my phone unanswered while I discuss a lesson with a teacher? These are difficult but necessary choices if more than lip service is to be paid to staff development. Commitment cannot be expected from teachers if they do not see a similar attitude displayed by management.

Delegation
Time can be made by creative use of delegation. Many tasks can, with careful forethought and discussion, be done by parents, ancillaries and pupils, thus lightening the burden on both head and teachers. We tend to have very traditional notions about roles and tasks in schools, and staff discussion of the grounds on which these are based can often lead to more open, democratic and responsible institutions. Once again, the ideas of all staff on this issue are needed.

Training
The skills required for active listening, careful observation and fruitful discussion need to be developed by both headteachers and staff. Once acquired, all of these processes are likely to take less time. As with all other tasks, it is the *quality* of the time invested rather than the *quantity* that determines consequences. Time invested in developing skills must therefore be perceived as time well spent.

Extra hours
Judicious use of extra hours can enable time to be found for staff development activities. Headteachers can also consider in what ways their INSET budget could be used to create more opportunities.

Bearing in mind all that has been said about climate-setting, Mr Jackson contacted a colleague, the head of a nearby average-sized primary school to discuss the ways in which she had set about this task. The school in question for many years had a reputation with the LEA for using innovative methods of language teaching and had frequently been asked to exemplify these to teachers in local schools. It was with some surprise, therefore, that the new head found staff morale at a low ebb when she took up her post. As a consequence of this, the first few months were spent talking to individual teachers and listening to their grievances in an attempt to build up a picture of the school and its specific problems. It became clear from these discussions that, though the previous head had been active in involving his staff in INSET, the decision about the courses to be undertaken had, in the main, been made by the head. Staff remarked that the previous head had rarely consulted staff either collectively or individually and had tended to issue instructions which had been disliked. On their return from INSET courses, staff had not been invited to talk to their colleagues formally about their experiences.

The new head considered that her first task in these circumstances was to boost the teachers' confidence and try to heighten staff morale. So, frequent staff meetings to review the curriculum were held with meetings being chaired by the relevant curriculum leader. Many of these meetings took place in the classrooms of individual teachers, thus providing them with opportunities to talk on their own territory about the work they were doing. This proved to be an excellent means of encouraging the less forthcoming teachers to describe what they were doing and why, with concrete aids in the form of children's work and classroom displays helping to anchor the discussion in the teachers' immediate concerns about the work being produced.

Another way of boosting staff confidence was to delegate responsibilities to all members of staff along with the authority to make decisions where necessary. A comment from one of the teachers may best illuminate staff reaction to this:

> *everyone likes the way she (the headteacher) gives responsibilities to people and doesn't interfere . . . this shows she has respect for the teacher . . . the atmosphere in the school has changed completely, her attitude to staff means she has total co-operation and one hundred per cent commitment from all of us.*

Responding to teachers' requests so that they came to feel that they had some real influence over decision-making proved to be another important strategy in sustaining motivation. This led, for instance, to the headteacher taking classes to enable staff to visit schools to talk with teachers and observe the implementation of different schemes and approaches in the teaching of mathematics. It also resulted in the area for specific review and INSET in the coming year being identified by teachers despite the fact that the headteacher considered that the focus should have been elsewhere. At this stage, the importance of enhancing teachers' feelings of value and influence by adhering to this whole staff decision was considered by the head to override any personal concerns she had about the curriculum.

Clearly, in this school the seeds of teacher confidence, openness and trust are being effectively, if informally, sown. It is worth noting that it is the gradual pace adopted that is important in bringing about the improved climate. Creating time to listen, observe and become familiar with teachers' concerns has enabled the head to build up a picture of individual differences and the stage of development of each member of staff. As a consequence, communication with individual teachers is grounded in their own situation and thus becomes more meaningful and useful. Also, teacher confidence and motivation is enhanced by praise, increased responsibilities and the capacity to influence decisions. In this school, according priority to staff development is beginning to reap rewards.

Issues for consideration

a) Read through sections 4.3.1 to 4.3.5. How would each factor relate to individuals on Mr Jackson's staff?
b) Can Mr Jackson rely on his 'experienced' teachers to take the lead and extend professionally his newer members of staff?
c) How would individual staff respond to Mr Jackson's making frequent visits to classrooms?
d) How can Mr Jackson delegate effectively without appearing to overburden staff or offload his own work on to others?
e) Can Mr Jackson afford the time to take a 'softly softly' approach to climate-setting?

5 Identifying needs

5.1 Needs and change

Chapter 4 considered the kind of climate that will increase the likelihood of a meaningful and effective staff development programme emerging in a school. It has been suggested that such a climate must be teacher-centred as there can be no school improvement without teacher development. But central though this focus on individual teachers must be in staff development terms, the process has wider connotations. It is also about whole staffs considering and assessing all aspects of the life of the school:

- in terms of their potential for promoting pupil learning;
- in the context of social change and new legislation, eg Educational Reform Act, equal opportunities;
- in relation to technological developments, eg computer-assisted learning;
- in respect of changing external influences, eg parental involvement and expectation; changes in governing bodies.

Discussion of needs is complicated, therefore, by the fact that education is a process in which many parties have an interest (and often an opinion!). Thus, schools do not exist in a vacuum. However, although all these factors exert an influence on the educational system, it cannot be overemphasised that the educational implications of changes for schools must be worked out in classrooms and are the professional responsiblity of the teacher. School improvement is achieved when the insights of thinking, reflective teachers are used to provide the professional perspective on the educational validity, desirability and feasibility of any changes proposed. In this way, the professional integrity of the teacher is acknowledged, teacher confidence is maintained and pupils are protected from the imposition of changes that have questionable educational value.

5.1.1 Whose needs?

Teachers' needs must be placed in this wider context. The range of interests that are involved in the needs identification process is indicated in Figure 5.1. If schools are to be adaptable, responsive, developing institutions, then all of the interests signified in Figure 5.1 have to be kept in balance in the needs identification process. Unfortunately, this is something which is more easily stated than achieved. Nowadays, with limited INSET budgets and external pressures to

Figure 5.1 Range of interests to be considered in the needs identification process

National priorities	These are set out annually in the Government's LEATGS circulars. Recent national priority areas have included: management training for headteachers: training in school teacher appraisal; training for the National Curriculum – management, assessment and content; training in the teaching of Religious Education; training in the teaching of children in primary classes who are younger than 'rising fives'; training to meet the special educational needs of particular pupils.
Local priorities	Local education authorities will have their own priority areas for INSET. They may include: setting up and working in consortia; implementing the LEA's curriculum policy; specific curricular or cross-curricular initiatives.
School priorities	*Staff* development as opposed to personal professional development needs will relate to specific priorities of the school. They may include: developing policies on staff development, assessment, cross-curricular work; setting up specific curricular policies; establishing links with secondary schools; updating of skills and knowledge in new curriculum areas.
Individual teacher priorities	Improved understanding/knowledge in an area of particular responsibility; career interest/aspirations; personal interest.

implement changes quickly, the needs of schools are frequently dictated by national priorities which often take precedence over those of individual teachers. Clearly, this is something which should be avoided. If teachers are to be effective, then it is imperative that their own views about both their own and their school's development are valued and recognised. Awareness of these different levels of interest is important as it is very likely that the method of needs identification adopted by a school will in some way reflect the priority accorded to the different interest groups.

5.1.2 Needs or development?

Is the use of the word 'needs' itself the most appropriate one to use in the context of staff development? Or does its very use, implying as it does that something is lacking and requires remedying, lead to a deficiency-based model for staff development? This is not the kind of foundation on which teacher self-esteem and confidence can be built.

An alternative viewpoint sees staff development as a process of organic growth and development out of the existing situation. Dependent upon the head's perspective, the two different positions are likely to influence the way in which the needs-identification process is tackled in a school. With the first approach, questions like 'What are our strengths?' and 'What are our weaknesses?' are addressed in coming to decisions about staff needs. By contrast, when 'development' is the focus, the questions are more likely to be 'What are we doing now?' and 'What can we learn from this?'

Change is thus perceived as *evolutionary*, rather than *revolutionary*, building gradually on existing practice. This does not mean, though, that such development is not influenced by an awareness of the external context and its requirements.

5.2 Methods of needs identification

There are many methods of needs identification available to a head in initiating the staff development process and, as already suggested, the choice is likely to be influenced by the following considerations:

- the school's attitude to the 'needs' or 'development' issue;
- whether the focus is on National/LEA priorities, institutional, functional, group or individual needs;
- the characteristics of the school (eg size, stage, location);
- the experience of the staff with this kind of exercise.

Whatever method (or methods) are selected, it is imperative that all staff are involved in the process. The commitment of teachers is rarely total if they do not play an active role in decision-making. In fact, the process of discussing the present situation and planning an INSET programme is in itself a valuable form of staff development.

Many methods of assessing the needs of schools, groups within schools and individual teachers are available. These range from the formal to the informal and include the following:

- checklists
- questionnaires
- interviews
- self-evaluation
- peer evaluation
- consultancy
- other methods.

The decision about which method to use will depend on the kind of information required. However, before a final selection, schools need to ask of each method:

1 How can it be used?
2 What kind of information will it provide?
3 What are the advantages/disadvantages of using it?

With these questions in mind, let us now look at some examples of these methods.

5.3 Checklists

Many LEAs have produced checklists for use in school-based reviews; of these, the most well known is probably ILEA's *Keeping the School Under Review.*

5.3.1 'Keeping the School Under Review' (The Primary School)

In the introduction to *Keeping the School Under Review*, the authors claim that it is designed 'to assist a school to examine its organisation, its resources, its standards of achievement and its relationships' (ILEA, 1982). To this end it is structured in seven sections:

1 the children, their parents, the governors, the community;
2 teaching organisation, school staff, responsibility structure, non-teaching staff, staff development;
3 the curriculum, continuity, assessment, extending the curriculum;
4 organisation and management;
5 the building and the general environment;
6 questions for the individual teacher;
7 questions for the headteacher.

The questions extending over twenty-two pages are numerous, detailed and wide-ranging.

How could such a checklist be used? It is possible that a school would want to use a checklist of this kind where it was felt that staff would benefit from becoming aware of the range of areas and type of questions that can be addressed when evaluating a school. The questions should be seen as 'triggers' for discussion. Some advantages and disadvantages of the checklist approach are given below.

Advantages	*Disadvantages*
• Provides comprehensive coverage of issues relevant to schools	• Length is daunting; could be dispiriting to teachers
• Issues are updated at intervals	• Categories and issues included are externally selected by LEA
• Addressing statements focuses staff discussion	• Real concerns of schools might not be represented
• All staff are involved in the process	• Provides no way of translating discussion into action

5.3.2 DION (Diagnosis of Individual and Organisation Needs)

A different kind of checklist is represented by DION, which is presented as a list of sixty-six statements to which teachers are encouraged to react immediately rather than through discussion. Each statement is designed to elicit a teacher's view on one of the eleven pre-identified school issues like:

- leadership and staff
- resources
- teamwork.

The combined responses from individual teachers are used to indicate areas for future attention and provide a foundation on which an INSET programme can be planned. There are a number of advantages and disadvantages to using DION. These need to be considered carefully before this approach is used with the whole staff.

Advantages	*Disadvantages*
• The checklist is extremely quick to administer • Provides information on individual and whole school needs • Provides quantitative data on which future developments can be planned	• All of the statements in the list are negative • Responses obtained are 'gut' reactions, not based on careful reflection • Categories and issues are externally derived • Little obvious connection with classroom practice • Statements need to be updated to take account of recent changes

In summary, checklists have their uses in suggesting starting points for discussion and in providing preliminary indications of teachers' views. However, they are equally likely to:

- overlook real areas of concern;
- be 'deficiency'- rather than 'growth'-based;
- offer no structure or process on which a proper 'developmental' programme for staff could be based.

5.4 Questionnaires

As with all questionnaires, the ones used for needs identification purposes can range from the highly structured, in that they elicit teachers' responses in pre-identified areas, to the unstructured where teachers are themselves invited to identify the areas of concern. The latter tend to be used more in teachers' self-evaluation exercises and will be discussed in a later section. Questionnaires can also be classified in terms of responses sought. For example, an LEA can issue a questionnaire to all of its schools to obtain a comprehensive picture of INSET needs. Alternatively, a functional group within a school might wish to use a questionnaire to identify areas in need of attention. The two examples of questionnaires now discussed are included because both incorporate procedures for enabling schools to act on the information obtained. It is often more appropriate, however, for staff to design their own instrument.

5.4.1 GRIDS (Guidelines for the Review and Internal Development of Schools)

The GRIDS questionnaire differs from other similar approaches in that it gives guidance about how the whole process of needs identification should be conducted as well as suggesting areas which should be covered. The process starts with a review of the whole school under the following headings:

- curriculum
- pupils
- external links
- management.

The questionnaire elicits responses from staff which indicate whether they think that the area under consideration is a strength or a weakness in the school. In the discussion which follows this survey of staff opinion, the priorities which have emerged from the questionnaire responses are debated and negotiated. Once an area for specific review is established, a co-ordinator is appointed whose responsibility is to

Figure 5.2 Planning an INSET programme using the GRIDS cycle

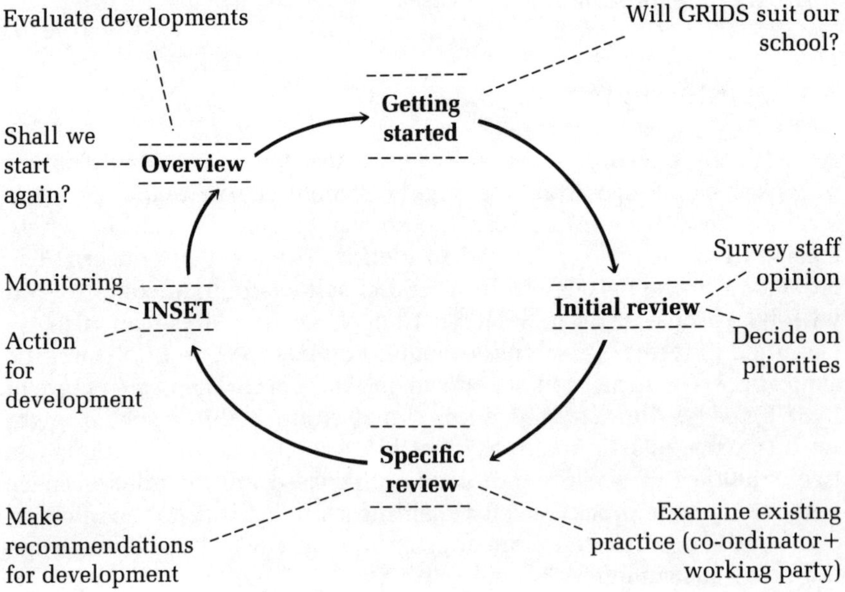

look in detail at the school's existing practice, examine how this can be developed and present recommendations to the whole staff. In a small school, it is likely that the whole staff will be involved in this exercise. An INSET programme is then planned and implemented (see Figure 5.2) and the whole programme is carefully monitored. Decisions about whether to retain any of the changes that have been introduced are then made and then (provided the staff have found the process helpful and wish to retain it) the whole cycle restarts.

Intrinsic to the whole GRIDS programme, and basic to its philosophy, is the principle that all staff consider whether it is a system of needs identification that they are happy to adopt. The following list of advantages and disadvantages could well form part of a school's deliberations.

Advantages	*Disadvantages*
• All staff are involved in decisions about priorities	• Pre-identified categories could be limiting
• Provides a system for moving from discussion into action	• Needs initially identified are broad rather than specific
• Stresses the importance of monitoring and evaluation	• Invitation to identify weaknesses implies a deficiency-based model for staff development
• Emphasises cyclical, on-going nature of staff development	

5.4.2 Training and Development Needs Questionnaire (NDCSMT, 1987)

The GRIDS questionnaire has subsequently been developed by the National Development Centre for School Management Training in co-operation with Dudley LEA so that its functions are now extended. The format of the original questionnaire has been modified so that it is now designed to:

- provide LEAs with the information they need as the basis for INSET planning;
- encourage individual staff and institutions to identify their INSET needs and feed them into the LEA's total picture;
- enable individual, group and school needs to be identified.

The questionnaire differs from GRIDS in that, instead of being asked to comment on strengths and weaknesses, teachers are requested to state against each of the topics presented the priority they would accord them in terms of training and development over the next twelve months. They are also asked to indicate, from the following options, the method of INSET they would prefer to undertake in order to address their relevant needs:

- school-based activity;
- external short course/workshop;
- visits to other schools;
- secondment to another job/institution;
- extended long course in own time;
- extended long course full-time or part-time;
- other forms (please specify).

Responses from the questionnaire provide information about INSET needs at three levels, the individual teacher, the school and the LEA. They also indicate the teachers' preferred methods of training. The amended GRIDS questionnaire serves a different purpose to the original and thus has different kinds of advantages for school staff to discuss and consider.

Advantages	*Disadvantages*
• LEA planning can be based on teachers' identified needs	• Designation of topics to address could be limiting
• Assures better co-ordination between LEA and schools	• Used alone is crude tool providing only brief outline information. Needs to be followed up with discussions (group and individual)
• Provides direct measure of individual teacher's needs	
• Information from teacher can be used as basis for interview with head	
• Talks of 'priorities' rather than 'weaknesses'	
• Could provide basis for further discussion in school	

While questionnaires have their uses when large amounts of information have to be collated (as in the case of LEAs), they must be seen as having limited use in a staff development programme predicated on the development of individual teachers. This is because:

1 They pre-specify and thereby limit teachers' choice of areas of need.
2 They suggest to the teacher that the specified areas are the most important ones.
3 They tend to be 'deficiency'-based in that the teacher is often requested to identify 'weaknesses' in the area specified.
4 They ask for needs to be specified in broad areas and general terms

(eg art and craft, science, teaching methods). An individual teacher's concerns, however, tend to be far more specific.
5 The relationship between the need identified and classroom practice is not always clear or obvious.

Another method is to centre on the teacher and allow the needs identification process to be guided by, and built on, his or her professional concerns on an individual basis. This is an approach we will explore more carefully in Chapter 6.

5.5 Interviews

Interviews with teachers on an individual basis present an extremely valuable avenue for discussion of a wide range of issues. Interviews

- provide an opportunity for teachers to discuss their own personal concerns privately and confidentially;
- provide information about individual needs or interests which differ from those of the whole school and which may not be revealed in other needs identification strategies;
- provide an opportunity for teachers to negotiate targets for the future and to review the extent to which previous ones have been achieved;
- 'personalise' the process of staff development; handled in a sympathetic, sensitive way, interviews can enhance confidence, heighten morale and create the sense of belonging, achieving and being valued that is at the root of all effective staff development programmes;
- constitute an integral part of the appraisal process and thereby offer a routine opportunity for review and forward planning.

5.5.1 The conduct of interviews

Interviews should be discussed in a much wider context than in relation to needs identification alone. However, regardless of their ultimate purpose, similar questions about the conduct of the interviews will be provoked:

1 Who should conduct them?
2 Where and when should they take place?
3 How often should they occur?
4 What questions should be addressed?
5 How should the agenda be constructed?
6 What should happen to the information obtained?

5.5.2 Who should conduct the interview?

In a small primary school the interviewing is likely to be the responsibility of the headteacher and there are strong arguments for suggesting that this should also apply to larger primary schools:

- It demonstrates to teachers the importance that the headteacher places on the event.
- It can be instrumental in forging a professional, supportive and trusting relationship between the head and individual teachers.
- The headteacher is perceived as having the status and authority to implement action on points arising from the interview.

On the other hand, this is a role which has been filled successfully in secondary schools by teachers appointed as staff development co-ordinators. Given the increasing administrative demands being made on headteachers, it is possible that the deputy heads or a senior staff member in primary schools could assume the responsibility. The choice would depend very much on the priorities of the head, the ethos of the school and the experience of the staff with staff development and should therefore be made by each school individually.

5.5.3 Where, when and how often?

Answers to more practical questions of where, when and how often will possibly contribute to the decision about who should conduct the interviews, as one of the difficulties is often that of finding a suitable time and place. This can be especially difficult for small schools when the only time available to a teaching head is likely to be outside teaching hours. For larger primary schools some of the schools LEATGS budget could be used to buy cover to release the head and teachers for interviews if it is considered these are important enough to take place within school hours. For most schools, however, this would be seen as beyond the scope of the INSET budget. Whether scheduled to take place in or out of school hours, the venue chosen should be comfortable and the time allocated undisturbed. It is likely that in the majority of schools, interviews will be conducted annually and it would be sensible for these to fit in with the overall strategy for needs identification of both school and LEA so that the information obtained can be taken into consideration in the forward planning of staff development and INSET.

5.5.4 What questions should be addressed?

It is difficult to distinguish between an appraisal interview where the primary focus is to foster the professional growth of the teacher and an interview which is designed to identify a teacher's needs. Both are concerned with reviewing and forward planning in a supportive and constructive way and both are likely to address the issues under a number of general headings. The headings listed below can be taken as fairly typical and offer a possible framework for structuring the interview:

Job description – to include changes as a result of:
- changes in conditions of service
- national legislation (eg requirements of the National Curriculum)
- teacher's own changing definition of the requirements of the job
- changes within the school (eg new head)

Self-appraisal
- review of targets previously set
- findings from self-evaluation

Career
- stage in career
- personal ambitions
- constraints and possibilities

Within these general areas how should the agenda for the interview be decided? The most important thing to remember here is that the interview is not intended to 'catch out' or surprise the teacher. It should be conceived in terms of a professional discussion in which both sides present their own perspective on the situation and, as a consequence, negotiate professional targets which are both realistic and attainable. If this is to be the case, then Wragg (1987) suggests that the following kind of preparation is essential:

The interviewee needs to

- be given at least one week's notice of the meeting;
- be reminded of its purpose;
- be asked to think back over all aspects of his work during the previous year;
- select areas that he feels to have been particularly worthwhile;
- admit to those of comparative failure;

- consider the contributory factors behind both of the above;
- suggest areas where in-service training might be helpful;
- suggest ways in which his talents may be better utilised;
- consider how the management has assisted/curtailed his progress.

The interviewer should prepare himself by reconsidering

- the job description;
- previous meetings both formal and informal;
- the above, in relation to targets agreed at previous meeting;
- contributions made by interviewee at various meetings;
- overall potential of the individual.

The agenda for the meeting can then be constructed on the basis of both parties' preparation. It has been the experience of many schools that a pre-interview meeting to draw up the agenda can be immensely beneficial in establishing a good rapport and relationship and in defusing any negative feelings that the teacher may have about the interview. This is important because it should not be assumed that all teachers feel positive about a situation in which they are being asked to talk about their personal and professional development. Opportunities for promotion have been severely curtailed in recent years and this can create difficulties in cases where teachers have reached middle-age with little change in their circumstances. Also, the effect of current legislation concerning the National Curriculum and assessment has left many teachers feeling that their own views are unimportant and that their job has become one of implementing an agreed syllabus. Feelings of frustration and powerlessness are not ones on which a fruitful discussion of 'needs' can be built. It is essential, therefore, that teachers' views and feelings on these matters are discussed openly, realistically and positively and that areas of conflict are addressed (even if not resolved) and not ignored.

Mismatch can clearly occur between 'needs' as identified by teachers, whether they be personal or professional, and those which the headteacher perceives as necessary for the school as a whole and this has led Bolam (1982) to suggest that a distinction should be made between 'needs identification' and 'target-setting'. This means that the headteacher must agree to provide all the support and in-service training necessary to meet targets that can realistically be set for the coming year, taking into account whole school requirements, other teachers' needs and available resources, but does not promise that all identified needs will be met. This is a situation which requires tact, diplomacy and skill in negotiating what is, and is not, desirable and possible in a way which does not leave the teacher feeling that his or her concerns are not being recognised.

All of the processes engaged in during interviews:

- reviewing achievement and engaging in mutual self-evaluation;
- negotiating realistic future targets;
- assessing and balancing interests and resources;

must be accomplished in such a way that the teacher's confidence is increased and self-esteem enhanced. The interviewer must, therefore, have at his disposal a wide range of skills which will increase the likelihood of the event being a positive experience for both sides. The kinds of skills that are widely considered to maximise the effectiveness of interviews have been listed by Gane (1986). They include the ability to listen actively, to question appositely and sensitively and to focus the interview appropriately. These skills are elaborated below.

Listening is improved when the listener:
- checks facts and clarifies points as the interview progresses
- notes and records key points as they arise
- paraphrases what has been said and seeks confirmation of correctness
- summarises main points at end of interview
- uses non-verbal signals to encourage a response

Questioning is more effective when:
- prompts are used to encourage the interviewee to elaborate or expand a point
- open questions allow the interviewee to respond more freely
- questions are used to steer the interview in fruitful and promising directions

The focus of the interview should:
- centre on examples of behaviour, *not* personal traits
- concentrate on remediable issues that the interviewee can do something about
- link to major issues
- emphasise the positive statements made by the interviewee

Many of the skills listed above are also required by teachers who should not see themselves as passive recipients in the situation but as active creators of contexts in which their own needs can best be met. Changing the terminology and calling interviews 'professional discussions' could be beneficial in that this would describe more accurately a situation in which the interviewer and interviewee are conceived as equal partners in the task of creating optimal learning environments for all staff and pupils.

Advantages	*Disadvantages*
• Introduces personal dimension into staff development process. Can enhance feelings of value and increase self-esteem • Provides opportunity for negotiation of a) personal targets b) individual vs school interests • Provides an opportunity for teacher to ask questions	• Process is very time-consuming. Particularly difficult in primary schools where 'cover' is always a problem • If handled insensitively could decrease confidence • Could, in leaving any conflicts unresolved, produce negative attitudes

5.6 Case study: using a consultant to identify needs

The case-study school is a suburban primary school with a staff of twelve. It is not untypical in its experience of INSET and staff development. Individual members of staff attend externally based INSET events in areas of personal interest, usually in their own time. No systematic procedure for school review exists.

After attending a day conference on staff development in primary schools, the head and deputy of the school decide to invite the conference organiser to work with the staff in setting up a programme of staff development. The invitation is accepted and, after a meeting between the head and the consultant, the following programme is agreed. Sessions are to be held on Monday afternoons from 3.30 PM to 4.45 PM.

5.6.1 Session one

This session focused on the importance of teachers' own development in the process of school improvement. It was agreed that the programme should arise from the current concerns of staff.

Question *There are twelve staff. Each of us has different concerns. They may be totally unconnected. Won't this produce a fragmented programme?*

Response (from staff as a whole): *An important aspect of staff development lies in the sharing of experiences. We should try to select/prioritise an issue on which all staff could work together.*

Decision *Before the next session teachers will identify their own current classroom concerns.*

5.6.2 Session two

The objectives of this session were:

- to discuss the classroom concerns identified by each teacher with a view to prioritising one or two for co-operative attention;
- to reflect on the process of working and reaching decisions as a group.

Teachers spent time listing their own personal areas of concern. These were read out and recorded by the whole group. As each point was raised, staff commented both on the importance that it had for them personally and for the school as a whole. This produced a lengthy and interesting debate which highlighted one of the difficulties of this approach: teachers' views on the importance of each issue varied considerably.

The debate was useful but the decision about what to focus on had to be left until Session three.

5.6.3 Session three

The list of staff concerns was presented on a flipchart. Staff were asked to reflect on the previous week's discussion and then rank the importance of each concern a) for themselves, b) for the staff as a whole. The list of identified concerns is shown in Figure 5.3.

A frequency count of the responses yielded the following scores:

1 Sharing courses (7 votes)
2 Classroom management (5 votes)
3 Record-keeping (5 votes)

After further discussion, it was decided that:

1 Sharing courses should be accomplished in report-back sessions after courses had been completed but that the ideas should not be

Figure 5.3 Staff concerns identified as a result of INSET session

Concern identified	*Personal ranking*	*Whole staff ranking*
• classroom management – creating time for practical activities		
• sharing INSET courses		
• development of group working		
• parental interest in/contact with the school		
• using the school environment		
• record-keeping		
• special needs		
• development of memory training/listening skills		
• children's reluctance to write/record		
• project work overlap		
• training to use resources		

pursued in depth unless they fitted in with the theme to be identified as a priority.

2 The issue to be identified should be one with which all staff (from reception to fourth year juniors) could identify and become involved. On this basis, it was agreed that classroom management with a focus on developing group work should be the priority area as this would not only enable all to be involved but would also provide insights into the different problems raised by differing age-groups in promoting effective group work.

This final session left everyone with a sense of achievement. An issue had been identified which had relevance for the whole staff. It would be misleading to suggest that all staff had participated equally in the debate; some views were expressed more forcefully than others and those of the staff teaching the junior age-range tended to command support. The headteacher took a back seat throughout the proceedings. This was both helpful in that it encouraged staff to express themselves freely but had drawbacks in that it meant that staff could not be sure of the support their activities would be likely to get. What was important was that everyone's concerns had been recognised, discussed and assessed in terms of their importance to all staff and that the final decision acknowledged the importance of identifying an issue with which everyone felt comfortable. As a consequence, the level of staff motivation and commitment to investigating the identified issue was promisingly high at this stage.

It could be argued that many of the concerns expressed by the teachers are those that already appear on many published questionnaires and checklists, but this is to ignore two important considerations:

1 Issues are far more meaningful to teachers when they are independently selected, rather than suggested.
2 Teachers using this approach for the first time will begin by using labels and categories for describing teaching that are currently available and commonly used.

Deeper understanding and fresh interpretation of the teaching process emerge with continual use of self-evaluation and group analysis and it is through this activity that classroom practice comes to be redefined.

During the following weeks, every member of staff collected data on the management of time, the composition of groups, the nature of group activities and children's involvement in group work using watches, field notes and observation of children and groups. The findings were talked over and analysed at meetings and suggestions were made as to how practices could be modified and monitored. Inevitably, value questions and individual differences and the impact of external pressures on teaching were raised and discussed during these sessions.

Some of the teachers' comments indicate the meaning that this particular attempt at staff development had for them.

> *For the first two sessions I could not see the point of what we were doing. It seemed a waste of time to be talking about things like how we were getting on together at meetings when there were so many other things to do. It was not until much later when we started collecting information about our own classrooms and discussing this together that I began to see how important it is to record in some way what is happening and see how this compares with what other people are doing.*

> *I feel as though I have more confidence – I am always worried whether I am doing the right thing and we are often told by advisers, HMI, that we should be doing things differently. I have enjoyed sharing what I have found in my classroom . . . and am pleased to realise that many of our difficulties are similar.*

> *I've learned to listen more and see that we can discuss things together without only arguing our own case.*

> *It has been rewarding to hear the comments of the infant staff.*

5.6.4 Comment

What do we learn from this case study?

1 Most importantly, we see that staff came to perceive that their 'needs' were their 'concerns' – they were not something external to their everyday classroom experiences but arose from, and were informed by, that experience.
2 Of the concerns identified, not one specific subject area is mentioned by any teacher. Staff are concerned with more wide-ranging, cross-curricular issues.
3 In addition to formal staff discussion, much informal conversation in the staff room came to centre on individual teachers' discoveries through the use of self-evaluation.
4 The 'climate' for staff development was being established through engaging in the process. Significantly, this was not achieved by the intervention of the head but by the decision of the staff to co-operate on an issue of common concern.
5 The whole process evoked values and provoked questions about what was actually happening in the classroom and how this could be improved. The staff development process thus became much more than an exercise in uncritically implementing new ideas or using a new work scheme.
6 Throughout the process, all staff remained committed to investigating an issue that they had identified themselves.

Thus, a new approach to needs identification and staff development has been tried at this primary school. It remains for the headteacher to build on this by providing an organisational structure and support system that will enable it to flourish.

5.7 Case study: planning the staff development programme from identified needs

In this second case-study school, the head and deputy recognised from the outset that the design of a programme based on identified needs would inevitably bring about a variety of responses from the staff, many of whom had always regularly attended externally based INSET. The school had several new members of staff, one of whom was a probationer. To accommodate this range of known and unknown variables the deputy, who had been given the position of co-ordinating the school's INSET programme, devised a checklist that was presented and explained to all members of staff (see Figure 5.4). This checklist contained similar areas to that used in the 'GRIDS' questionnaire but it had been modified to suit the school's own unique situation.

Figure 5.4 Responses to the needs identification checklist in the case-study school

*Numbers indicate the *total* number of responses from twelve staff. Two responses of 3, one of 2 and four of 1 give a total response of 12.

Please read through all categories included on this checklist. You should then indicate your preference for INSET in each category by placing numbers 1, 2 or 3 in the box opposite where:

1 means that you are fairly happy with this and INSET in this area is a low priority;
2 means that you feel INSET in this area would be beneficial; and
3 means that you regard INSET in this area as a high priority.

LANGUAGE

	*
1 Children reading in school	4
2 Children reading with parents	2
3 Children's writing (general)	7
4 Poetry	10
5 Spelling	9
6 Listening skills	5
7 Fiction-centred/Picture-book approach	5
8 Language awareness	9

MATHEMATICS

9 Problem solving in mathematics	23
10 The role of calculators	17
11 Mathematical games	23

SCIENCE

12 Content	16
13 Organisation	20
14 Environmental studies	15

OTHER CURRICULUM AREAS

15 History	2
16 Geography	3
17 Aesthetics	16
18 Handwriting	2
19 Music	11
20 Welsh	5
21 RE	7
22 Health education	8

COMPUTERS

23 Logo	20
24 Control	15
25 Design and Technology	22

PE/GAMES

26 PE lessons (from floorwork to apparatus)	11
27 Drama	12
28 Dance	10
29 Outdoor strategies/Team games	3

CLASSROOM MANAGEMENT

30 Group work	12
31 Record-keeping	21
32 Assessment (with objectives in mind)	23
33 Multicultural education	10
34 Equal opportunities	13
35 Planning special needs programmes	18
36 Marking – a common approach	20
37 TV programmes	2
38 Parents in school	4

In addition, please could you indicate on a scale from 1–3, with 3 as your main priority, if you are interested in the following strategies that have emerged from this year's INSET and Evaluation.

Visiting other schools to see examples of good practice	22
Practically based INSET with workshop sessions	27
Lecture-type INSET	0
INSET with parents to explain school procedures, aims, curricula, etc	20

The first modification concerned the staff identifying areas in which they personally felt a need for INSET rather than a perception of overall school needs. This allowed all staff the same perspective and was therefore as meaningful to new members of staff as to existing members. As such, it was essentially non-threatening and intended to promote a positive response.

The second modification asked staff to indicate on a scale from 1 to 3 their personal response to each of the categories itemised in the checklist. A response of '1' indicated that a teacher felt happy with a particular category whilst '2' indicated that the teacher would like to attend arranged INSET sessions in the area. A '3' response showed that the teacher considered the category one of personal priority.

In addition to an explanation of the checklist, all members of staff were informed at the outset of the system of funding INSET and the considered importance of providing INSET in areas perceived as priorities by the majority of staff. It was the opinion of both the head and the deputy that this essentially 'open' democratic approach would help to establish a participatory management style that would be ultimately transmitted to the children via teachers' greater combined and individual level of expertise.

Teachers completed and returned their checklists which were then collated by the deputy. From this position certain areas emerged as clear priorities and these were itemised. At this stage the deputy attempted to plan a programme for the following three terms, taking into account the money available for this process and the cost of buying in consultants for the identified priority areas. An outline of the programme for the year is given in Figure 5.5.

The actual order of the INSET sessions was to some extent dictated by the availability of suitable consultants and pressures created by the busy parts of the school year. The plan was presented to the staff along with a summative sheet of staff responses. The proposed plan was accepted as part of the overall staff development programme for the

Figure 5.5 A proposed outline for INSET for the year

The programme below is based on the returns for the INSET needs checklist issued earlier this term. Categories with the highest responses from staff were:

Problem solving in mathematics	(23)
Mathematical games	(23)
Assessment	(23)
CDT	(22)
Record-keeping	(21)
Science organisation	(20)
Logo	(20)
Marking	(20)

As agreed, sessions will be held on Wednesday evenings between 7.30 PM and 9.00 PM. Consultants have had to be booked in advance. It will not be possible to change dates or times. We will review the practicability of evening INSET sessions before next year's programme is finalised.

AUTUMN TERM	
1st Half Term	
Logo	4 hours with an invited consultant
Assessment/Record-keeping/Marking	3 hours in-house
2nd Half Term	
CDT	4 hours with an invited consultant
EASTER TERM	
1st Half Term	
Maths games/Problem solving	4 hours with an invited consultant plus 2 hours with own staff
2nd Half Term	
Maths games/Problem solving	2 hours with own staff led by curriculum co-ordinator
Assessment/Record-keeping/Marking	2 further hours in-house
SUMMER TERM	
1st Half Term	
Assessment/Record-keeping/Marking	A final 3 hours in-house

Total time: 24 hours *Total cost:* £238

Throughout the year as appropriate it is hoped to arrange visits in school time to see examples of good practice as they occur in other schools, notably in science organisation.

year but before arranging the actual dates staff were again consulted as to the most convenient and beneficial starting time for the sessions.

To maximise the available funding it had already been decided not to arrange this school-based INSET in school hours but the staff were still asked whether or not they would prefer the sessions at the end of the school day or in the evening. The staff unanimously decided to return in the evening and the first term's sessions were arranged in this way. (This plan was always conditional on each individual consultant's agreement to meet this requirement.) A breakdown of teacher directed time hours is given in Figure 5.6.

Figure 5.6 Teacher directed time – a suggested outline

Personal administration

30 hours (to include display)

Development work

10 hours Related to policy documents with specific reference to objectives. Additionally this time allocation will include the presentation of the policy documents to the new governing body.

School management and organisation

22 hours 10 hours to be set aside for parents evenings/consultations. 12 hours for staff meetings.

Staff development and INSET

30 hours

Further pupil involvement

12 hours Concerts throughout the year

Contingency

12 hours

11 hours approximately to be negotiated with each staff member for other school events, eg liaison meetings, sports events, etc

The first five sessions took place at two-weekly intervals and after the final session each staff member was asked to complete a simple evaluation schedule designed by the deputy. This asked a variety of questions concerning the method of presentation, the content of the sessions, the timing of the sessions and the implications for the school (children, teachers and resources). Teachers also had the opportunity to add any comments which they considered relevant either to this particular INSET or which might help the planning of future events.

Teachers were very forthcoming in their evaluations and generally considered that while the presentation, content and timing were all satisfactory there was a definite need to reappraise the school's equipment, materials and approach to particular areas of the curriculum.

The second term's INSET followed a similar pattern with the only real change being a slightly modified evaluation schedule to encompass two separate areas covered by different consultants. The format remained the same again in the third term with the initial plan being closely followed.

Towards the end of the third term teachers were once again asked to complete a checklist although, like the evaluation schedule, this had been modified to include several extra categories that referred to the methods of INSET delivery and the opportunity to visit other schools to see examples of good practice.

From the collated results it was clear that several areas had emerged as priorities. Additionally, it could be seen that teachers were in favour of workshop-style INSET with some form of practical involvement rather than lecture-style INSET. Teachers also valued highly the opportunity to visit other schools wherever this could be arranged.

The programme for the second year was, once again, a response to the majority of staff and appeared to bode well for the future. The only problem or drawback encountered was the reduction of money provided for school-based INSET by the LEA and the increased consultancy fee. This effectively reduced the number of consultancy hours in the programme. Nevertheless, the model for identifying INSET and its subsequent evaluation had proved efficient, effective and straightforward to manage and operate.

5.8 Conclusions

We have tried in this chapter to find ways of identifying needs around which a programme of staff development can be designed. In doing this, questions have been raised about the nature of 'needs' and the suggestion made that these can be determined, to some extent, by referring to the criteria by which they are assessed. Are they, for example, decided on as a response to new theories or ideas, changing legislation, external advice or do they arise as a consequence of close analysis of classroom practice? In reality, decisions about needs are likely to be influenced by all of these factors as teachers are generally aware of the importance of all these dimensions to their overall effectiveness. In fact, if the needs identified are to provide the foundation of an effective staff development programme they must:

- arise out of teachers' concerns;
- be appropriate in terms of the stage of development of the teacher and the school;
- relate to external considerations/pressures;
- be decided on collaboratively;
- be congruent with teachers' values.

The criteria by which needs can be assessed offers one way of looking at the process. Another is to look at the variety of methods available for the task. In examining the range of methods, it is significant that we have been involved in exploring the concepts and issues which underlie the whole process of staff development like those of:

- corporate decision-making;
- self-evaluation;
- sharing of experiences;
- explication of values.

In other words, deciding on the focus for staff development must be seen as part of the whole process; the methods employed at this stage must be those which will characterise the whole programme.

Which method should a school select from those available? This question in itself could constitute the start of the process. Staff need to be aware of the methods that could be used and encouraged to consider which would best suit their needs. In order for this to occur, headteachers need to be active in informing teachers about methods and their purpose and considering along with staff their appropriateness. It is likely that a range of methods will be used, depending on the stage of the process reached. But ultimately, the only way in which a school will know what is best will be by monitoring and evaluating the method and making adjustments which will increase its effectiveness.

Issues for consideration

a) What might be the needs of each individual member of staff at Greenbank School as indicated by the pen pictures given in Chapter 3?

b) Might these individual needs conflict in any way with the needs of the school or with national priorities?
c) How would individual staff respond to different needs identification strategies?
d) How could time be found for individual interviews to be held?
e) How would individuals respond in an interview situation as outlined in section 5.5 (this may be effectively drawn out using role play in training situations)?
f) How would staff at Greenbank respond to a consultant being brought in to facilitate a needs identification exercise as described in section 5.6?
g) To what extent could/should the head take a 'back seat' when teachers are openly discussing whole-school needs?
h) Which method should Mr Jackson choose to identify needs in his school?

6 Self-evaluation

6.1 Self-evaluation and change

We have stressed that there can be no real development in schools unless individual teachers continually monitor and improve their classroom practice. No staff development scheme can be fully effective, therefore, if teacher self-evaluation is not an integral part of the process. A number of questions are provoked by this statement:

1 What is the relationship between self-evaluation and school improvement?
2 How do the concerns of individual teachers relate to the external pressures for change to which schools are expected to respond?
3 How do teachers set about evaluating their practice?

There are no simple answers to any of these questions. However, we will now examine some of the possible consequences of self-evaluation schemes.

Before embarking on this, it is helpful to consider what is implied by the term the 'self-evaluating teacher'. And here we must begin by emphasising that the teacher who is actively involved in reflecting about and improving practice is one who is concerned that the education experienced by the pupils is of the best. At the same time, decisions about what is 'best' cannot be neutral. They inevitably involve the teacher in making a number of value judgements. Such judgements will be influenced by a wide variety of situation-specific factors (location of the school, needs of the child, resources available, personality of the teacher, etc). Underpinning these will be a number of fundamental concerns common to all teachers. These are:

- *moral* – the concern that each individual is equally valued and respected with all the implications that this has for the promotion of equal opportunities in relation to gender, race and class;
- *social* – the need to be aware of changing social patterns and values;
- *political* – the concern to uphold democratic values;
- *educational* – the concern to provide maximum opportunities for the enhancement of pupils' learning and understanding.

> Each individual is equally valued and respected.

The self-evaluating teacher is not one who is unaware of external pressures for change or the context (political and social) in which these arise, but is one who considers what these mean in the context of her own school, values and practice. In other words, proposals for change are evaluated in terms of aims as well as methods. This view of teaching preserves the notion of teachers being active in their own development while remaining aware of, and making judgements about, the educational implications of external developments and pressures.

But what does all this mean in practical terms? Staff development is about whole-school improvement as well as individual teacher development. This means that *all* staff must be involved in the process. How then can the two be brought together?

6.2 Self-evaluation and whole-school development

Pollard and Tann (1987) suggest that one approach would be to start from the point of an individual teacher having identified through self-evaluation an issue which has implications for the whole school. With this as a starting point, the following stages may then be considered:

1. Focusing colleagues' attention on the issue and achieving agreement regarding its importance and the practicality of change.
2. Analysing the issue in detail.
3. Analysing factors constraining change and factors which will facilitate change.
4. Considering ideas for innovation and deciding collectively on a

coherent programme of actions to introduce change.
5 Monitoring the change process – being prepared to amend plans and even to redefine the problem.

(Pollard and Tann, 1987)

The first stage is considered to be the most difficult in this process as it involves laying the foundations for change from which all else follows. It is at this stage that the teacher needs to be active in forming alliances and gaining support for the proposed change.

Another possible starting point could be the mutual sharing among the whole staff of concerns or experiences. Easen (1985) suggests a practical strategy for use in such an approach:

1 Teachers *individually* describe two situations in their school which lead them to think that school-centred INSET might be helpful.
2 The results of this exercise are taken to a group meeting where they are described and listed.
3 Teachers individually rank all the items listed in terms of their importance for the school.
4 The group comes to a decision about the ranking of these items. During this process it is important that teachers
   - avoid arguing for their own individual judgements;
   - avoid changing their mind only in order to reach agreement and avoid conflict;
   - avoid, if possible, techniques such as majority vote or averaging;
   - view differences of opinion as helpful rather than a hindrance in clarifying the group's thinking.

(Easen, 1985)

Once a group has decided on an issue, staff then define it in more specific terms before going on to consider the constraints on change and appropriate ways of tackling the problem.

The important feature of both these approaches is that the agenda for action arises out of concerns identified by *teachers.*

6.3 Self-evaluation and the teacher

We have just considered how teachers' concerns (as they arise out of their classroom experiences) can be used as a basis for whole-school evaluation. We need now to ask more specifically: a) What do we mean by teacher self-evaluation? b) How can teachers benefit from becoming involved in the process? c) How can it be accomplished?

The process of self-evaluation can be conceptualised in a number of ways. First, it can be described as the teacher's appraisal of him- or herself as a teacher, involving a careful examination of values and attitudes and the influence that these have on actual practice. For example, there are likely to be differences in emphasis between the practice of teachers who believe that the purpose of education is to equip children with skills deemed socially or economically useful and those who regard the process of enquiry and learning as sufficient justification in itself.

A second approach to self-evaluation is one which focuses directly on the activity of teaching itself and aims, by close analysis of specific episodes, to obtain a better understanding of process and consequences. If this perspective is adopted, teachers are provided with opportunities to develop tentative themes about the educational process.

More recent approaches to self-evaluation have developed out of the notion of 'the effective teacher'. These are predicated on the assumption that teachers can evaluate their practice against pre-indicated criteria which are considered to be characteristic of good teaching.

Whichever approach is adopted, the important feature of self-evaluation is that it engages teachers in active investigation and in an analysis of their values and practice. This constitutes the foundation on which decisions about future activities can be made. None of this suggests that teachers are not routinely involved in making decisions; clearly, this is an integral part of the teaching task. However, self-evaluation is widely considered to offer an added dimension to this aspect of teaching. Using evidence which is based on systematic investigation and reflection, it provides teachers with a valuable decision-making tool.

6.4 Why self-evaluation?

We have already alluded to the many reasons why self-evaluation is beneficial to teachers. But, of these, the most important aspect is that a teacher capable of self-evaluation is the one who is most likely to meet the current needs of pupils. With the changing nature of education in recent years, the process is now conceptualised as one in which pupils are encouraged to think for themselves and master the art of learning, and the focus has shifted from teaching to learning; from the passive acquisition of facts and routines to the active application of ideas to problems. If teachers are to help others to think for themselves, then a similar reflective process must predominate in their own learning. But, apart from the benefit to pupils, there is much evidence to indicate that the personal learning and development of pupils is best accomplished when pupils are engaged in reflecting on, and finding solutions to, issues that are self-identified. It thus provides a sound basis for improving teaching. If, as we have already argued, there can be no school improvement without teacher development, the case for self-evaluation becomes irrefutable.

6.5 Methods of self-evaluation

There is now a burgeoning literature on ways of carrying out self-evaluation. However, regardless of the method eventually adopted, learning may have little meaning if needs are defined by someone else; defining these needs is difficult and constitutes a learning process in itself. For self-evaluation to work effectively, it is important, therefore, that teachers develop the necessary skills and confidence to exercise independent judgement. A sympathetic and supportive school climate is indispensable here.

6.5.1 Self-appraisal questionnaires

One possible starting point for a teacher is to use a self-appraisal questionnaire. These are usually very broad in their coverage and encourage teachers to think in a general way about their teaching. Easen (1985) offers the following possible format for this kind of self-evaluation, which is typical of the questionnaires increasingly being used to provide information regarded as relevant for annual interviews between headteachers and staff members:

1 What do you consider to be your key activites as a teacher? Try to list them in order of importance.
2 Do you anticipate any significant changes in any of these activities during the next year or so? If so, try to specify them.
3 What aspects of your work give you the most problems at present? Try to list them in order of importance.
4 Consider and note what, if any, were the reasons preventing you from coping with these aspects to your own satisfaction.
5 Are there any areas where you feel that the school could make better use of your experience and talents? If so, try to note what those areas are and what you think that you have to offer.

6 What extra help or guidance do you feel you need to:
- meet the challenge of changes mentioned in (2);
- deal with the problems mentioned in (3);
- help you to use your experience and talents in the context of this school?

7 Which of these approaches would be most relevant to you? Indicate the order of priority by ranking from 1 to 6, 1 being the most relevant:
- secondment for a course at a higher education institution;
- short LEA courses on specific issues;
- visits to other schools;
- reading;
- school-based workshops/meetings;
- working alongside a colleague.

Another kind of model for self-evaluation is one which is based on the assumption that if the characteristics of an 'effective' teacher can be identified, individual teachers can measure their own performance in relation to these. Moyles (1988) has produced a model for self-evaluation which makes this assumption and this is made explicit when she states that:

> The principle behind the model is a fairly simple one: it is essentially a specialised checklist of identified basic characteristics of the effective teacher . . .
>
> (Moyles, 1988, p. 12)

Her checklist is organised into sections under the following headings:

Section 1 Curriculum content
Section 2 Relationships with children
Section 3 Children's progress and achievements
Section 4 Discipline and child management
Section 5 Classroom administration, organisation and display
Section 6 Teachers' professional attitudes and personality.

Against each statement in these sections the teacher rates him- or herself by giving a personal estimate of his or her own strengths and weaknesses on a continuum ranging from 'very inadequate' ('score' of zero) to 'excellent' ('score' of 10). Below we have an example of the kind of items included on the checklist.

In relating to children, I am able to:

- recognise and enhance the need in every child for a positive self-image;
- acknowledge and encourage children's ideas and contributions to activities;
- interact with individual children every day;
- thoroughly understand the personality needs of individuals and groups of children;
- participate in activities alongside children;
- understand when, and when not, to intervene in children's tasks;
- communicate with children easily in verbal and non-verbal situations;
- recognise the growing influence of the peer group on children's attitudes and behaviour;
- be essentially positive and encouraging in all dealings with children;
- provide a suitable adult 'model' for children;
- make myself aware of the child's background and other relevant information;
- use a variety of types of questioning to elicit thoughtful responses;
- make time to listen to children;
- recognise the need for awareness of equal opportunities for boys and girls;
- recognise the need for awareness of equal opportunities for children from all ethnic and cultural backgrounds.

The teacher is encouraged not to take long in responding to each item but to react immediately. It is not anticipated, therefore, that this will be a time-consuming exercise. Once each section is completed, and scores computed, the teacher is able to compile a histogram like the one shown in Figure 6.1 which will indicate areas of strength and weakness in general terms.

On the basis of this profile, teachers can decide:

- what they are doing effectively;
- where their strengths lie;
- where their weaknesses lie and what in-service requirements they have;
- what modifications are needed in classroom practices;
- the issues which they perhaps need to take up with the headteacher or other colleagues.

How useful are checklists of this kind in identifying teachers' real

Figure 6.1 Histogram of teachers' estimate of areas of strength and weakness

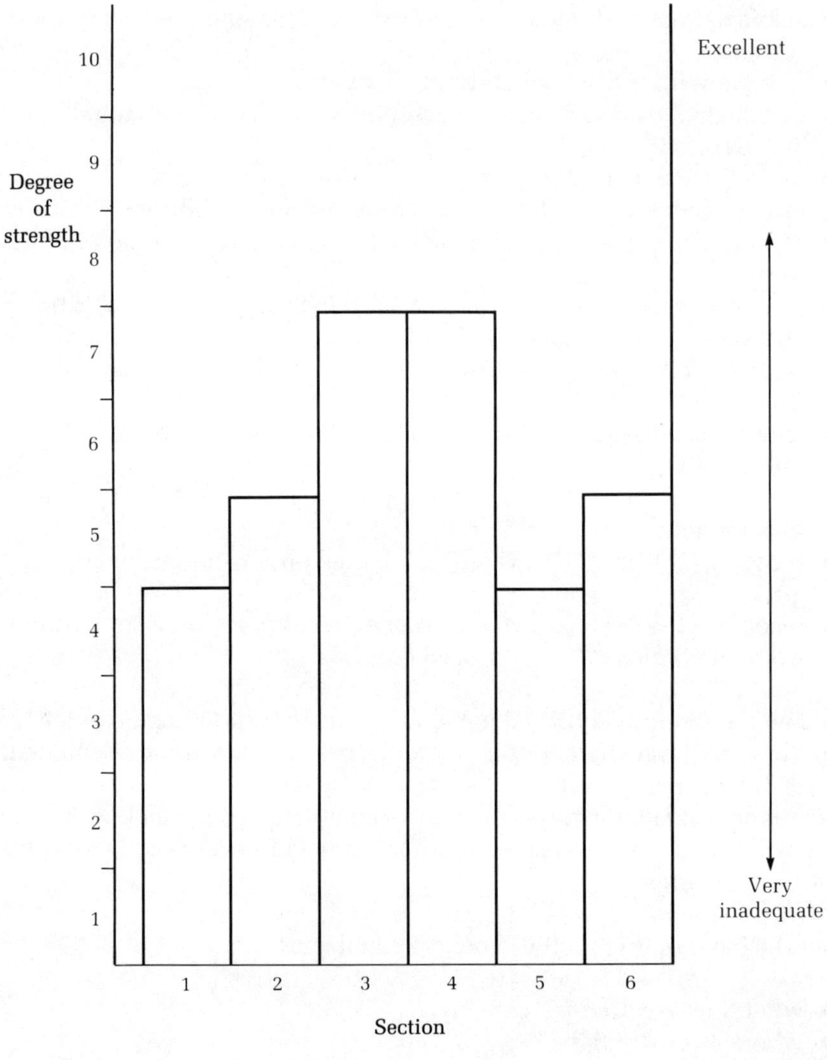

needs? The answer to this must really relate to how precisely you wish to have 'needs' specified and how closely these arise out of actual classroom practice. They are helpful in focusing teachers' thinking in relevant areas and in indicating generally where further classroom investigation on INSET provision may be required. However, it is difficult to see what they can achieve. They are really tools for raising self-awareness about teaching and do not provide a means of involving the teacher directly in the evaluation of classroom practice. They are more likely to confirm existing thoughts and impressions than provoke disturbing new ones.

Nevertheless, there are contexts in which checklists of this kind might be helpful and the following list of advantages and disadvantages may help to clarify which these might be.

Advantages	*Disadvantages*
• Can focus teachers' thinking on aspects of teaching which have been identified by fellow professionals as important • Provide a speedy way of reviewing a wide range of aspects of teaching • Provide quantified information	• The range of items covered could be daunting • Teachers may think these are the most important aspects of teaching • Teachers' real concerns may not be addressed in the list • Could encourage superficiality in that it asks teacher to review her teaching without much evidence

6.5.2 Self-evaluation in the classroom

Self-evaluation occurs when a teacher is actively involved in researching his or her own classroom practice and in making improvements in the light of the data obtained. This is done by using methods like questionnaire, interview, tape-recording, video recording, photography and the analysis of documents. The needs that are identified as a consequence of such self-evaluation arise directly from the information obtained by the teacher on what is actually happening in the classroom, how the learning process is being facilitated and what all this implies for future development.

Classroom-based self-evaluation can be undertaken in a number of ways and be used for a variety of purposes. For example, if a teacher has already identified an area of concern (eg relationships in the classroom) then he or she will want to employ investigatory procedures which will give further information about these. Clearly, the views of children and teachers are necessary here. A possible starting point might be to use an instrument like *My Classroom Inventory* (Frazer and Fisher, 1984) which gives pupils the opportunity of making their own observations on classroom life by responding to statements like:

	Answer
Some pupils are not happy in class	Yes/No

Some of the children in our class are mean	Yes/No
Many children in our class like to fight	Yes/No
In my class everybody is my friend	Yes/No
The pupils enjoy their schoolwork in my class	Yes/No

In addition to the inventory, children's views about the teacher, discipline, class rules, work and play should be obtained to provide as full a picture as possible of classroom relationships. The teacher then has evidence not only to aid understanding of the existing situation but also as a basis for decisions about future practice.

Many methods for obtaining information about classroom practice are available. These include tape recordings, video recordings, photographs, observation schedules and interviews. Further information on the use of these methods may be found in books on educational research methods such as those by Hopkins (1985); Bell (1987) and Walker (1985).

6.5.3 Needs identified by use of self-evaluation

So far we have considered evaluation in circumstances where the issues to be considered have already been identified. It is, however, possible for issues to be raised and needs identified as a result of careful analysis of what exactly happens in a lesson.

One way of doing this is to make a video of a lesson which should include a focus on the teacher, small group work and individual pupils. The video can subsequently be used as the focus of a wide range of activities with a group of teachers. The activities should be designed to encourage the viewer to observe, reflect on and interpret what exactly is going on in the lesson. Suggestions as to possible ways of structuring these activities have been made by Wragg (1987). They include exercises like:

- asking teachers to make freehand notes of whatever occurs to them as significant about the lesson and using these notes as the basis for subsequent discussion with the whole group;
- recording notes under headings such as 'class management', 'relationships', 'questioning and explaining', 'pupil response and participation', 'appropriateness of topic and teaching strategies' – or whatever is devised;
- using a checklist to determine either the existence or frequency of the teacher's classroom practices (eg the kind of questions asked by the teacher, the range of classroom management techniques employed);

- making notes in such a form that these can be given to the teacher as both a basis for discussion and a record.

It would be equally possible, of course, for the teacher to carry out all these activities on his or her own. (Initially, this might be perceived as less threatening.) However, if the analysis is conducted as a group activity it could be followed up by:

- discussing what the different approaches used have revealed about the teaching process;
- what implications the findings have for future development.

The important feature of a method such as this is that the agenda for action arises directly out of observation, discussion and reflection on the teaching situation. Furthermore, it is likely to raise issues that may not be easily labelled and which do not appear on checklists.

Issues for consideration

a) What differences of opinion are likely to arise between members of Mr Jackson's staff over issues of policy?
b) Are these differences likely to lead to overt 'conflict'?
c) How might this conflict be predicted and avoided?
d) How would Miss Grove, Miss Morris, Mrs Scott and Miss Pugh respond to the self-appraisal questionnaire reproduced in section 6.5.1?
e) How could Mr Jackson encourage the use of classroom self-evaluation methods as listed in 6.5.2?
f) What reactions might individual staff make to suggestions that they use tape or video recordings to obtain information about classroom practice?
g) How should Mr Jackson go about introducing the notion of teacher self-evaluation?

7 Designing the programme

7.1 Putting the programme in context

Having identified the staff development needs of the teachers in the school and prioritised them in the ways described in Chapters 5 and 6, the staff development co-ordinator or headteacher now has to devise a programme that will most effectively meet these needs.

The easiest way of doing this is to draw up a list of INSET activities which match the list of identified needs. The co-ordinator may spend some time at home or in school drawing up such a programme. It is not uncommon for heads or staff development co-ordinators to appear one morning with a sheet of paper outlining the programme for the year. If the co-ordinator is sensitive to the needs of the staff, the programme will reflect their requirements and there will be a good deal of support for the activities. However, if the co-ordinator treats the design of the programme as a purely mechanical management exercise, staff will have little ownership of the programme; they may feel a lack of involvement in its design and respond with a lack of commitment to its implementation. Stories of 'INSET detentions' abound. However, one should pity the poor consultant, brought in to deliver a staff development session, who is faced with a group of 'detainees' at 4.00 PM on a Tuesday and is charged with the responsibility of motivating them on the head's chosen topic!!

In the designing and running of programmes, therefore, co-ordinators should ensure that:

- staff see that it is *their* programme;
- the programme clearly reflects the identified needs of staff;

- staff feel involved in the choice of activity;
- staff feel involved in the choice of venue;
- staff feel involved in the choice of activity leader;
- staff feel involved in the evaluation process;
- staff feel involved in the follow-through to classroom practice;
- the programme remains flexible, with staff having the power to adapt it.

> Staff should have ownership of the programme.

The design and implementation of the programme is no less complex than the other stages in the staff development process. Sections on staff development in various checklists produced for school self-evaluation give some indication of the complexity involved. For example, a working party on in-school evaluation in Avon (1980) suggested that primary heads address the following questions on staff development:

> ... Are teachers' skills being developed and supplemented through a planned programme of in-service education both formal and informal?
>
> Is it possible for all staff to gain experience and confidence over a wide age range and across a broad curriculum?
>
> Do I ensure that teachers with curriculum responsibility have opportunities to influence their colleagues?
> - Informally?
> - Through staff meetings?
> - Through in-service days?
> - By working with pupils alongside a colleague?
>
> Are teachers who attend a course required to communicate to colleagues what they have learned from the course?
>
> Are there regular opportunities for the exchange of ideas both within the school and between schools?
>
> Do we have contact with playgroups, universities, colleges of education and other institutions?
>
> What additional expertise or interest is needed to improve the balance of the combined talents of the staff?

The ILEA (1982) document, *Keeping the School Under Review*, poses many more questions. Amongst them are:

> How are opportunities provided for staff who have been involved in INSET to share their knowledge and experience with colleagues in the school?
>
> Has the school an explicit policy and practice for staff development?
>
> Who is responsible for co-ordinating and implementing this policy?
>
> Does it include the provision of opportunities to discuss with all staff their professional progress?
>
> Does it include the needs of the school as well as the personal professional needs of individual teachers?

To gain maximum effectiveness from the programme a number of questions must be asked from the outset:

1 Why is the programme being run?
2 Who is it for?
3 What is the role of the head/staff development co-ordinator?
4 Who should co-ordinate staff development in the school?
5 What training is needed for the staff development co-ordinator?

7.2 Why is the programme being run?

'The simplest question is the most deceptive.' The truth of this statement is borne out by the fact that many schools have run so-called staff development programmes under the LEATGS 'umbrella' without having a clear understanding about why the programmes have taken place. For many teachers both the reasons for running the programme and its outcomes have been confused and a sense of direction lacking.

So what are the reasons for running a programme? O'Sullivan, Jones and Reid (1988) outlined three forces acting on the running of staff development programmes: political, professional and pragmatic.

7.2.1 Political forces – how you must *run staff development programmes*

These emanate from central government who, through their allocation of funding put direct pressure on LEAs to 'promote more systematic and purposeful planning of in-service training' (LEATGS Circular 6/86). By setting up National Priority Areas, controlling funding allocation and maintaining strict regulations on expenditure, central government clearly determines that part of staff development which is met through the training grants scheme. At the time of writing it would appear that LEAs will retain control over the LEATGS budget when other finances have been devolved to schools.

Acting under close scrutiny from DES and Welsh Office, LEAs have a duty to ensure that the INSET budget is spent effectively and, through their own policy statements, to encourage schools to formulate their own INSET policies and to utilise their INSET budgets accordingly. There is, therefore, pressure on schools to:

- formulate a staff development policy;
- identify needs of staff;
- manage and resource staff development programmes;
- monitor and evaluate their programmes;
- assess value for money of the programmes;
- address centrally identified National Priority Areas (specifically, the National Curriculum and its assessment implications).

7.2.2 Professional forces – how you should *run staff development programmes*

Professional forces emanate from the pundits in education: HMIs, higher education institutions and the teachers themselves. There is a growing body of theory relating to staff and professional development in schools. Much of it focuses on the management of institutional change and philosophies associated with implementing effective change. Others focus on the centrality of the individual and address ways of overcoming resistance to change. The credibility gap that often exists between philosophical approaches to individual professional development and what actually happens in school is always the most difficult for heads to bridge. *Professional* pressure is therefore put on schools to:

- make staff development programmes meaningful for the individual as well as the institution;

- follow a cyclical/process model of staff development;
- ensure that the staff development programme is *coherent*, not a package of unconnected activities;
- ensure that the staff development programme is seen as a process rather than a product;
- look to the future rather than overemphasise present or past needs;
- see staff development as a continuing process of teacher education;
- build reflexivity into the programme (ie encourage teachers to *think* about what they are learning and also put into practice what they have learned).

7.2.3 Pragmatic forces – how you probably will *run the staff development programme*

Regulations may be laid down by the DES and LEAs; theories and rational observations may be made by writers and thinkers in education; but schools are still managed and staffed by busy people with rising workloads and apparently diminishing time. No two schools will interpret guidelines in the same way; no school will follow guidelines to the letter. Inevitably, heads and teachers will find it difficult to carry out what they know to be right. Theory does not translate easily into practice where people are concerned. Staff development programmes are arguably easier to put into practice now than they were in the early 1980s because teachers have come to accept INSET as part of their professional duty; directed time has made management of whole staff groups a reality; providers and LEA support groups are increasingly geared to provide school-based activities or to meet common needs identified through LEA needs identification strategies.

However, for heads or their staff development co-ordinators, the forces of pragmatism often work against the ideal requirements. *Pragmatic* pressure exists on schools to:

- concentrate on the *how* rather than the *why*;
- provide instant solutions to immediate problems;
- provide in-service *training* rather than in-service *education*;
- provide INSET activities rather than staff development programmes;
- run a series of one-off INSET activities rather than a coherent staff development programme;
- work cheaply within small budgets;
- avoid systematic needs identification and evaluation procedures;
- manage the programme 'from the top';
- avoid day-time release because of lack of supply cover;
- look for 'courses' for staff to attend;

- avoid requesting feedback for danger of over-burdening staff.

To manage an effective staff development programme the aims must be clear. There may be conflict between LEA priorities and school priorities; between the perceived priorities of the head and those of the staff and between the staff as a whole and individual teachers. Co-ordinators will need to balance the political, professional and pragmatic pressures if the programme is to reflect the requirements of the main parties involved.

7.3 Who is staff development for?

Again, a simple question; often answered with the response: 'the pupils, of course'. Staff development should enable teachers to provide a more effective curriculum for the pupils in their care. There is no doubt that teachers exist to provide a broad, balanced, relevant and

Staff development is for the pupils.

differentiated curriculum for pupils. In the same way, staff development programmes exist in the first instance for the teachers. The programmes themselves should be broad, balanced, relevant and differentiated: *broad* enough to cover the pastoral and academic requirements of teachers; to provide the language specialist with experience of science and vice versa; to give experience of issues which teachers as full professionals need to consider but which would not normally present themselves through day-to-day experience; sufficiently *balanced* to enable training in the skills of teaching as well as giving a deeper perspective into why the methods are successful; to allow more time for the immediate problem without neglecting other less pressing issues; to provide opportunity for personal needs as well as school-focused needs and to meet these needs through off-site as well as school-based activities; sufficiently *relevant* to enable teachers to appreciate that the activities are meaningful to them as individuals as well as to their current roles within a particular school; and *differentiated* in recognising that teachers are at different levels of intellectual ability, at different stages in their personal and career development, have differing needs and interests, different perceptions and philosophies of education and differing levels of commitment towards in-service education.

The design of the staff development programme must therefore take into account the needs, interests and abilities of its participants. Morant (1981) identified four types of INSET need: induction, extension, refreshment and conversion. Figure 7.1 shows these. Each requires a different type of staff development provision.

Figure 7.1 The four types of INSET need

Teacher in-service need	*Nature of requirement*	*Appropriate staff development activity/ process*
Induction	1 *Teachers new to the profession:* induction programmes may be provided by the LEA and schools may elect to send new staff to them. New staffing arrangements under LMS (local management of schools) and the possible introduction of licensed teachers add a new dimension to induction. The use of a 'mentor' in school may fail to provide the invaluable links with new teachers in other schools which may be found at the moment.	• frequent personal contact with head/mentor; • opportunities provided to talk with experienced teachers and observe their lessons; • formal and informal discussions on topics such as classroom management, methodology; • meetings with other probationers, advisers/ inspectors, schools psychological service, etc; • inviting new teacher to attend PTA, governors' meetings; • inviting new teacher to impart new ideas, skills, knowledge and objective comments.
	2 *Experienced teachers new to the school:* the most experienced teacher may struggle in the short term when moving schools – new regimes, new traditions and practices; new pupils/ parents/colleagues.	• informal counselling by head/deputy to ensure smooth entry to school system; • induction into new routines; • familiarisation with school policy, etc; • invitation to impart best examples of good practice from previous institution.

Extension	1 *'Thinking teachers'* who reflect on practice often express a need to extend themselves intellectually. This need may be stimulated by self-evaluation, observation of colleagues, or by an INSET activity which raises questions rather than presenting solutions.	• supporting teachers' attendance on long courses (eg MA or MEd courses); • enabling teacher to feedback from that course to others on the staff; • encouraging classroom-based research (possibly stimulated by a series of INSET sessions with higher eduation consultant); • working with a consultant in school; • using student teachers to provide opportunity for observation of classes; • working as a trainer in other schools.
	2 *Career extension* – potential deputy/ headteacher.	• involvement in management of school; • 'job shadowing'; • delegation of responsibilities; • simulated interviews for deputy/headship.
Refreshment	1 *Updating in curriculum areas* to meet National Curriculum requirements.	• attend awareness raising INSET course within or outside local area; • lead school-based INSET session; • visit other schools with different approaches.
	2 *Updating in new approaches* to methodology, resources.	• observation; • training course(s) to master specific skills, eg information technology.
Conversion	*Adaptation* required following change in role (lateral) or promotion (vertical).	• INSET course; • shadowing experienced teacher; • contact with those having similar responsibilities in other schools.

We can design and manage the programme more effectively if we make the assumption that by enabling the teacher to develop there must inevitably be a 'knock-on' effect to pupils. In many ways it is a dangerous assumption to make. There are many prepared to testify that a great deal of money has been wasted providing educational courses which produced thinking teachers but had little effect on practice. Similarly, the 'value for money' of short, skills-training courses cannot be doubted. The profession will, however, become impoverished if the INSET curriculum becomes imbalanced towards training. The importance of evaluation becomes evident here; this is addressed in more detail in Chapter 9. For this reason we must keep in the front of our minds that staff development is primarily for teachers; that changes in pupil learning, classroom organisation and school effectiveness have to be brought about through teachers; that, although benefits to pupils will be an important consideration in programme design, if the programme does not initially meet the perceived needs of *teachers* it stands less chance of success.

Staff development is primarily for teachers.

We can take this question one step further. The design of the programme should reflect the different *sets* of needs existing within the school, that is, the needs of the *individual teacher*, *'functional groups'* (for example, teachers of infant or upper junior age classes) and staff as a whole.

7.3.1 The individual

For morale to be high, and for the programme to be credible, the requirements of individuals must be seen to be met. It is too easy to relegate the needs of individuals when resourcing whole staff priorities. The aphorism 'All staff development programmes are a compromise: *you* just happen to be unlucky' should not have a direct relevance to any one member of staff. Many teachers already feel let down by the ending of full-time secondments and the increasing necessity of following personal professional development courses in the evening; some consideration should be given where possible to those who bother to attend such courses in their own time. At its most basic, a simple attempt to show interest is often all that is required – 'How is your course going?'; 'Is there anything that I or other staff might be interested in?'; 'Spend thirty minutes with me tomorrow telling me what you have been doing on your course.'

All staff development programmes are a compromise;
you just happen to be unlucky.

7.3.2 The functional group

Within the larger primary school are sub-sets of teachers with common interests: nursery, reception and infant staff; staff with a management role; staff with interest in particular curriculum areas (music, art, science, etc); staff with skills in a particular area (computers, drama, sport, etc). The staff development programme should cater effectively for these functional groups (there may be as few as two teachers involved in a group). Staff development programmes for functional groups should pay dividends since the isolation often felt by the individual in learning and introducing innovation to the school is minimised. Staff learning together may support each other in their learning and provide moral support when attempting to introduce the innovation into the school. The staff development programme should acknowledge this and the programme design should facilitate group initiatives.

7.3.3 Whole staff

Many staff development issues will be identified by the staff as a whole: the introduction of the National Curriculum, assessment and record-keeping, information technology across the curriculum and classroom management are but a few. The programme will obviously use these issues as its core, with staff development for groups and individual staff development forming large and small satellites moving around it.

7.4 What is the role of the staff development co-ordinator?

The normal assumption is that the head will fulfil the role of staff development co-ordinator. As will be seen later, there are other alternatives to autocratic management of staff development in primary schools, but before we address the question of *who* should co-ordinate the programme we need to consider what needs to be co-ordinated and what the role of the co-ordinator entails.

7.4.1 What needs to be co-ordinated?

Like headship, the role of the staff development co-ordinator is an endless task. Any attempt to itemise the detailed requirements of the role soon overspills the time and space available and the task becomes daunting. It is nevertheless useful to highlight some of the more fundamental aspects of what the staff development programme entails. Figure 7.2 summarises some of the main aspects of the role. These can be expanded as follows:

Figure 7.2 Some aspects of the role of the staff development co-ordinator

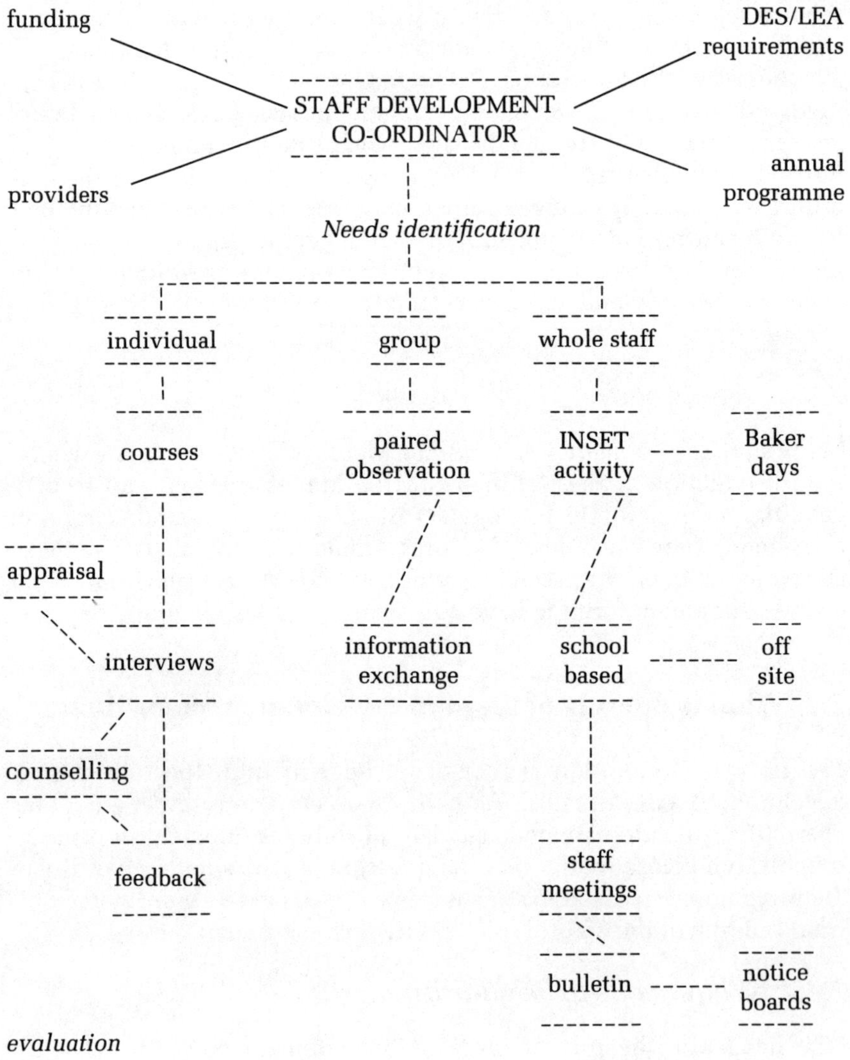

Managing the budget
Maximising the value from what is usually a very small school-focused INSET budget. 'Overspending is a crime; underspending is a sin.' The calendar year, academic year and financial year are, inconveniently, different. The programme has to be flexible yet funds have to be committed in advance if planning is to be effective.

> Overspending is a crime; underspending is a sin.

Linking with DES and LEA over policy
This requires a knowledge of national and local priorities. There will be heavy pressure to build these into staff development programmes. They may or may not reflect the identified needs of staff in the school.

Identifying and liaising with providers
Requires knowledge of the different providers available within the locality and regionally. INSET directories are useful, as are recommendations from other schools. Many organisations have mailing lists enabling co-ordinators to keep up to date with local expertise.

Liaising with other schools
Requires an active knowledge of what other schools are doing and how they are moving. The telephone is useful but there is no substitute for visiting other schools and conversing with heads. It may extend to arranging for teachers from other schools to deliver INSET sessions. It may involve a complex bartering system of staff with expertise from your own school.

Identifying and analysing needs
Of individuals, groups and whole staff. Requires knowledge and understanding of different strategies, time and status to implement them. Effective prioritisation is essential, as is the communication to staff of what has been prioritised and why.

Managing staff
Requires sensitivity, tact and diplomacy as well as firmness in setting clear goals.

Communicating with staff
Often forgotten but essential to the smooth running of any programme. Communication channels should flow freely two ways – co-ordinator to staff and vice versa.

Providing resource support
Time has to be created for staff development. This may involve

arrangement of internal cover or use of supply teachers for day-time release. Negotiation of after-school or evening attendance within, or sometimes outside, directed time may be necessary. Training materials need to be arranged for programmes and activities to run effectively. Schools should have access to the following: video playback facilities; overhead projector and screen; acetate (for writing and photocopying) and pens; flipchart, paper and pens; slide projector; cassette recorder; video camera, if possible. Support materials also need to be available for staff (library books, current documents from DES, LEA, etc, newsletters from curriculum agencies, eg NCC/SEAC, HMI reports on local schools or highlighting good practice . . .).

Setting out a clear staff development policy for the school
Whatever the views of the head on unnecessary bureaucracy, pressure is increasing on schools to provide evidence of coherent, planned structures for staff development to operate. An *ad hoc* approach to staff development is no longer permissible. Arguably, bureaucracy will replace adhocracy. At worst, staff development policies will be drawn up, filed and brought out on special occasions for HMI, LEA inspectors, etc. At best, the thought which goes into formulating a policy statement will crystallise ideas and result in action which might not otherwise have taken place. Staff development policies are looked at in more detail in section 7.5.

Co-ordinating the full programme
The staff development programme is more than a series of INSET activities. The whole is greater than the sum of its parts. It will require formal and informal communication; planned and incidental activities; core and support events; short- and long-term considerations.

Designing individual activities
Poorly designed activities can set back teacher support and impair motivation. Section 8.5 gives more detail on this.

Monitoring and evaluating the programme and ensuring follow-through
This links in with the identification of needs. It extends to formative and summative, formal and informal arrangements.

7.4.2 Who should co-ordinate staff development?

The answer to this question will depend on how the school is run. If the head traditionally takes full control of initiatives, the head will automatically assume the role of staff development co-ordinator. This has advantages and disadvantages:

Advantages	*Disadvantages*
• gains authority and respect; • eases links with appraisal of staff; • part of head's role anyway; • confidentiality; • career advice may be more appropriate/informed; • full background information on staff is accessible; • credibility; • only viable option in small school; • no fragmentation of authority – coherent approach to staffing.	• may unduly influence staff perception of needs; • may be undemocratic; • use of subjectivity, giving staff no recourse to higher authority; • job overload – too little time to do the role justice; • role conflict – appraiser counsellor developer.

Bearing in mind the diversity of responsibilities which fall under the staff development 'umbrella', many would argue that delegation is essential, and, as is stated later, delegation in itself is a staff development function.

Some models of management of staff development are shown below:

School A Head traditionally manages all activities. Oversees whole of staff development programme.

School B Head appoints deputy to be in charge of INSET (administration of INSET activities and support service) but retains responsibility for staff development (appointments, allocation of grades and responsibilities, career advice, interviews, etc).

School C Whole staff form a staff development committee with a policy-making brief. The chair is democratically elected. Responsibilities are shared. The head is a member of the committee with the same voting rights as other staff.

School D A small working group is elected to manage the INSET programme. Head retains the main staffing function; working group adviser on the staff development programme.

7.4.3 What training is needed for the staff development co-ordinator?

Whether the responsibility for co-ordinating the programme lies with the head or with a delegate, the co-ordinator requires training in the role. The following areas of training need have been identified:

- how to identify teachers' staff development requirements;

- how to analyse and prioritise these;
- negotiation skills;
- interview skills;
- counselling skills;
- approaches to appraisal;
- how to set up staff development programmes;
- balancing individual school and national requirements;
- strategies for effective teacher education;
- training skills;
- budgeting and cost effectiveness;
- methods of evaluation;
- presentation of evaluation reports.

Training may be provided through the LEA or may be available through local centres of higher education. Staff development co-ordinators with the responsibility for providing training and professional development for others often forget about themselves. In one authority for example, a group of primary headteachers and staff development co-ordinators booked a conference room in a local hotel and drew up their own training programme.

Courses on the management of staff development are becoming more common, many carrying recognised qualifications. Some examples of 20-hour courses on staff development in primary schools are given in Figure 7.3.

Although the concepts underpinning staff development are the same for all sectors, experience has shown that there is a marked difference in emphasis in the way these ideas are put into practice in the primary, secondary, further education and higher education sectors. Courses on staff development for secondary and further education co-ordinators may be of interest to primary schools, but the scale of operation (often 70+ staff in a school/college as opposed to (typically) less than 10 in a primary school) necessitates a more bureaucratic style of management. The limited number of books and courses available relating specifically to primary schools is remarkable when compared with the extensive bibliography and in-service support for co-ordinators in other sectors (see Bibliography). The most difficult problem for an LEA INSET co-ordinator is the sheer number of primary schools compared with secondary and further education establishments. This makes the training of co-ordinators difficult to manage. Primary heads/staff development co-ordinators must therefore take control themselves in many cases and, through clusters or federations, provide their own training. Most primary staff development co-ordinators will find their colleagues at secondary level very helpful in supporting training in the manage-

Figure 7.3 Examples of 20-hour courses on staff development in primary schools

EXAMPLE A
Level 1 (training level)
8 sessions at 2½ hours
Aim: to equip staff development co-ordinators in primary schools with the skills necessary to effectively manage the LEATGS programme in their schools.

Session 1 Defining the role: who does it?; what is entailed?; drawing up a detailed job specification.
Session 2 Identifying needs: analysis of different approaches; how to do it.
Session 3 Interviewing skills: simulation work, conducting a staff development interview.
Session 4 Designing a coherent staff development programme: what to look for.
Session 5 Running school-based INSET activities: making sure the programme runs effectively.
Session 6 Monitoring and evaluating INSET: why evaluate?; how to evaluate.
Session 7 Budgeting and administration: ensuring efficiency; maximising cost-effectiveness.
Session 8 Drawing up a school staff development policy: drawing together sessions 1–8; making staff development explicit.

EXAMPLE B
Level 2 (appreciation level)
8 sessions at 2½ hours
Aim: to give staff development co-ordinators in primary schools an insight into some of the professional issues underlying staff development.

Session 1 Background to INSET: James Report, TRIST, LEATGS, etc.
Session 2 Evaluating INSET: why?; what?; for whom? etc.
Session 3 Identifying needs: whose needs?; merits and demerits of different approaches.
Session 4 Teacher self-evaluation as the basis for staff development (1)
Session 5 Teacher self-evaluation (2): participants carry out research in own schools.
Session 6 Running a balanced staff development programme: alternative strategies.
Session 7 Teachers as adult learners: in-service *training* and *education.*
Session 8 Transfer of training: evaluating the effects of staff development on pupil learning.

ment of staff development. Formal or informal support groups may be set up in which staff development co-ordinators from local primary schools, secondary schools and tertiary colleges can discuss issues related to their common role.

7.5 Drawing up a staff development policy

7.5.1 The need for a workable policy

The trend towards increased accountability has resulted in a growing bureaucracy. Secondary schools and further education colleges, because of their very size, find the production of policy statements useful and necessary to give structure to the work they are doing. Heads of many primary schools, on the other hand, find the time-consuming nature of producing written guidelines a distraction from the work they feel they should be doing. They argue that curriculum guidelines or staff development programmes can be communicated easily without having to resort to paperwork. Anti-policy heads resent:

- spending time on 'paper exercises';
- producing a policy for 'show', ie a piece of paper which will only be referred to when inspectors call;
- producing a 'tablet of stone', ie once the policy is written, few will want to change it;
- producing a document which will look good in theory but bear little relationship to actual practice.

However, for a number of reasons, the need for staff development policy formulation is inescapable:

1 DES/Welsh Office regulations require each LEA to have a staff development policy which reflects practice in their schools.
2 LEAs require a written commitment from schools to the principle of staff development.
3 Teachers are entitled to know the procedures underlying the management of staff development in their schools.
4 The construction of a staff development policy may be a staff development exercise in itself if drawn up by a working group of interested staff.
5 Information on how teachers are supported in their professional development has to be communicated to others not on the staff (governing body members, for example).
6 Continuing professional development of teachers is no longer an

option. The contractual obligation of directed time for INSET and the use made of INSET days needs to be spelled out formally.

Heads may well look upon policy-making cynically and file policies away once written. This is bureaucracy at its worst. The alternative is an approach to staff development which is unsystematic and lacks coherence. This has been called adhocracy, and is equally as bad. The purpose of a staff development policy is to bridge the gap between bureaucracy and adhocracy. Good policies will do this effectively. Policies should be reviewed frequently so that they serve this function and reflect reality.

> Good staff development policies should fill the gap between bureaucracy and adhocracy.

There is no single way of presenting a staff development policy. The local authority may provide guidelines for schools to follow; clusters or consortia may agree a common approach; alternatively, schools may 'go it alone' in devising policy statements. Whatever style of presentation is used, however, for the policy to be an effective tool for the management of staff development, it should have some or all of the following attributes:

- be arrived at through a process of consultation (either with all staff affected or with a representative group). It should not be 'handed down by the head';
- be publicly available to all teaching staff, governors and other interested parties;
- derive from good practice within the school and elsewhere;
- be reflected in the practice of the school, not stand apart from what goes on;
- be 'user friendly' and jargon free;
- not be long-winded. Detail may be presented in point form;
- be well presented (typed), legible and easy to read;
- be unashamedly domestic (ie it should reflect what goes on in one particular school, not be an abstract document);
- link with the staff development policy of the LEA/cluster;
- link with school policy on curriculum and management;
- have a built-in review procedure.

7.5.2 Policy structure

There are many suggestions as to the form a staff development policy should take. The West Midlands Advisory Council for Further Education and Training (1988) suggests that policy formulation is concerned with:

- defining staff development
- clarifying roles and responsibilities
- defining structures in the management of staff development.

It uses a wide variety of examples of staff development policy documents drawn from further education colleges in the West Midlands. At first sight they seem to lack relevance for the primary sector. On closer reading, however, it is apparent that the structure of a policy document in further education may be similar to that of a primary school. The policy structures may be the same; the implementation will be totally different. In one example, interested staff meet to draw up a policy document. They address a series of questions, and these are shown below, together with responses which specifically relate to the primary school experience.

1 What is staff development for?
   (• to improve teacher performance;
   • to improve career and personal development;
   • to improve the quality of educational provision in the school, thereby directly helping pupils)
2 What does staff development affect?
   (• pupils;
   • curriculum;
   • staff;
   • resources)
3 How does staff development affect individual members of staff?
   (• improves performance;
   • enables reflection;
   • encourages self-evaluation;
   • improves motivation;
   • enhances personal and career development)
4 How will staff development be implemented?
   (• designated staff development co-ordinator;
   • staff development plan;
   • staff development interviews;

- school-based activities;
- day release;
- supply cover;
- directed time)

5 How will staff development be evaluated?
(• course feedback;
- classroom observation;
- questionnaire;
- interview feedback;
- formal report)

The policy document which was eventually drawn up was set out under the following headings:

1 *What is staff development?* (brief explanation)
2 *Identifying your staff development needs* (flow diagram showing how needs are identified and analysed)
3 *Programme outline* (timeline for a typical staff development programme)
4 *Monitoring and evaluation* (guidelines and requirements, eg access to classroom)
5 *Responsibilities* (of co-ordinator and curriculum leaders)
6 *Policy review* (procedure for changing policy and process).

A framework for setting out a staff development policy document is provided by Hewton (1988), who uses the acronym ASPECT to illustrate the elements of a staff development policy. They are

Aims – why staff development? A brief indication of the purposes of staff development should be given.
Structure – who co-ordinates and how? What are the responsibilities and relationships of the head, staff development co-ordinator, curriculum co-ordinators, classroom teachers?
Programme – what will be the pattern of staff development? An outline of the nature of provision should be given, for example, expectations of teachers in directed time, in-house support and typical arrangements for staff development days.
Evaluation – how and when will the programme be reviewed? Who will evaluate? How and to whom will the results of the evaluation be presented?
Cost – what are the resource implications? Supply cover costs, evaluation costs and general costs of provision should be broadly indicated in relation to the likely budget for school-financed INSET.

Timing – what can realistically be achieved in a year? What activities are ongoing? Which have highest priority?

As stated earlier, the construction of policy documents can be a staff development exercise in itself. Staff development co-ordinators (heads and/or deputies) from groups of schools have found it useful to meet, share experiences of managing staff development, draw up an outline structure with common elements (for example, a section on aims will be common to most schools) and return to their schools to complete the individual elements of the document. Some schools have typed or word processed their finished versions on A4 sheets. Others have been more creative in their presentation. For example:

- use of coloured paper (all staff development memos, programmes, reports, etc might be 'colour coded' on green or blue paper);
- use of computer graphics (desk-top publishing may be used to produce diagrams such as the staff development cycle or flow charts which explain the process more clearly);
- construction of a small booklet which matches other school documents (for example, booklets for parents of new intake children, curriculum policy documents, booklets for student teachers).

We live in an age where marketing is important. The psychology of 'packaging' cannot be understated. The credibility derived from a well presented staff development policy document will pay dividends when the policy is implemented. The programme must then live up to the policy.

7.6 Planning the programme

It is almost impossible to guarantee that a staff development programme has one hundred per cent success. INSET activities which work well in one school may flop badly in another; consultants and providers with impeccable reputations often 'fail to deliver'; staff with many years' experience may attend courses or conferences but be less successful at feeding back what they have gained. Even the most carefully planned activities, arranged to take place when other commitments are minimal, suffer from the effects of teachers being constantly busy. Only full INSET days allow staff the luxury of giving the whole of their attention to the activities that have been arranged.

It is also the case that some teachers are professional cynics. They lie in wait to complain (not formally but usually loudly enough to be heard) about time being wasted on INSET when they could be teaching or putting up displays; of money being frittered on incidentals (for example, training equipment and resources) instead of books for the children; of teachers 'indulging themselves' on INSET days when children are at home losing a day's schooling. The response given by many to this attitude is:

> It is not the amount of time spent in the classroom which is important but what goes on in that time.

Justification of the time spent on staff development is not difficult, but it does depend very much on the effectiveness of the programmes being offered. If teachers are constantly subjected to badly planned or badly organised activities then INSET does become a waste of precious time. The staff development co-ordinator carries the responsibility for ensuring the credibility of INSET.

The keys to successful programmes lie in careful planning, even better communication, efficient co-ordination and honest, open, participative evaluation.

Careful planning
Staff should know what the programme is intended to achieve (different aims and objectives for different components and, for individual development, for different staff). Involve staff throughout in the planning of their personal programmes.

Effective communication
Staff need to be aware of the aims, content and implications of the programme well in advance so that they can be sure the programme reflects their identified needs; and, if they have been involved in the planning, this stage should serve as confirmation rather than providing new information. A staff development bulletin or newsletter is a useful way of reinforcing plans; a well kept staff development notice board is an absolute must (see Figure 7.5).

Efficient co-ordination
Dates and times should be adhered to; careful organisation should enable activities to run smoothly; staff should not 'see behind the scenes' unless they show an interest in what happens there. However, a basic understanding of the constraints on staff development co-ordinators may provide some explanation of why the programme follows a particular format, and at the same time reduce misconcep-

tions and even generate some sympathy for the difficulty of the co-ordinator's task.

Participative evaluation
The best answer to critics of time and money spent on teacher development is to emphasise the benefits gained from the activities. Evaluation should involve all who participated in the programme, should accentuate the positive and be open about the negative. The evaluation report should be made public (with copies at least to staff, governors, LEA INSET adviser, and used as the basis for discussion of the programme for the following year. (It should not be a lengthy document – brief comments will have more value than long, wordy paragraphs.) Chapter 9 gives more detail on this.

Figure 7.4 Example of a staff development notice board

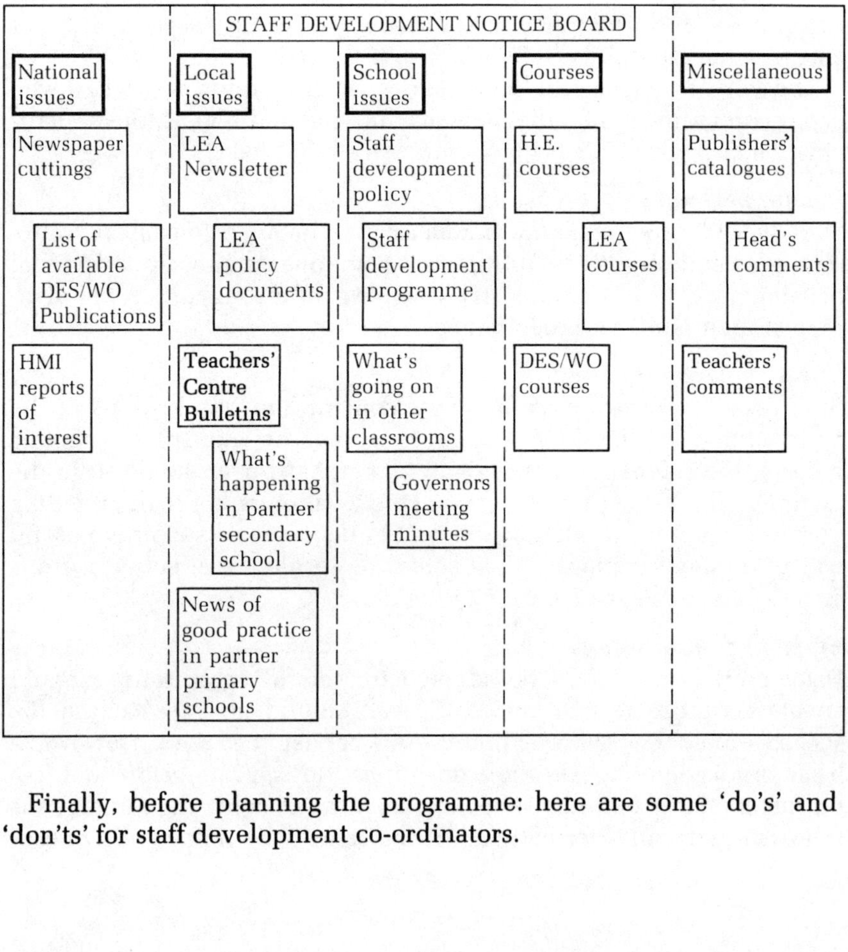

Finally, before planning the programme: here are some 'do's' and 'don'ts' for staff development co-ordinators.

DO

For the programme as a whole

- involve all staff in the programme design;
- negotiate specific roles/responsibilities for individual staff;
- conform with the school's staff development policy;
- recognise and build on the strengths/expertise of individual staff;
- extend these strengths through the programme itself;
- set achievable aims and objectives for the programme and for individual components;
- discuss aims and objectives with staff before finalising them;
- communicate the final arrangements to staff;
- ensure that the programme is seen as a whole, not as a series of fragmented activities;
- clarify and make explicit any commitment required of staff during or after the programme (eg will teachers be expected to try out ideas in the classroom?; will individuals who have attended courses be expected to 'cascade' what they have learned back in school?);
- build in an evaluation procedure and criteria for evaluation from the beginning;
- ensure that monitoring and evaluation are seen as part of the programme, not separate from it;
- vary the type of activity as much as possible;
- use a notice board, bulletin, handbook, staff meeting agenda, etc to keep staff up to date with plans;
- calculate the real costs carefully and aim to get maximum cost effectiveness;
- take account of hidden costs, eg disruption of classes, and build these into the evaluation;
- look for examples of good practice locally (consult with advisory service, local heads and co-ordinators, local higher education providers);
- obtain as much information as possible about local providers of primary INSET;
- utilise *free* support services (LEA-provided centres, advisory teachers, etc) for inputs or resource materials;
- negotiate with higher education institutions (eg if *you* take students on teaching practice, can *they* arrange for the supervising tutor to spend time running INSET in the school? Can they offer accreditation for school-based courses?);
- get on the mailing lists of organisations which produce relevant educational material;

- ensure that *all* staff have access to DES/Welsh Office publications sent to the school (write off for extra copies if necessary).

For individual activities

- produce documentation 'professionally' (typed/word processed documents are more effective than hurriedly handwritten sheets produced on a spirit duplicator);
- circulate appropriate reading/documentation *before* the activity where necessary;
- confirm date and time well in advance;
- ensure date of activity doesn't fall in busy period (eg two weeks before Christmas);
- ensure that time of day and length of activity are appropriate;
- if follow-up is required, make the commitment clear before the activity gets under way;
- ensure purpose of activity is understood by all who will be involved (including any external providers);
- confirm all details in writing with provider (if used);
- ensure a suitable venue/learning environment (comfortable yet work-oriented; coffee and biscuits available, etc);
- set up the room before the activity begins (ensure overhead projector works as small inefficiencies can spoil the learning process);
- negotiate the evaluation with the provider/activity leader.

DON'T

For the programme as a whole

- impose the head's priorities on staff in the guise of a staff development programme;
- pressurise unwilling staff to attend – negotiate carefully to avoid negative reactions;
- run needs identification exercises and not follow them up in the programme (unless more urgent issues emerge during the year in which case re-run the needs identification exercise);
- reprioritise staff's needs by top-down interference;
- ignore group needs (eg nursery/infant teachers);
- ignore individual needs (try to meet them in some way within the broader staff development programme);
- confuse 'wants' with 'needs' (see Chapter 5);
- pander to the 'professional course-goer' at the expense of the teacher who needs support but will not come forward;
- make the aims and objectives of the programme too broad or impossible to achieve;
- overspend;

- underspend;
- ignore existing staff expertise;
- expect staff to lead successful INSET activities without some moral or resource support. Advice on training skills may be needed;
- communicate only through indirect methods (notice board, bulletin, etc). Talking to people works better;
- bolt-on the evaluation at the end of the programme;
- forget to put into practice what has been learned;
- abandon all reference to a topic once the INSET activity is over.

For individual activities

- allow the activity to proceed at a slow pace but at the same time ensure the sessions are intensive and productive;
- overburden staff with paperwork or reading matter;
- run activities in smoke-filled staffrooms;
- leave providers with the task of setting up the room (chairs, OHP, screen, etc);
- use the same format (eg discussion groups for all activities);
- use people you don't know to deliver INSET without clarifying your objectives beforehand;
- forget that teachers attending an INSET activity are adults in a learning situation. Build on good classroom practice;
- expect curriculum co-ordinators to be expert 'trainers'.

Issues for consideration

a) Which of Mr Jackson's staff would most benefit from induction, extension, refreshment and conversion activities as listed in Figure 7.1?

b) What functional groups (7.3.2) exist within Mr Jackson's staff? How might their staff development needs be catered for?

c) Should Mr Jackson himself take on the role of staff development co-ordinator or should he delegate?

d) To whom could he delegate the role of staff development co-ordinator?

e) How might Mr Jackson ensure that:
   - the staff development co-ordinator received appropriate training?
   - all staff were aware of the co-ordinator's role and their own responsibilities in supporting that role?

f) What might a suitable programme for the staff of Greenbank School look like?

8 Approaches to staff development

8.1 What goes on at the moment?

Many heads and staff development co-ordinators, when asked to report on what staff development programme exists in their schools, often 'miss the wood for the trees'. A great deal of normal practice has staff development outcomes, often much more effective than formally organised activities. One of the most appropriate forms of staff development, conversation in the staffroom, is perhaps the one most under threat as the demands of the job pull people away from what is wrongly seen as time wasting. Teachers frequently 'talk shop' in staffrooms. Ironically, one survey has shown that teachers are becoming more reluctant to go into staffrooms in some schools since the unloading of new ideas often creates stress. Some have the attitude: 'stay in the classroom, ignore what is being said, hope it goes away!'

Staffroom conversations *may* have the following staff development outcomes:

- sharing views on pupils/families (pastoral exchanges);
- sharing views on difficult children/groups and how they are handled (behaviour modification);
- sharing views on successful lessons (methodology exchanges);
- sharing views on teaching materials used (resource exchanges);
- sharing views on topics which may be followed up in other years (curriculum exchanges);
- sharing views on the implications of recent government educational documents (political/educational exchanges);

- sharing views on the DES/advisory service/head/deputy (management exchanges);
- sharing views on the staff development programme (staff development exchanges).

It is unfortunate that the most honest evaluation of activities and processes within education often takes place in such informal situations and is then lost. This 'bike shed' evaluation is one of the leakages to the system and needs to be harnessed if negative 'gossip' is to be

Figure 8.1 A classification of staff development activities

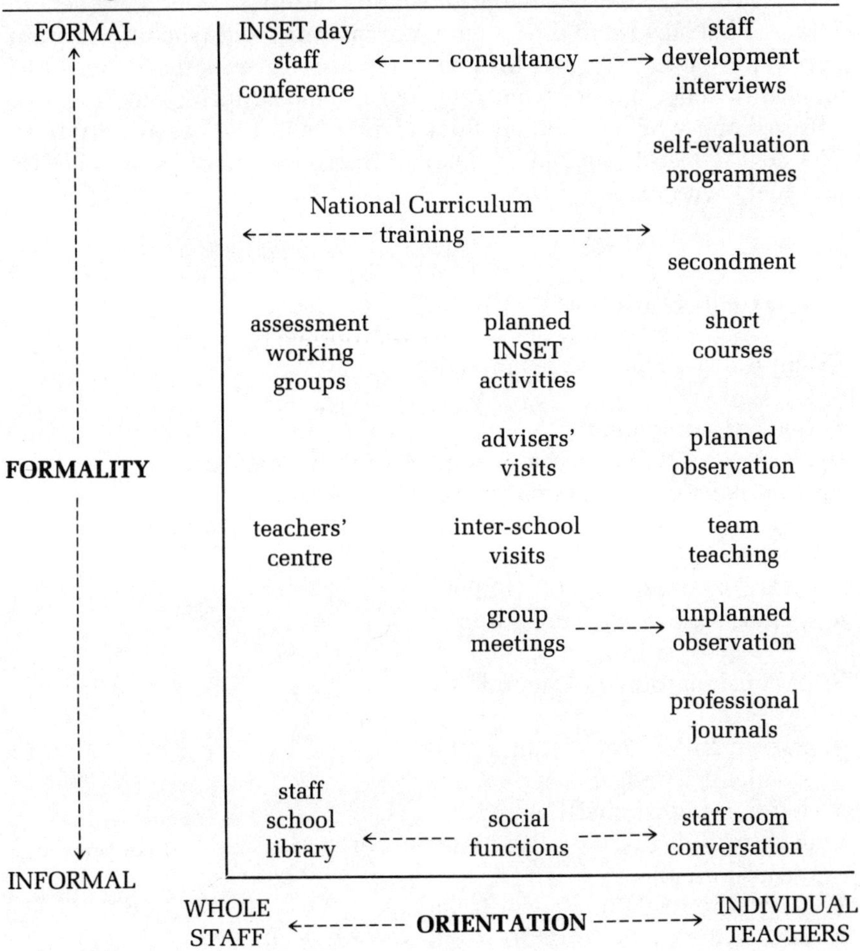

turned to positive effect. Some ways of doing this are considered in the next chapter.

'Bike shed' evaluation is a leakage to the system

Any analysis of what staff development activities teachers do as part of their job will obviously differ from school to school. The primary school where closed-door classroom teaching is the norm will have a much lower exchange of ideas than a more open school, where there is constant staff interchange. Some activities with staff development outcomes are shown in Figure 8.1. We can differentiate between INSET activities which take place out of school and those which are school based. A balanced staff development programme will take into account both types of activity, and for maximum effectiveness there should be an acknowledgement of what goes on in schools (during out-of-school courses) and what goes on outside schools (in school-based activities). The next two sections look in detail at the two types of INSET activity and their overlap.

8.2 Out-of-school activities

Examples of such activities include:

- one-day conference;
- single-session activity after school (eg at teachers' centre);
- short course over eight or ten evening sessions;
- visit of teacher to another school to discuss with/observe other teachers;
- formal meeting called by LEA;
- membership of working group.

Prior consideration will include:

- assessment of cost of course (fee, travel, subsistence) in relation to total INSET budget;
- determining who will meet that cost;
- deciding whether activity should be part of directed time or personal commitment;
- ascertaining whether cover is available (if day-time activity);
- assessment of the appropriateness for individual member of staff

(career potential; relating to present role, etc);
- assessment of the appropriateness for school (high on identified staff development priorities?);
- calculating the benefits likely to accrue to individual, whole staff, pupils;
- deciding whether one or two staff should attend (feedback is more effective if the experience is shared);
- making a decision about how the INSET will be evaluated;
- establishing what feedback/follow-through will be required (written report? display? cascade to all staff? arrangements for other staff to observe classroom application?).

Most of these points will need to be covered in discussion with the member of staff concerned. Although it may be inappropriate to talk in terms of a formal 'contract', it is less than fair to expect teachers to run feedback sessions for other staff if they have not been given prior warning of this. It also enables teachers to attend the activity armed with questions of a school-focused nature, thus maximising the value of the activity for them.

One way in which the benefit of an out-of-school INSET activity can be maximised is given below. Typically, an *ad hoc* situation has operated in schools, where a member of staff attends a course but has no opportunity to share the experience that has been gained (except, perhaps, for a loosely-structured 'feedback' session in a staff meeting). The example given below shows how one primary school fully integrated the attendance of the science co-ordinator on an out-of-school course with a detailed school-based programme of INSET for science. The steps in the procedure were as follows:

1 Booklet advertising local short courses arrives in school.

2 Staff development co-ordinator photocopies contents page or summarises courses available and
   - posts list on staff development notice board;
   - approaches interested staff directly.

3 School science co-ordinator is informed of a 20-hour course on **'Primary Science for the National Curriculum'** – one evening a week for 8 weeks.

4 Staff development co-ordinator discusses feasibility of the science co-ordinator attending the course (see above). There is agreement that:

- the cost of the course and all expenses will be met by the school/LEA;
- it will count against the teacher's directed time (20 hours) (though there will be common agreement that the full implications of attendance will exceed the allocated hours);
- the school will arrange for two half days of cover to enable the teacher to prepare feedback materials for staff INSET;
- objectives are set which relate to the *school's* intended benefits from the course, as follows:

By the end of the term, staff as a whole will:

i) be aware of the requirements of the science component of the National Curriculum;
ii) under the guidance of the science co-ordinator, discuss the implications of the science 5–16 guidelines for reception, infant and junior age-groups;
iii) begin to identify ways of building in progression in science from reception to junior age-range;
iv) through the science co-ordinator, be informed of how other schools are approaching this work (from the co-ordinator sharing views with other course participants);
v) be exposed to ways of teaching science at primary level;
vi) use ideas on teaching science in the classroom with pupils and discuss the outcomes (with other staff).

5 These objectives
- commit the science co-ordinator to getting as much as possible out of the course;
- commit the science co-ordinator to cascade the ideas obtained on the course;
- commit the staff to using some of the ideas and discussing the practice.

It also helps the course leader who asks, in session one of the course, what the participants expect and what they would like from the course. The objectives stated above are not incompatible with what the course leader intends to do.

6 Science co-ordinator attends the course. After four sessions she has sufficient information and understanding to hold the first staff feedback session on the National Curriculum requirements. The programme runs as follows:

Weeks 1–4	Science co-ordinator attends sessions 1–4 of course (one session per week for 4 weeks).
Week 4	School-based INSET session led by co-ordinator looking in detail at National Curriculum requirements. Co-ordinator given cover for afternoon to enable preparation for session. Objectives i to iv above are covered. Co-ordinator takes issues back to course for discussion. Staff request course leader to come to one of their INSET sessions.
Weeks 5–7	Staff focus on teaching science. Science co-ordinator invites staff to observe her working with her class. The presence of a student teacher in the school enables some staffing flexibility. Student teacher also asked to contribute ideas from college on teaching science. INSET sessions in weeks 5–7 after school. Science co-ordinator sets up equipment in one of the classrooms. Staff discuss ways of teaching science at all levels. Staff agree to try out ideas with their pupils.
Week 8	Science co-ordinator reports back to course leader (this forms part of the course evaluation). Course leader agrees to attend one of the school-based INSET sessions.
Week 10	INSET session held in week 10. Course leader present ($1\frac{1}{2}$ hours) to share ideas and focus on classroom application. Teachers report back on classroom experience. INSET session in week 11 consolidates progress so far.
Weeks 11 and after	Science co-ordinator produces a *brief* report on progress in science. Reception, infant and junior staff contribute short descriptions of work with pupils. The report is typed and copies sent to all staff, governors, course leader, science adviser. Science co-ordinator in consultation with the staff development co-ordinator arranges future INSET sessions (two per term) to 'keep the pot boiling'.

8.3 School-based activities

Examples of such activities include:

- school-based INSET day;
- one or a series of sessions run in school by 'consultant' (advisory teacher, higher education lecturer, etc);
- activities run for cluster of primary schools with venue shared by participating schools;
- 'in-house' INSET led by school curriculum co-ordinators;
- two teachers from a working group (eg on assessment) report back to the rest of the staff;
- teacher from local school sharing ideas with staff.

Prior consideration will include:

- finding providers who will be able to meet the specific needs of staff within budgetary limits;
- finding provider who is credible with staff and has appropriate training skills (college lecturers may lack credibility or be considered over theoretical; practising teachers may be poor at communicating ideas to peer group);
- matching school needs without compromising provider's perspective (someone with expertise in language work may hold views on reading schemes which are contrary to those of your staff);
- acquainting provider with the 'culture' of the school (hidden agendas, expertise of teachers, advice on grouping for activities if required);
- giving individual teachers moral and resource support to lead INSET sessions;
- ensuring, where possible, two rather than one teacher having responsibility for the session;
- negotiation of time, venue, cost and content;
- ascertaining resource requirements (handouts, materials, equipment, etc);
- arrangements for monitoring, formative and summative evaluation to be built in;
- arranging time and venue with staff;
- publication of programme/prior reading/information on provider, etc, if required;
- negotiation of 'after care' (what will be classroom outcomes?; will provider return to observe outcomes?).

8.4 Support for individual teacher development

This is the broader interpretation of in-service education as professional development. Examples of such activities include:

- *job shadowing* (deputy works closely with head; grade A allowance teacher works closely with the staff development co-ordinator);
- *delegation* (specific roles of responsibility are negotiated with individual staff);
- *observation and participation* (where cover allows, making classroom observation and participation a common, natural and non-threatening occurrence);
- *visits to other schools* (to include observation and participation where possible);
- *staff development interviews* (not to be confused with appraisal interviews, though the two have common elements);
- *personal support* (identifying career aspiration and facilitating career development. An example of this is a simulated job interview given to a teacher applying for a headship in another school);
- *using teachers as trainers* (involving teachers in the delivery of INSET to colleagues and others is a very rewarding form of staff development);
- *involvement of students* (ensuring that teachers maximise the benefits of having student teachers attached to their classes.) Teachers may learn from the student's objectivity and recent experience and may also benefit from an extra pair of hands, freeing them to try out new ideas with smaller groups. The student's college tutor may also be used. More detail on how to extend this triangular relationship, known as IT-INSET, is given in Ashton *et al* (1983).

One example of such individual support is the *staff development interview*. Essentially, this is a formal or semi-formal discussion between the staff development co-ordinator and an individual teacher. It is important that: all staff go through this process; the 'interview' is held at an appropriate time (3.30 PM on the last day of the summer term is *not* appropriate!); the interview lasts for at least 30 minutes; some record is kept (preferably by both participants) of the conclusions reached and any action which needs to be taken.

Since interviewing requires certain skills (understanding body language, opening and closing the interview, avoiding unintentionally threatening behaviour, avoiding making promises which won't be upheld, etc) some training in interviewing skills should be made available to staff development co-ordinators. This is best provided through the LEA as a centralised course.

The 'culture' of the school will affect the credibility and nature of the interview. Some heads will conduct it themselves on a strictly formal basis with a leaning towards appraisal (what aspects of your teaching need to be developed?); others will make one interview serve a number of purposes (identifying individual and school needs, ascertaining expertise which can be utilised for staff as a whole, obtaining evalua-

Figure 8.2 The staff development interview

Depending on the degree of formality required, the interview can be fully or semi structured. If it is formally structured, both interviewer and interviewee should have sight of the questions to be addressed. If it takes place as an informal 'dialogue', the purpose of the occasion should be clear to both participants and the areas to be covered should be agreed beforehand.

PROMPTS

The job as a whole?

1 What aspects of your job have given you most satisfaction this year?
2 What do you consider yourself to be particularly good at?
3 What would you say were your main areas of interest?
4 Which aspects of your job have given you most frustration this year?
5 What training/staff development support would help to reduce this?

The staff development programme

1 How, in your view, is the programme going?
2 Has it helped you in any way?
3 Have you been able to contribute to the programme?
4 Could you contribute to the programme?
5 How could the programme reflect your personal interests more effectively?

The future

1 What support would you like to receive:
   - to develop your classroom work?
   - to develop your work in the school in general?
   - to enhance your own professional development?
2 What expertise/interest do you think you could share with colleagues?
3 Would you be prepared to share your ideas?

Action plan

Points for action for
- the staff development co-ordinator;
- the teacher.

tive information on the staff development programme, etc). Heads may use it as an opportunity to motivate staff by showing interest and support for their ideas; or they may prefer to use the term 'dialogue' rather than 'interview'. Some heads will delegate the task to an INSET co-ordinator, preferring to keep staff development separate from appraisal.

An example of a staff development interview schedule is given in Figure 8.2.

8.5 Designing the activity

The following guidelines will be helpful in designing INSET activities. Although they may appear over-formal for activities with only a small group of staff, they are nevertheless important to bear in mind so that the activity has some direction and purpose. There is little that is more frustrating to staff than an INSET session which is confused in its purpose, follows a format adopted many times before, is uninspiring in its creativity, and which covers content or issues which could have been addressed in half the time. The credibility of the programme as a whole, and of the staff development co-ordinator, often rests on the success or failure of individual sessions.

8.5.1 Set clear objectives for the activity

These should:

- relate to identified needs of staff;
- link, where possible, with national, LEA or school priority areas;
- express clearly what may be expected from the activity;
- be understood and accepted by all participants;
- be understood and accepted by the activity leader;
- be realistic and achievable;
- be linked to the process of evaluation (ie how will we know if they have been achieved?).

Training objectives should not be long-winded or too vague. There is little point in informing staff at 3.45 PM after a busy day that the purpose of their INSET activity is 'to enhance the educational provision for pupils by enabling staff to reflect on . . . etc, etc'. It is more important, for example, to distinguish between measurable outcomes and gains in awareness. An external 'provider' invited to work with staff on, for example, assessment and record-keeping, will benefit from clear objectives being drawn up for INSET activities. The ultimate objective may be *to draw up a school policy on assessment and record-keeping*. There will be a number of steps required before this is achieved. The first may be *to clarify what is meant by the terms: assessment, formative, summative, skill, concept, diagnostic, attainment, etc.* A second may be *to share experiences on the ways in which pupils are assessed now (by teachers within the school and by examining examples of good practice in other schools)*. A third may be *to discuss these different ways of approaching assessment*. A fourth, and main, objective might be *to agree on a common approach to assessment*.

It may be left to a small working group to draw up the school policy statement at this point, but the policy will need to be shared, understood and implemented. A fifth objective may therefore be *to examine the draft policy statement on assessment and record-keeping and agree on ways in which it can work in practice*. Figure 8.3 illustrates how the objectives relate to a structured INSET programme on assessment.

Figure 8.3 Outline of an INSET programme on assessment

SESSION 1 INFORMATION AND AWARENESS RAISING

Objectives
- to clarify terms and expressions relating to assessment;
- to examine the implications of assessment within the National Curriculum.

Venue (combining with neighbouring primary schools) at the local higher education college/university

Time 4.00 PM to 6.00 PM (or 6.30 PM to 8.00 PM)
Negotiate time

Method
1 *Input:* What do we mean by assessment?
(HE lecturer; 30 minutes)
2 *Input:* The National Curriculum and assessment.
(HE lecturer or adviser; 30 minutes)
3 Tea and biscuits (15 minutes)
4 *Input:* Assessment and the first year in the secondary school; implications for partner primary schools.
(Head of first year at the local secondary school; 20 minutes)
5 *Discussion groups:* How can primary schools respond?
(25 minutes)
Structured questions relating to:
- implications for yourself and pupils;
- implications for your school;
- implications for liaison between primary schools in your area;
- implications for primary/secondary liaison.

SESSION 2 EXPLORATION OF ALTERNATIVE STRATEGIES

Objectives
- to share ways in which we assess pupils at the moment:
  i) in our own school;
  ii) in other schools.

Venue Teachers' Centre

Time 4.00 PM to 5.30 PM

Method
1. Brief input from selected teachers – 'how I assess my pupils' – with *honest* and *open* evaluation of suitability and effectiveness.
   (20 minutes)
2. Examination of published resource materials and examples of good practice from other schools (organised by the Teachers' Centre warden or LEA adviser responsible for assessment).
   (40 minutes)
3. Discussion: What ideas should we take back to school?
   (30 minutes)

SESSION 3 APPLICATION OF KNOWLEDGE AND IDEAS TO OUR SCHOOL SITUATION

Objectives
- to share views and ideas on assessment gleaned from Sessions 1 and 2;
- to agree on a common approach to assessment.

Venue School (infant classroom)

Time 3.40 PM to 4.45 PM

Method
1. In groups (junior, infant), discuss the issues raised in the previous sessions with specific reference to own classroom/school.
   (15 minutes)
2. Groups put forward suggestions as to:
   - what to assess;
   - how to assess;
   - when to assess;
   - how to record what has been assessed;
   - how to pass on the information.

   (20 minutes)
3. *Plenary*: Combine the responses of each group and highlight areas of difference and commonality.
   (25 minutes)
4. Establish a 'working group' (two or three teachers) to draw up a statement of policy working to the agenda outlined in 3.
   (5 minutes)

SESSION 4 POLICY FORMULATION AND ANALYSIS

Objectives	• to examine the draft policy statement on assessment and record keeping drawn up by the working group; • to agree on ways in which it can work in practice.
Venue	School (J2 classroom)
Time	3.40 PM to 4.45 PM
Method	1 Working group presents draft policy (handouts available). (30 minutes) 2 Discussion and amendment as necessary. (35 minutes)

The objectives may take a series of weeks to fulfil successfully. They may be tied in with a particular aspect of curriculum development (for example, assessment in primary science). They should, if made explicit *before* a particular INSET activity, leave provider and teachers in little doubt of what is expected from the session. They *should not* be totally inflexible. One of the disadvantages of setting objectives, as with objectives-led teaching, is to destroy the 'voyage of discovery' which is such an important part of child and adult learning. However, the advantages to busy teachers are obvious – we must meet deadlines, so let's get down to business!

8.5.2 Ensure an appropriate learning environment

Why are so many INSET activities carried out in school staffrooms where teachers need to be prised out of their armchairs to engage in group work then struggle to find space between ashtrays and coffee cups? Staffrooms are not, on the whole, good learning environments for formal INSET activities. Classrooms are. They should contain bright, stimulating display work and allow greater flexibility for arrangement of furniture (though suitably sized chairs may need to be imported into the nursery or infant areas). To hold an INSET session in a classroom gives other staff time to study the resources used by that class and to look at the display work of their past or future pupils. It also gives the class teacher an incentive to re-organise the room and change display work which has been on the walls for too long! Clear warning must be given if classrooms are to be used as venues to enable this 'refurbishing' to be done with as little panic as possible.

The choice of venue should reflect the nature of the activity. In addition to classrooms, possible venues include:

- classrooms, laboratories or workshops in another school (primary or secondary);
- teachers' centre;
- computer centre;
- institute of education resource area or lecture theatre;
- museum/art gallery/library/information centre;
- hotel, conference centre;
- training centre of a local large firm.

It is obviously not practicable or advisable to hold each activity in a different venue, but teachers might find the change of venue outlined in Figure 8.3 stimulating.

8.5.3 Build in appropriate and varied learning strategies

INSET methods of delivery have moved from the sublime to the ridiculous. Before 1980, most in-service work was in the form of a lecture by a higher education provider to a passive audience of tired teachers. Seminars were also common: those who enjoyed talking were given the floor for an hour, allowing the other teachers to switch off and recharge their batteries. Then came the 'new INSET': professional 'trainers' travelled the land involving teachers in experiential learning activities. Flipcharts were everywhere, together with group work, role play and empathy. These combined to test the patience of teachers, who just wanted to know *how* to do what was required with the pupils in their classes.

The problem for staff development co-ordinators was how to achieve a balance between the 'traditional' and the 'progressive' INSET methodology. The problem is, in fact, an exact parallel to the teacher's problem in promoting effective learning with pupils. Its solution requires an understanding of how adults learn (andragogy) as opposed to how children learn (pedagogy), but the methods in many ways are similar. This issue is considered in more depth in Part Four.

> Effective INSET requires an understanding of andragogy.

The skill of the staff development co-ordinator will be put to use in planning the delivery of each activity. Over a series of INSET sessions there will be a mixture of:

- formal input (talk or lecture);
- visual stimulus (overhead projector, transparencies, videos);

- handouts containing information;
- discussion work in pairs, threes, small groups and plenary;
- problem-solving activities;
- resource-based activities (analysis of curriculum materials);
- demonstration and hands-on experience;
- debate and decision-making;
- testing of ideas in class and report-back;
- role-play exercises.

The key to successful INSET is to use the appropriate method for different activities. Staff development co-ordinators should have some experience of training skills if they are to plan the delivery of INSET effectively. If cascade of training is to work, these skills must also be passed on to teachers.

8.5.4 Plan relevant and systematic follow-up

School-based INSET is trivialised when it becomes detached from the day-to-day activities of teachers. To 'use up' INSET time by inviting a succession of speakers on issues unrelated to teachers' identified classroom needs is to invite boredom and frustration. In the same way, to abandon one topic because it is time to move on to the next item in the programme is to reduce the credibility of individual activities and the programme as a whole. Topics should not be seen as transitory. It would be unhelpful for a head/staff development co-ordinator to plan ten separate one-hour INSET sessions on ten different topics, ranging from assessment to science, display, mathematics, language, etc. Teachers need to take part in INSET activities, take away what they have learned, use ideas in the classroom where possible, and bring back to future sessions comments on how these ideas worked in practice. Follow-up activities include:

- report-back sessions;
- display of work resulting from the INSET activity in the school foyer or corridors;
- pupils being used to demonstrate activities to teachers;
- teacher observation of lessons;
- parents' evening with speakers, display and demonstration;
- written report circulated to governors, advisers, etc;
- display in teachers' centre, local shop window;
- article and photograph in local newspaper.

8.5.5 Incorporate appropriate methods of evaluation

There is always a danger of over-evaluation, 'paralysis by analysis' as it is known. Evaluation will occur naturally throughout the INSET activity and programme; the job of the co-ordinator is to extract these comments and make them meaningful. If negative comments emerge when there are still parts of the programme to run, it is better to face the issues as they arise rather than ignore them and hope that people will 'come round' to your way of thinking eventually. The importance of setting out a clear programme outline is emphasised here. Teachers will have a much clearer view of the relevance of individual sessions if they can relate them to future sessions in the programme. It may, of course, become apparent that after two sessions much more work needs to be done on one part of the topic before continuing with the planned programme. The staff development co-ordinator should be sensitive to this and be prepared to amend the published programme after full consultation with staff. The tail should not wag the dog.

The processes of monitoring and evaluation will be considered more fully in the next chapter. At this stage, it can be noted that evaluation should be built-in rather than bolt-on; that the staff development co-ordinator should be sensitive to statements being made about the INSET programme and respond to them where possible; and that a climate of co-operative learning should exist in which teachers can make honest, professional comments about the effectiveness or otherwise of the programme.

Issues for consideration

a) What staff characteristics should Mr Jackson or his staff development co-ordinator bear in mind when designing school-based INSET activities?
b) Using the plan of Greenbank School (Figure 3.1) suggest ways in which a staff development programme could be accommodated.
c) What support would Miss Morris, the science co-ordinator, need to run a similar activity to that outlined on page 105?
d) What in-school staff development activities, outlined in section 8.4, would be of most benefit to individual teachers at Greenbank?
e) What learning methods might suit different members of Greenbank staff?
f) Which staff have interests in common which may help them in their learning of new ideas and skills?

9 Evaluating INSET

9.1 Evaluation as a continuous activity

Implicit in the whole process of staff development and needs analysis is the notion that evaluation is integral to it, an on-going and vital element of the dynamic process. From the outset, it is essential that the participants address the following questions:

1 Does the INSET programme meet the declared needs of the teachers?
2 Is it worth the time and resources invested in it?
3 Is it worth the money it is costing?
4 Is it eventually going to have a beneficial effect on:
   - the teachers' practice;
   - the pupils' performance?

These questions are crucial. They make it clear that the cycle of INSET evaluation does not end with the INSET programme; it has to extend further, to the teaching and learning that goes on in the classroom as a consequence. It may be useful, therefore, to think of INSET evaluation in two phases: the short-term evaluation of the INSET programme itself and the longer-term evaluation of the effects of INSET on teachers' practice and pupils' performance in the classroom:

Short-term evaluation of INSET	*Long-term evaluation of INSET*
Evaluation of: • individual INSET sessions; • the INSET programme as a whole.	Beyond the INSET programme: • effects on teachers' practice; • influence on children's learning.

In the case of both short- and long-term processes, schools will need:

- to have established a suitable climate for evaluation;
- someone to be familiar with evaluation techniques.

The main intention in this chapter is to describe some of these evaluation techniques and suggest ways in which they may be adapted for the primary school. Those evaluating INSET programmes will need to apply some creative thinking to the task in hand. They will need to be flexible and adaptable, prepared to make mistakes and to learn from them.

First, we need to establish a context within which to frame our evaluation methodology. The following checklist for planning INSET evaluation identifies some of the issues that are germane to the evaluation process in schools.

1 What is the purpose of the evaluation?
2 Who needs the information?
3 Who will carry out the evaluation?
4 When will the evaluation be carried out?
5 How will the information be collected?
6 What will happen to the information collected?

Before we examine each of these questions in turn, it may be as well to consider one more, the nature of evaluation itself.

9.2 What is evaluation?

In the literature about evaluation the terminology can sometimes be confusing: commentators do not always agree in their interpretations, and we often encounter what Rowntree (1974) referred to as 'tortured educational semantics'. To begin with, a comparison of evaluation and assessment can help to clarify meaning.

We make *informal* evaluations all the time, not only when we are teaching, but in the normal course of our everyday lives. In the classroom, these judgements may manifest themselves in the merest raising of any eyebrow or a reassuring nod of the head. The distinction between *evaluation* and *assessment* may be made in the following way:

Assessment	*Evaluation*
• implies the use of measurement and/or grading, based on certain criteria; • provides information about pupils' levels of attainment and abilities.	• is more general and looks beyond the children to the style, circumstances and materials of the teaching and learning; • is to do with reviewing the quality and provision of a school and its methods of work.

Evaluation is part of a general process that includes *observing, monitoring, recording, analysing and reviewing*. It is to do with the nature and worth of something. In addition to *formal* and *informal* evaluation, we need to distinguish between monitoring and evaluation, and between formative and summative evaluation.

Eraut (1988) notes the frequent confusion over the use of the terms monitoring and evaluation, and offers the following definitions:

> MONITORING is to check what has happened and the extent to which things have gone according to plan.
>
> ADMINISTRATIVE MONITORING confines itself to the administrative aspects of these questions (for example, are the rooms we are using suitable for the INSET being provided? Are we sticking to our budget?).
>
> PROFESSIONAL MONITORING is also concerned with customer satisfaction and with qualitative aspects of INSET processes (are the INSET activities meeting the identified needs of our teachers?).
>
> PROFESSIONAL REVIEW goes beyond monitoring to ask more fundamental questions and to examine the assumptions which underpin practice.
>
> The term 'evaluation' covers both professional monitoring and professional review. We would not normally use it to describe administrative monitoring alone. So when people make a distinction between 'monitoring' and 'evaluation' we shall assume that it is only administrative monitoring to which they refer.

The distinction between formative and summative evaluation is less complex.

Formative evaluation	*Summative evaluation*
• carried out *during* the programme, to improve it as it runs; • influences the direction the work takes.	• carried out at the *end* of the programme, often in the form of a final report; • reflects upon the effects of what has been done.

The difference between summative and formative evaluation is based not so much on *when* the evaluation is undertaken as *for what purpose* it is being done. This leads us to our next question.

9.3 What is the purpose of evaluation?

In the words of the 1986 Government, the purpose of evaluating INSET is:

> 'to assess how far it has contributed to more effective and efficient delivery of the education service'.
>
> (DES, 1986)

When schools are obliged to respond to such official directives there is a risk that the evaluation of INSET may be viewed more as a chore that has to be done than something that has an intrinsic role in the educational cycle of staff development. Nevertheless, it must be acknowledged that, increasingly, schools are having to be accountable to the 'paymasters'. Headteachers have to show LEAs that their INSET programme is giving value for money. It can be costly, especially if external consultants are involved; fees and expenses must be paid, and, possibly, extra materials provided. It is of the utmost importance that the school knows whether this investment has been of value to its staff and, ultimately, to its pupils.

The main purpose of evaluation is to provide information for improvement: improvement in the quality of the INSET programme itself and also in the educational provision of the school. Holly (1987) adds further dimensions to the purposes of evaluation:

> Evaluation *of* INSET (making value judgements about activities or programmes);
>
> Evaluation *for* INSET (using the information derived from evaluation to identify future needs);

Evaluation *as* INSET (teachers involved in the process of evaluation have, by necessity, to reflect on the INSET and this reinforces the learning that has taken place).

Those who are engaged in the evaluation need to be quite clear about why they are doing it, otherwise the outcomes will be confused and evaluation will be seen as a time-consuming exercise with minimal benefits.

9.4 Who needs the information? Who will carry out the evaluation?

It is appropriate that we address these two questions together because, for at least some of the time during the evaluation process, the people who will carry out the evaluation will also be the ones who need the information. Gone are the days when INSET was seen as something organised exclusively *by* others *for* teachers. The school-based approach to INSET depends largely on the degree of commitment, enthusiasm and involvement of the teachers themselves. Even when the INSET involves a contribution from an external provider, it is important that teachers feel a sense of ownership towards the activity, so that they will take a professional responsibility for its evaluation. It gives teachers a personal stake in the process.

Other partners in the collaboration might be consultants, 'critical friends', parents, governors, LEA officials and members of the wider community. All these parties might usefully contribute to INSET evaluation; certainly, many of them will have an interest in the information that is collected.

Finally, and perhaps most importantly, there are the children. They will naturally be involved, not only as the ultimate beneficiaries of improved educational provision, but in providing evidence during the information-gathering stage in the long-term evaluation of INSET.

9.5 When will the evaluation be carried out?

The evaluation should be carried out:

- at the beginning of the INSET activity;
- during the INSET activity;
- after the INSET activity.

Evaluation of INSET, just like all educational evaluation, is a continuous, cyclical, reflexive process. It is not something that happens at the end of an INSET course, merely to pay lip-service to a government or local authority edict.

9.6 How will the evaluation be carried out?

The task of evaluating INSET can seem a pretty daunting prospect. To make it manageable, the most useful thing to do initially is to try and break it down into distinct parts, thus avoiding it becoming a perfunctory paper exercise, to be discharged as quickly as possible, with little or no benefit to the staff or the school.

The process has two main phases: phase 1 the evaluation of the staff development programme itself, and phase 2 the evaluation of the effects of INSET in the classroom. Figure 9.1 illustrates the distinction between the two phases.

Figure 9.1 Evaluation of INSET and its effects: the two phases

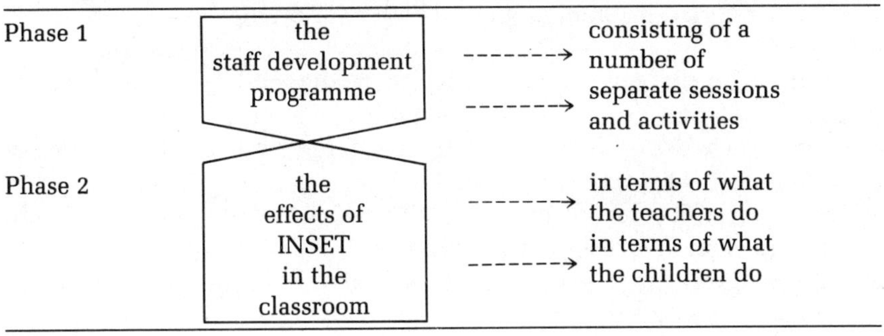

In practice it may be difficult to separate out these phases. The effects of INSET are quite likely to be felt in the classroom while the programme is still running. An idea may fire a teacher's imagination and be spontaneously integrated into her or his practice. However, for the sake of clarity, we need to look at each phase in more detail.

9.7 Evaluation of the staff development programme: phase 1

We have already noted that the staff development programme will consist of a number of separate sessions, all of which will need monitoring and evaluating (formative evaluation) while the programme itself will need to have a summative evaluation made of it. Figure 9.2 gives an overview of the evaluation process for this phase.

Figure 9.2 Overview of the evaluation process (Phase 1)

↑	*Monitoring*	• Are we carrying out our plans?
	Formative evaluations	• How are we carrying out our plans? • Do we need to adjust them?
The staff development programme	*Summative evaluation*	• Was the programme worthwhile? • If the activities were to be repeated for others, how should they be changed? • How will the INSET change my teaching? • What do I intend to do as a result of it?
↓	*Review*	• Do we need to change our aims, priorities, approach?

In practice, of course, the staff development programme may well be more complex than a series of 'in-house' workshops run by the same person. It might consist of any or all of the following:

- informal/formal staff discussions, led by the INSET co-ordinator;
- teachers/INSET co-ordinator researching official documents or other literature before or during the running of the course (eg LEA policies, school policies, HMI reports, etc);
- teachers/INSET co-ordinator making visits to other schools where good practice has been identified;
- external consultant being called in to give a 'foundation' presentation and/or to conduct some 'in-house' sessions;
- teachers/INSET co-ordinator enrolling for relevant courses based in centres other than the school (eg local institute of higher education, teachers' centres) to increase expertise and then provide 'feedback' to staff.

Further examples are provided in Chapter 8. These are all possible elements of an INSET programme which will require reflection, evaluation and action. The evaluation will be undertaken by different people for different purposes. For instance, in the case of the teachers' centre course, the provider (probably an adviser or advisory teacher) will need to know how to improve the course, as well as what the teachers learned from it. The course members will need to evaluate its usefulness in terms of the staff development programme running at their schools, and communicate their conclusions to colleagues.

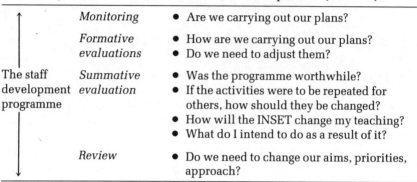

Because of this diversity of provision and purpose, it is not possible to give a blueprint for evaluation. However, the INSET co-ordinator may like to consider some of the following points, and think about how they might be adapted for specific situations.

Informal evaluations

We have already noted that informal evaluations will be made constantly. For instance, as teachers walk into the room where the INSET session is to be held, they will notice whether it is ready for them or whether the provider is still rushing around, red faced, trying to find an extension lead for the projector. Immediately, an impression is being shaped in teachers' minds of the sort of person the provider is (if not a colleague). Throughout the session there will be little signs and signals going backwards and forwards from provider to participant, establishing relationships or building up resentments. The participating teacher may be thinking:

THINKS . . .

> Who is this person telling me what to do and how to do it when I've been teaching thirty-two years. Barely out of college. He's assuming certain things which have no foundation. He thinks we've been living in the dark ages until he came on the scene. I don't like the way he keeps jingling the change in his pocket when he talks – I can't hear half of what he's saying. I wish we could *do* something instead of just sitting here listening. I can feel my eyelids getting heavier and heavier . . .

OR

. . . THINKS

> He seems quite nice. I like the way he's got everything prepared. He seems to have his finger on the button. I've got confidence in him. He realises we've got a lot to offer, too, and asks our opinion about things. He admits he hasn't got as much experience as we have of infant teaching. He's honest. I trust him. He knows we've been working hard all day – he appreciates that. He's quite amusing too – it's good to have a laugh at the end of the day.

If the providers are sufficiently sensitive, they can learn a great deal about how things are going simply by observing the behaviours and taking careful note of the responses of the participants. In workshop situations, or perhaps over a cup of tea during a break, teachers can be engaged in conversations which often tell providers far more about how things are going than a more formal evaluation at the end of the session.

Formal evaluations

Let us focus our attention to begin with on formative evaluations, where participants and providers need to check on progress and development. There can be two approaches: *oral* and *written*.

The oral approach

This is perhaps the most viable approach in the school-based situation where the INSET session may last for just an hour, probably at the end of the school day. There is not much time, and it will have to be kept fairly simple:

- What have we done?
- What have we learned so far?
- What has been particularly useful?
- What has not been relevant?
- Do we need to adjust what we had intended to do next, in the light of what we have just done?
- Do we need any support for this?

The procedure could be:

1 By open discussion. This needs to be handled skilfully, otherwise an inaccurate impression of the group view may emerge as a result of contributions from the more forceful members.

2 By going round the group, one by one, encouraging individual responses.

3 By asking teachers to discuss their responses first in pairs or groups (depending on the size of the staff) and then reporting back orally to the assembled staff. This will take more time.

Someone (the provider) will need to make a record of the oral responses: this may be done in writing or, if it is not thought to be too inhibiting, by tape recorder. Sometimes, an immediate response straight after the activity is modified by teachers as they discuss the course in the period between INSET sessions. Consequent adjustments to the next session, or even a change of direction for the whole programmes can be made accordingly if that is the consensus view. If an external consultant is involved, then he or she will need to be contacted in good time before the subsequent session. These periods of informal discussion/evaluation between sessions are crucial, because they are often more likely to get to the heart of teachers' needs than anything else.

The difficulties of conducting oral evaluation should not be understated. One systematic way is to conduct a 'round'. Participants sit in a circle and, one by one, give their professional opinions of the activity. It is known by trainers as 'creeping death'! The initial comment often sets the tone for the round. It is difficult to be critical when you are looking someone in the eye, however professional the atmosphere might feel. It is even more difficult when the value of the activity has been lessened because of some personal attribute of the provider, rather than points which can easily be remedied. (For example, the provider may be a poor speaker or may have difficulty in relating theoretical issues to classroom practice.) The climate set by the staff development co-ordinator is all-important here. Relationships between staff and co-ordinator, co-ordinator and provider, and provider and staff must be sufficiently open to enable professional statements to be made in as non-threatening a way as possible.

The written approach

Written approaches can vary considerably in detail and complexity. Those responsible for their design should remember that the important thing is for the written approach to be appropriate to the situation in hand. Here are a few examples:

The 'graffiti sheet'

Large sheets of paper are pinned around the room, headed with the beginning of a sentence, such as:

- I hoped that this session would . . .
- What I found valuable was . . .
- What I found of little use was . . .
- What I would like to know more about is . . .

One disadvantage of this method is that some teachers may be reluctant to make public what they really think in private. Another disadvantage of the graffiti sheet is that it invites the staff-room wags to show off and make facetious comments which may not always be helpful. On the other hand, if handled appropriately, this can often help to lighten the atmosphere.

Index cards
These can be passed around at the end of a session for comments. Suggestions for using them are as follows:

1 Leave blank, just ask for 'comments'.
2 Give out three cards with sentence beginnings:

What I found MOST useful . . .	What I found LEAST useful . . .	What I need to know more about . . .

3 Give out one card, bearing different messages front and back. On the front, participants are invited to write succinct comments about the course so far. On the back, course members are again asked to respond succinctly.

Index cards can also be used for a summative evaluation at the end of the course. This strategy has three stages:

Stage 1 All course members are given two cards, one pink and one blue. The pink cards represent warm, positive feelings and the blue cards cold, negative feelings. Staff write any appropriate comments on these cards. The condition is that any comments written on both cards must be justified. Respondents are asked to say *why* they think as they do.

Stage 2 Course members get together in groups to discuss the comments they have written down. If any individual's negative comments do not have the full support of the group, they are discarded. Only the comments that are shared by all the members of the group are kept.

Stage 3 All groups convene for a plenary session in which they feed back their conclusions. This evaluation session can be very threatening for the provider. Sometimes comments can be (unintentionally) destructive and unhelpful. Therefore, it is necessary to emphasise that constructive criticism is particularly welcome here. On the other hand, it is perhaps more frustrating when 'bland' comments are made ('not bad', 'enjoyable', etc), which give little information to the provider. To avoid wasting time, directions should be clear: 'please comment specifically on the following aspects . . .'.

Questionnaires
These can vary from a few simple questions to a complex arrangement

of statements with boxes for ticking or numbers for circling. There are many books available about questionnaire design (see for example Hopkins (1985) and Bell (1987)), but perhaps the most important rules can be summarised in the following way:

1 Decide at the outset exactly what it is you want to find out, and why.
2 Make it as succinct as possible. Only ask the most *essential* questions.
3 Ensure that all questions are unambiguous.
4 Keep the questionnaire as simple as possible.

For a summative evaluation of an INSET programme, the questions would probably fall into the five following categories:

- what the teachers thought of the course (and provider);
- how the course might be improved;
- what insights the teachers have gained;
- in what way those insights will influence how they teach;
- what support teachers might need to implement any new ideas.

The format of the questionnaire can take a number of forms:

1 Closed-ended questions.
Example: Did the course meet your requirements? Yes/No

2 Open-ended questions.
Example: What new skills do you think you have learned?

3 Questions with a matrix that call for a tick.
Example:

	very satis- factory	satis- factory	unsatis- factory	very unsatis- factory
How satisfactory was the accommodation for the course?	☐	☐	☐	☐

4 Statements with a matrix.
Example:

	YES!	YES	NO	NO!
The accommodation for the course was satisfactory	☐	☐	☐	☐

5 Statements with numbers to be circled.
Example:
Circle the numbers below according to your response. Use the following guide:
4 – Strongly agree
3 – Agree
2 – Disagree
1 – Strongly disagree
During the course I felt
clear about the objectives 1 2 3 4

The use of a four-point rather than a five-point scale commits teachers to a positive or negative response.

Questionnaires with lists of statements are the most time-consuming to compile. On the other hand, they are quicker to analyse, because they are easier to process.

Example 70 per cent of teachers thought that accommodation for the course was unsatisfactory.

It is much more difficult to analyse people's responses to the more open-ended questions. However, it is this information which helps to illuminate the more quantitative analysis, and gives a fuller picture of respondents' views. It is very frustrating to arrive at the conclusion that 70 per cent of teachers thought that the course accommodation was unsatisfactory, without knowing *why* they found it unsatisfactory. Was it size? heating? seating? poor visual aids? It is important to build these detailed responses into the original questionnaire.

Summary of phase 1 of INSET evaluation

One final word about this phase of INSET evaluation before moving on to the question of what happens next. We have described a number of strategies and techniques which may be used formally or informally, for the purpose of making formative or summative evaluations. Those with a particular interest in the immediate outcomes of the INSET evaluation will be:

- the provider;
- the participants.

The provider will need to know what teachers thought of his or her performance, with a view to improvement. The participants will need to reflect on what they have learned and think about how it will influence their teaching. Evaluations vary. They need to be 'tailor made' for each INSET course, just as every INSET course needs to be 'tailor made' for each given situation. Figure 9.3 shows some questions that may need to be asked in a summative evaluation. They can, of course, be broken down further, depending on precisely what information is needed, and in how much detail.

Figure 9.3 Example of a questionnaire for summative evaluation of an INSET course

Please answer the following questions. Give reasons to explain your answers where appropriate.

1 In your opinion, did the course fulfil its aims/objectives? Yes/No
2 Did it meet your requirements? Yes/No
3 Was the general level of presentation: too high/just right/too low?
4 Was the standard of presentation: satisfactory/unsatisfactory?
5 What was the most valuable aspect of the course?
6 Was there a session you gained little from?
7 How do you think the course might be improved?
8 What insights have you gained?
9 What new skills have you learned?
10 What do you intend to do now as a result of the course?
11 What support will you need in order to do this?
12 What further INSET do you feel you need?
13 Please add any further comments (overleaf).

You may give your name if you wish

Name: ____________

Thank you.

There is, of course, a danger of over-evaluation. Long questionnaires take time to fill in properly. If they are not filled in properly the information is often not worthwhile. There is a danger that evaluation will take up valuable activity time (twenty minutes of the final one-hour session for instance). If no action occurs on the part of the provider or of the staff, that time will have been spent to little effect.

9.8 Evaluation of the staff development programme: phase 2

Let us assume that the staff of our model school, Greenbank School, have evaluated the INSET programme that was initially set up in response to their identification of needs exercise. They have considered:

- what it was they did;
- how the programme was delivered;
- how relevant it was to them;
- what they learned as a result.

The next obvious question for each member of staff is:

- What do I intend to do now?

and

- What is there about my practice that I intend to change as a result of the INSET programme?

In our experience, teachers don't always wait until the end of the INSET programme. They discuss whatever topic is raised during the course of the session, and internalise it, process it, and either spit it out or file it away for possible further use. The more receptive and open-minded the teacher is, the more dynamic this process is.

Next question:

- How do I know whether the changes in my teaching are having a positive effect on my pupils?

Now we are getting to the more complex stage of the INSET evaluation process. The chain of activities which leads from the initial INSET session to eventual changes in pupil learning is long. Sometimes it is too long to evaluate with any validity. However, if a healthy climate of staff development, staff appraisal and teacher self-evaluation has been established in the school, then the monitoring and evaluation of INSET will naturally go on as the teacher develops professionally. Information will be required relating to the change in her/his practice as a result of the INSET activity. This information can be gathered by means of:

- discussions

- interviews
- questionnaires
- observations
- field diaries

Discussions
We have already said that teachers begin immediately to assimilate information as it is being presented on the INSET course. They naturally discuss it with their colleagues, especially in the situation of school-based INSET. They will relate it to their own situations, their own teaching methods, their own pupils. Informal discussions will be on-going.

Interviews
The staff development co-ordinator may at this stage wish to interview members of staff individually to capitalise upon individual responses made in the summative evaluation of the course. This needs to be done as soon after the event as possible: striking while the iron is still hot. The substance of the interview will focus on teachers' perceptions of the INSET activity, and what they intend to do next, in respect of their own practice. The co-ordinator will also need to find out what kind of support individuals will need at this stage in order to implement any innovations (for example, equipment, materials, resources, money, time, another pair of hands).

Questionnaires
If there isn't enough time available to interview members of staff individually at this stage, then questionnaires may be a more convenient way of collecting the kind of information that is required.

Observations
These will need to be undertaken over a period of time in the different classroom situations, and may be done by:

- the teacher her/himself;
- the staff development co-ordinator or another teacher;
- an external evaluator.

Increasingly, teachers are becoming used to having other adults in the classroom with them: ancillary helpers, parents, nurses and teacher-supports. However, there are still many teachers who work predominantly on their own, within the confines of their classrooms. They may feel threatened by the presence of another adult in class with them, particularly one who may be seen as having a critical function. It is therefore of the utmost importance that the following points are recognised:

1 The observer must be someone the teacher feels at ease with and can trust.
2 Appropriate criteria for observations must be negotiated by the teacher and observer beforehand.

These criteria will then be discussed from time to time with the teacher and used as a means of gauging development or improvement. The teacher and observer may between them devise an observation schedule, if that is appropriate. This will provide a means of recording information and act as an 'aide memoire' for subsequent discussion. Any issues generated by the post-session discussion may well provide further criteria for the teacher to focus on during successive activities.

Field diaries
It may be a good idea for the teacher to keep a field diary of her or his own observations and comments during the activity. This can either be kept on the desk, near at hand, and notes made 'on the hoof', or the teacher may prefer to write down comments as soon after the event as possible. Writing things down often helps to identify patterns and connections between things which might otherwise remain unarticulated or unnoticed.

Let us review our progress so far in this description of the evaluation process. First, Figure 9.4 suggests a possible sequence of events. The question of where to go next, and the necessary feedback and support for teachers, can be determined by having evaluation sessions at regular intervals. It is also helpful if teachers get together as a group from time to time to discuss how they see the influence of INSET on their teaching. School-based INSET activities allow for a shared experience by the school's staff as a whole. It is likely that most of the teachers involved will have much in common in implementing change. The mutual support system offered by this kind of group reinforcement has many advantages. It also allows for systematic and repeated feedback, which is a crucial factor in evaluation. It is quite likely that these regular evaluation sessions will also throw up other needs, which will in turn be the subject of further INSET.

Figure 9.4 Possible sequence of events so far

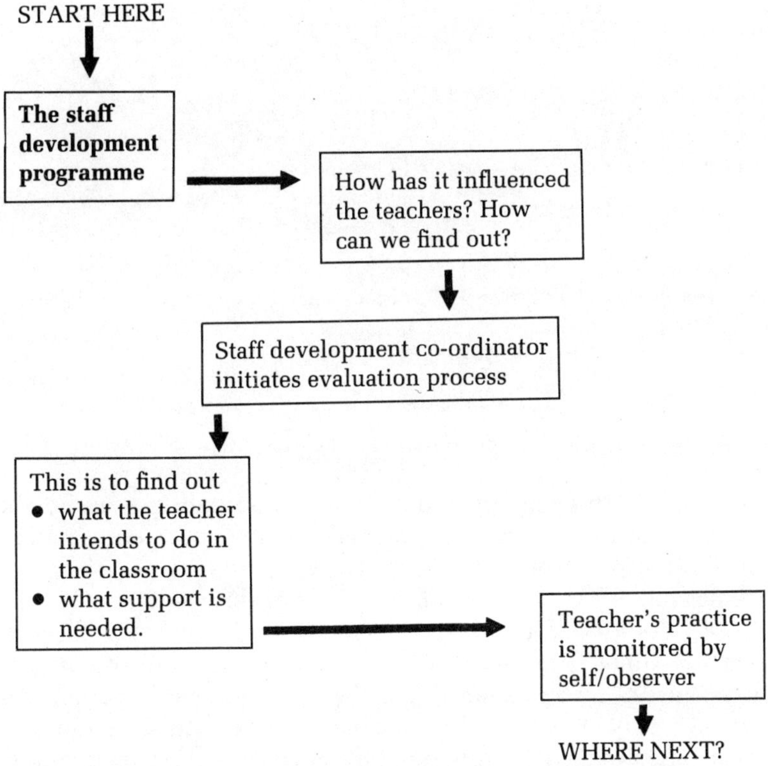

Gathering information about the effects of INSET on pupils' performance in the classroom

The techniques are similar to those outlined above, with the addition of one further source of information: the outcomes in the shape of children's work. Figure 9.5 lists some techniques for gathering this information. Space does not allow us to develop this further here, but there are a number of excellent books which deal with classroom research techniques in much greater detail. Details can be found in the bibliography provided at the end of this book.

Figure 9.5 Techniques for classroom research

Discussion	• teacher with pupil • observer with pupil • pupil with pupil
Observation	• teacher • observer
Field diaries	• teachers' perceptions • pupils' perceptions (if old enough to write – if not, try a tape-recorder!)
Assessment of children's work	• by teacher • by colleagues • by headteacher • by external evaluator • by pupils

Analysing the data and writing the report

The final stages in this lengthy and complex evaluation process relate to analysis of the information that has been gathered, making judgements about it and writing the report. The time required to complete this stage should not be underestimated. Filing cabinets in schools are full of INSET questionnaires which have never been analysed because of pressure of time! However, the process of writing the report is a valuable means in itself of analysing and making judgements, because it forces the writer to reflect on what has gone on, to examine any documents – diaries, interim reports or minutes, and questionnaires. A full picture is compiled from all these fragments. Three processes are involved, all of which influence each other:

Description
This gives a summary of what has happened, in what circumstances, and the work that has ensued. Written documentation may need to be augmented by photographs, video tapes, tape-recordings, etc.

Analysis
Reflecting on the information will allow significant issues and emerging patterns to be disclosed.

Judgement
On the basis of the information and analysis, certain conclusions will be drawn about whether the INSET programme was worthwhile or not, and who benefited from it.

Finally, Figure 9.6 summarises the evaluation process which has provided the substance of this chapter.

Figure 9.6

STAGES IN THE PROCESS OF INSET EVALUATION	EFFECTS
Formative evaluations of sessions *during* staff development programme	• May lead to a change in the direction of the programme in response to participants' views
Summative evaluation *at the end of the* staff development programme	• Allows teachers to make judgements about the quality of the staff development programme/activity • Guides teachers into thinking about any changes they might make to their own practice in the classroom
Review: interview with staff development co-ordinator	• Enables teachers to identify a strategy for the classroom as a result of the staff development programme • Establishes the kind of support the teacher is likely to need in order to implement the strategy (innovation)
Evaluation of effects of INSET in the classroom	• Provides opportunities for the collection of information about the way in which the teacher implements the innovation • Provides opportunities to monitor and evaluate the quality of children's learning in the classroom as a result of the innovation
Mutual support system: regular staff discussions	• Allows for feedback and support for teachers • Helps to analyse and make judgements about the information collected • Encourages further identification of INSET needs or other support
Writing the evaluation report	• Keeps all participants in the picture • May indicate whether INSET has met teachers' needs or not • May indicate whether or not INSET has been worthwhile – cost in time and money • May be responsible for generating further INSET based on teachers' needs

Issues for consideration

a) Who should evaluate Greenbank's staff development programme:
   i) as a whole?
   ii) as individual activities?
b) How much of the programme should be evaluated formally (ie with the production of a written report)?
c) How much time should be set aside within the programme for evaluation to be conducted?
d) How can evaluation be 'costed' into the INSET budget?
e) How will the evaluator(s) gain access to information on the effects of INSET on pupil learning?
f) With the exception of the staff, governing body and provider, who else should have access to the evaluation report?
g) How will longer-term effects on pupils' education be evaluated?

PART THREE
STAFF DEVELOPMENT AND THE CURRICULUM

Lawrence Stenhouse's (1975) belief that 'there can be no curriculum development without teacher development' neatly sums up the purpose of this next part of the book. In Parts One and Two we examined the stages in the process of staff development. In Part Three we take a number of curriculum areas and examine ways in which staff development programmes support the delivery of the curriculum in primary schools. Since it would be impossible to go into depth on any one curriculum area or, in a book of this nature, even to cover all core and foundation subjects of the National Curriculum, we have chosen to examine one or two examples of staff development activities in the core subject areas of English, mathematics and science and in two cross-curricular areas (display and special needs). We begin with a brief analysis of the role of staff development in laying the foundations for the introduction of the National Curriculum.

10 Staff development and the National Curriculum

10.1 The search for information

Staff development programmes in primary schools are built on the foundation of teacher-identified needs. Successful and effective programmes, we have been told, reflect the needs and priorities which teachers feel affect them most. In relation to this, two important issues have arisen since the introduction of the Education Reform Act in 1988:

1 Increasingly, the definition of priorities and needs has been determined centrally, rather than by the teacher. Deadlines for the introduction of National Curriculum programmes of study and assessment requirements were tight. They were also non-negotiable. The new tier of accountability in the form of more potent governing bodies ensured that teachers would reprioritise their individual needs to meet the demands of the Secretary of State.
2 Changing and often conflicting messages about the National Curriculum made planning difficult. Crude needs identification exercises produced little in the way of useful information. When teachers are asked to list their 'in-service needs', many respond with a bland list of their current concerns. Projecting future needs is more difficult. The aphorism associated with this is 'You don't know what you don't know'.

   This problem was accentuated in the build-up to the National Curriculum by the 'shifting goalposts', and lack of consistency during the debate. The interim reports for science and mathematics bore only a slight resemblance to the final document. The incorporation of profile component three (*Practical Application*) of the mathematics proposals into components one and two of the final document and a similar slimming down in the science recommendations (with the loss of the profile component entitled *Science in Action*) left many teachers wary of trying to plan too far ahead, for fear of further changes. The short supply of the relevant documents did not help. Teachers were unable to get hold of the subject working group reports and 'trainers' running in-service sessions on National Curriculum issues found it difficult to get even single copies of documents. Identifying needs, therefore, has often been a case of educated guesswork.

Anything written last week is already out of date.

The change which the National Curriculum brought about has needed carefully structured staff development programmes to support it at all levels.

The implications for primary heads/staff development co-ordinators were, and are, apparent.

What?
- Do we focus on National Curriculum content?
- – or the management of the curriculum?
- – or on assessment separately from content?
- – or on group-specific issues (junior, infant, reception, rising 5s)?
- – or on all of these in an integrated way?

When?
- Do we abandon all other identified needs and allocate school closure days exclusively to National Curriculum issues?
- Do we hold sessions in directed time after school?
- Do we have to wait until an appropriate 'provider' can be found?
- Do we plan backwards from specific government or LEA deadlines?

Where?
- Should we combine with other schools and commission joint courses at local colleges of teacher education?
- Should we operate as a consortium with other local primary schools?
- Should we join with non-local primary schools with a similar philosophy to ours (denominational schools, Welsh medium schools, etc)?
- Should we join with our local secondary school or with specific departments within that school?

- Should we 'go it alone'?

How?
- Should we plan a *training* programme (ie how to teach to specific attainment targets)?
- Should we build our INSET programme totally on LEA policy statements (a standardised approach)?
- Should we try to motivate teachers by emphasising their own responsibility for translating programmes of study into school-focused schemes of work?
- Should we spend time on the philosophy (ie the reasons *why* some approaches to the curriculum are more effective than others)?
- What methods/criteria should we use to evaluate the training?

Who?
- Should we buy in consultants from higher education?
- Should we use advisory teachers even if we have to wait for some time before they are available?
- Should we concentrate totally on cascading from our own staff?

10.2 Understanding the procedures for assessment

Closely linked with the content and management of the National Curriculum are the new requirements concerning assessment of pupils. The TGAT Report (1987) states that 'Assessment policy should follow from decisions about the curriculum' and that 'assessment of individual children must continue to be the responsibility of the teachers'. Since the publication of the TGAT Report, however, there have been a variety of statements from both official sources and other interested parties, which have either applauded or criticised the Report's message. The implementation of some of the Report's proposals has also proved practically or politically difficult, resulting in a change of emphasis away from the original recommendations.

Primary-school teachers need to know, understand and be able to implement the assessment procedures. Each school should now have on its staff at least one teacher who is conversant with the finer points of assessment. Each school now should also have an assessment policy setting out clearly the aims and procedures for teachers of all year-groups.

INSET on assessment will need to be on-going. The acquisition of knowledge will be relatively simple to achieve once the 'jargon' is understood. The TGAT Report itself provided a useful glossary of terms, a summary of which is produced in Figure 10.1.

Figure 10.1 National Curriculum assessment: the jargon (adapted from the TGAT Report, 1987)

Assessment	all methods customarily used to appraise performance
Test	any of a broad range of assessment instruments with standardised rules of administration and marking which ensure comparability of results
Standardised test	one published with marking instructions and data on the levels of response established for a national population sample
Criterion referencing	the performance of a pupil irrespective of the performance of other pupils
Aggregation	combining a pupil's marks or grades . . . to give a single mark or grade
Moderation	the process of checking comparability of different assessors' (eg teachers, national standardised test) judgements of different groups of pupils
Calibration	statistical rather than judgemental adjusting of results
Skill	ability to perform
Concept	a generalised idea or notion
Understanding	the ability to select and use knowledge and skills
Task	any activity in which a pupil takes part and which could be used for assessment
Project	an open-ended task sometimes requiring independent planning or research on the part of the pupil
Item bank	an orderly collection of test questions or tasks (from which users may select sets of tasks for particular assessment purposes)
Ranking	putting pupils' performances in order of relative quality
Rating	ranking pupils' performance against given criteria
Norm referencing	an assessment system in which pupils are placed in rank order and pre-determined proportions are placed in the various grades
Level	achievement of a particular set of performance criteria which have been defined within a 'profile component'

The TGAT Report's recommendations argued that national assessment should satisfy four criteria:

1 It should be *criterion-referenced.*
2 It should be *formative* (giving guidance for the pupil's next stage of development).
3 It should be *moderated* (using teacher and external assessment).
4 It should be *progressive* (giving a coherent picture of a pupil's progress over the years of compulsory schooling).

The main edition of the TGAT Report provided useful examples of a variety of tests which can be used with pupils. It is suggested that teachers use different methods, occasions and sources of information to assess pupils, using a combination of the results of teachers' internal assessments with the results of Standardised Assessment Tasks (SATs) to provide information on a pupil's progress at the key stages of 7, 11, 14 and 16. It is emphasised that these ages are *reporting*, not *assessment* ages, and that assessment should be continuous throughout a child's schooling. Assessment should be built-in rather than bolt-on. The implications of the assessment arrangements for staff development are clear:

1 Curriculum leaders will need to understand and communicate assessment procedures for their specialist areas.
2 One member of staff will be needed to co-ordinate assessment across the curriculum.
3 Cascade training will be needed to ensure that assessment is carried out efficiently.
4 Classroom management will need to be a major consideration if teachers are to look for 'assessment opportunities' rather than set a large number of formal testing situations.
5 Teachers will need to appreciate the diagnostic nature of testing if pupils are to benefit.
6 Teachers will need to appreciate the relative importance of curriculum and testing if the latter is not to dominate the former.

Staff development programmes on assessment will have to develop teachers' understanding of procedures as well as their knowledge of what to do and how to do it. The warnings to teachers who try to implement national requirements mechanistically are clear:

> . . . assessment is a means of improving teaching and learning and not a means in itself. What must be avoided is . . . [the setting up of] a long series of 'quality control' tests, with teachers continually nagging children about assessment and threatening them with the consequences of failure to reach predetermined standards.
>
> (Edwards, R. and Bennet, D. *Schools in Action*, 1985)

This is echoed in one of the responses to the Mathematics National Curriculum Working Group's Interim Report: 'The important must be made measurable and not the measurable important.'

> The important must be made measurable and not the measurable important

10.3 Staffing and training implications

The staffing and staff training implications are complex and long-term. The National Curriculum Council's report on Mathematics (December, 1988) stated that:

> . . . there will need to be an intensive training programme for those primary and secondary teachers who will be immediately affected and, subsequently, a rolling programme of in-service training to support the progressive extension of the new requirements to other age groups.
>
> (para 3.2)

The report added:

> . . . it would be reasonable to expect primary teachers . . . to be able to cope up to and including level 6 which is above the upper end of the spread of pupil performance around the mean expected of primary pupils. For some pupils who may be capable of level 7 and above additional arrangements will need to be made in some schools. Where a capable mathematician is already employed on the staff of a primary school, usually acting as the mathematics coordinator, such a person will need to ensure the delivery of work at level 7 and above. In some cases this will require the teacher with expertise in mathematics teaching the fourth-year junior class for this subject. In many primary schools, particularly smaller ones, such a teacher may not be available. To ensure that pupils are not held back it will be essential that supporting teaching is provided, for example through liaison with the mathematics department of a neighbouring school or college and/or through the provision of peripatetic teachers of mathematics. It may be that reference to such specialist provision should form part of the curriculum statement for a particular pupil.
>
> (para 3.4)

The staffing implications for teachers in primary and secondary phases are great. The suggestion is that secondary subject specialists act as consultants to their primary colleagues. In mathematics the support may need little resource allocation. In science, however, the resource implications are greater. Primary schools in general lack science equipment and laboratory facilities. Primary teachers are, understandably, putting increasing moral pressure on science departments in secondary schools to extend the usual tour of the school for new pupils to a working relationship which involves use of laboratories in free time (for example during and after fifth-year public examinations when the normal teaching timetable and laboratory use is suspended). This always seems a useful initiative to primary heads and is educationally commendable. Logistically, however, the secondary head of science (with no time specifically allocated for primary liaison) may have to deal with requests from five or six partner primaries.

Setting up a staff development programme in National Curriculum areas which require specialist staff or accommodation therefore requires close liaison between the teachers responsible for staff development in the secondary and primary schools. It has been found useful to arrange joint meetings between primary and secondary staff development co-ordinators (often on a consortium basis) to plan annual programmes, share expertise and set common goals. This type of meeting has become increasingly common.

A further dimension to the practicalities of in-service training for the National Curriculum is given by the general staffing shortages existing nationally. A Welsh Office survey of 770 primary schools in 1988 showed that almost half had gaps in their curricula due to staff shortages. In November 1988 the *Times Educational Supplement* reported the evidence of teacher shortage given to the Interim Advisory Committee on teachers' pay. It showed that:

- shortages were worse in primary than secondary schools;
- unfilled posts in English and Welsh junior, infant and nursery schools in January 1988 stood at over 2500;
- in Greater London, one in every 24 primary places was unfilled;
- at secondary level, an increasing number of staff were teaching subjects in which they were not trained.

HMI have already made sweeping criticisms of the ways in which new teachers are prepared for their tasks when they first enter the profession. Their report, *The New Teacher in School* (1988), though not itself without critics, stated:

> Given the great diversity of situations in which new teachers find

themselves, it would be unreasonable to suppose that initial teacher training could prepare all teachers for all aspects of professional work.

HMI identified a number of areas in which new teachers experience difficulties:

- classroom management and control;
- making explicit the aims and objectives of lessons;
- matching work to the varied abilities of pupils;
- using questioning and marking to help pupils;
- using computers;
- teaching under-fives;
- catering for children with special needs.

It is accepted that colleges of initial teacher education can never prepare the 'perfect' teacher. The concept of licensed teachers makes new entrants to the profession even less likely to possess the practical skills outlined above. If the National Curriculum is to operate effectively, these issues need to be carefully considered. The role of the staff development co-ordinator in the primary school will be increasingly important in the field of induction as it will be for more experienced teachers.

11 Staff development in language

Few areas of the curriculum have created as much debate and division in both theory and practice as English. Teachers differ strongly in their views on how to facilitate language development, literacy and reading skills. The different approaches to the development of reading skills is an example. Many schools will approach the teaching of reading through commercial, packaged reading schemes. Others will take a literature-centred approach. Some will use computer software to enhance their work. Others will use a variety of classroom-based and environmental stimuli to develop pupils' literacy and oracy.

The approach adopted by a primary school will depend very much on the views of the head, or of the language curriculum co-ordinator or of individual teachers, or the policies of LEA advisers and advisory teachers. Often, approaches have not been thought through carefully and, in the absence of any clear reason why a school is adopting any particular approach, teachers may fall back on the methods that have traditionally been used.

Many heads feel strongly that it is not enough to know *how* to teach the various elements of literacy and oracy; it is more important to understand *why* certain approaches are being adopted or rejected. It is also important that staff in the school feel comfortable in following a common philosophy so that progression of learning throughout the school may be achieved.

Figure 11.1 is an example of a school-based staff development programme in 'language'. The school (a primary school with twelve staff) currently uses a commercially produced reading scheme. Two teachers attended a locally run course on 'A Picture Book Approach to Literacy', and this so captured the imagination of the staff involved that it led to a considerable amount of staffroom discussion.

It emerged that:

1 Staff were divided on the merits of using the reading scheme.
2 Some teachers were taking short-cuts with the scheme, others were operating it mechanically.
3 Pupils reacted in a variety of ways. Some appeared bored, others spirited by the competition to reach the next level.
4 Parents reacted in a similar way to pupils, often with unpleasantness appearing as one pupil moved along the scheme faster than another. Many strongly defended the use of the reading scheme.

'Language teaching' emerged as the top priority in the school's needs identification exercise. The staff development co-ordinator (the deputy head) was given the responsibility of setting up a series of staff development activities on language. It seemed sensible to involve the two teachers who had attended the picture-book course. They advised the co-ordinator to contact the course leaders who had a good reputation for running school-based INSET activities on language development.

The staff development co-ordinator was invited to meet the course leaders to discuss the feasibility of running a series of sessions on language. The course leaders had also been approached by a neighbouring school and it was felt that a combined activity would increase interaction and make the sessions more cost-effective. A reasonable fee was negotiated which enabled the co-ordinators of the two schools to fund five one-hour sessions plus travel. The cost of producing any resources required would be borne by the schools.

It was agreed, after consultation with the second school, that the purposes of the programme would be:

- to raise awareness of the many aspects of language;
- to examine a series of classroom activities;
- to enable staff to formulate and agree a school policy for language development.

Sessions would be interactive and experiential rather than didactic.

The course leaders would concentrate on the application of language development in the classroom rather than go into depth on the theories of language development.

The programme was presented to staff as shown in Figure 11.1.

Figure 11.1 A school INSET programme on language development

________________SCHOOL
STAFF DEVELOPMENT PROGRAMME
Language development

Sessions will be held between 3.35 PM and 4.45 PM in Y6 classroom.

Aims

- to raise awareness of the many aspects of language;
- to examine a series of classroom activities;
- to enable staff to formulate and agree a school policy for language development.

Programme outline

Session 1 Introduction
2 What is language?
3 Ideas for teaching (1)
4 Ideas for teaching (2)
5 Ideas for teaching (3) and evaluation

In Session 1 the pyramid game was used to negotiate the programme with all staff. It is important that this session involves everyone (not just one person talking and the staff listening) and that everyone has a clear idea of what is expected in the following sessions. Figure 11.2 illustrates how the pyramid game might work in practice.

Figure 11.2 The pyramid game

Objectives

- to draw up a list of priorities to be addressed in the programme;
- to involve all staff in doing this;
- to begin to identify the many aspects of language work.

Format

1. *Input:* explanation of purpose and what is going to happen.
2. *Individually:* write down three areas of concern in language work.
3. *In pairs:* share your areas of concern; explain in detail what is meant by each; prioritise *three*.
4. *In fours:* share your areas of concern and prioritise *three*.
5. *As a whole group:* agree on three areas of priority to be addressed on this series of sessions.

The leader(s) move around the groups stimulating discussion. Keep asking for explanations (eg 'what do you mean by "listening"? "reading"? "writing"?' etc).

Agree on specific areas which need to be covered in the next four sessions.

The pyramid game resulted in the following topics being among those which emerged as priorities for consideration:

- group prediction;
- graphic and stylistic modelling;
- cloze procedure;
- reading;
- picture-book approach;
- poetry patience;
- sequencing;
- in-basket exercises;
- SQ3R (reading skills);
- comprehension;
- literature-centred English.

An example of the way in which a one-hour session on one of the above topics, graphic modelling, was delivered is given below:

Session Three Ideas for teaching (1)

Example: 'Graphic modelling'
Time: one hour

Purposes of session

1 To present an example of a teaching technique which aims to put into practice elements of the previous session on the theories of language acquisition and development and features of English in education.
2 To enable teachers to fully evaluate the technique by putting them in the position of learner and by experiencing the technique at first hand.
3 To demonstrate, by example, the role of teacher as facilitator in the learning process.
4 To demonstrate the cross-curricular application of the technique.
5 To demonstrate the application of the technique across age-ranges.

Note: Handouts explaining the technique and its use in the classroom are supplied at end of session. This is made explicit to teachers at the outset, so enabling them to fully participate in the experience itself. No need for note-taking during the experience!

Procedure

1 Teachers are introduced to the purposes of the session (as above). The nature of the teaching technique is described as follows:

> 'Graphic modelling' is a strategy which aims to encourage reading for a purpose, reading for meaning and the retention of information. It requires the reader to restructure a written text into an appropriate graphic form. This could include drawings, cartoon strips, graphs, plans, maps, diagrams, and so on, and may be usefully applied to both factual material and imaginative literature.

2 Group divided into two: Groups A and B.
3 Subgroups divided into pairs.
4 Example A (Figure 11.3) distributed among pairs in Group A. Example B (Figure 11.4) distributed among pairs in Group B.
5 The pairs 'graphically model' their texts, given the information that the finished models will be exchanged between groups. Each group will be required to 'read' off the information of the other, reconstructing the original text, as accurately as possible, from the predominantly visual information at hand. Headings, keys and minimal labelling is encouraged.
6 Facilitator circulates the groups giving help, advice and encouragement, as appropriate.
7 Groups exchange models, pairs discuss and explore them and one of the pair 'reads' his or her diagram to the whole group. Opposite pairs evaluate the success of their reconstruction on the basis of this response.
8 Both groups are asked to recount the content of their original texts to the whole group. (This usually demonstrates a high rate of information retention.)
9 The group as a whole evaluates the nature of the experience, eg:
- how it felt to be the learner in the experience, including an appraisal of the general approach;
- a consideration of the role of the 'teacher' in the experience;
- what they felt they *specifically* learned from the technique;
- how the experience related to the principles which emerged from the previous theoretical sessions.

10 Using the technique in the classroom: group discusses specific example of adaptations for non-readers; examples from early picture/story books; information books of varying levels; junior and secondary fiction.
11 Handouts circulated and explanation, clarification offered.

12 Teachers encouraged to develop other teaching techniques based on principles which have arisen from the session (ie to generalise rather than to see the activity in isolation – not a 'tips for teachers' approach).

Evaluation of this activity shows a high degree of positive response from teachers. They enjoy the experiential nature of the activity, can relate it to their own classroom situations and, most importantly, can extend the idea for use with classes across the age-range and, with application, across the curriculum.

Figure 11.3 Example A

Volcanoes

The name volcano comes from the island of Vulcano which lies to the north east of Sicily.

The crust of the Earth is relatively thin. Underneath the crust, temperatures are so hot that the rock is in a molten state. The molten rock is called magma. When magma pushes up through a crack or fissure in the Earth's crust a volcano may be formed. The magma is called lava when it reaches the Earth's surface.

Some lava is thick and runs very slowly, like treacle. It flows out onto the Earth's surface through a hole, or vent, but does not flow very far. A cone-shaped mound gradually builds up as more and more lava is forced out.

Sometimes the gases in the lava shoot it high into the air in an explosive eruption. As it flies through the air it cools quickly and falls to the surface as pine-cone shaped rocks called volcanic bombs. Some of the lava disintegrates into even smaller pieces of rock called volcanic ash.

Alternating layers of lava and volcanic ash build up to form a volcanic cone. The hole in the top of the cone is called the crater.

Figure 11.4 Example B

My Secret Hideaway

At the bottom of my garden is my secret home. I'll describe it to you if you like.

My father made it for me two years ago out of logs from trees which had just been felled. The frame is about two metres square and one and a half metres high and is built up on three sides. The little house leans against a tall grassy bank which is covered in dead leaves in winter and beautiful daffodils in spring.

The main frame is made out of tree trunks about twenty centimetres in diameter. The corner pieces have been set into the ground and joined by cross-pieces at the top and bottom. The top cross-pieces on both sides have been set into the grassy bank. You can't see the frame from the outside because it has been covered in branches from the fir trees in the wood nearby. These are tacked on to thicker branches which run from floor to ceiling and form the walls and roof. There is one small window on the sunny side of the house and another on the front next to the door.

There is room inside my house for a tree-trunk table and two tree-trunk chairs. I have placed one chair underneath the sunny window to keep me warm in the winter time. I have no one to share my house with me but I don't mind. I like being alone.

12 Primary mathematics: an approach through games

Mathematics in the primary school has always been an area of public interest. Parents and politicians seem to base their opinions of schools on the ability of pupils to perform the so-called basic skills of addition, subtraction, multiplication and division. Levels of numeracy will continue to be important performance indicators of school effectiveness for the public at large. Teachers, meanwhile, have to keep pace with the changing approaches to mathematics: are times tables in or out?; are commercial schemes worthwhile? It is not surprising, therefore, that providers of INSET for primary mathematics are heavily in demand.

Unfortunately, the requests for INSET support often show up the inadequacies of superficial needs identification systems. Schools frequently contact providers saying 'We have identified maths as our priority area this term. Can you help?' Further analysis is needed if the INSET is to meet the true needs of teachers. The precise nature of the INSET must be ascertained. Is it:

- the mathematics itself (how to do it)?
- the pedagogy (how to teach it)?
- the content (what to teach)?

Often, primary teachers need to develop confidence in handling mathematical concepts themselves. For this reason, it is useful to begin any series of INSET sessions in mathematics with something that will give teachers confidence. Mathematical games serve this purpose. They are fun, useful, may easily transfer from INSET to classroom use, and, most important, they are non-threatening. Games differ in sophistication and level of application. It will usually be left to the teacher to take the 'idea' associated with a particular game and adapt it for use with his or her own teaching groups.

The use of mathematical games as the first of a series of INSET sessions also breaks down barriers between teachers and provider. Such sessions also enable the provider to extract information about more detailed mathematical needs. An example of such a session is given below:

Staff development programme: Mathematical games

The aims of this session are to:

- form an 'ice-breaking' activity – exciting and fun;
- increase teacher confidence in mathematics;
- illustrate some basic mathematical concepts;
- acquaint teachers with materials which can be used in class;
- stimulate ideas for future classroom use;
- focus on the *aims* of mathematics teaching.

Throughout the session examples of games (commercial and 'home-made') are on display around the room. Time is made available for teachers to browse and discuss the value of individual games. The session could run as follows:

Input: the use of games in the classroom

Time: 20 minutes.
When talking to teachers about the use of mathematical games in the classroom, the same questions seem to arise.

Why should we use games in the classroom?
When is the best time to use games?
How do we organise the use of games in the classroom?
Which type of game should we use?

In trying to answer these questions, it must be remembered that the attitude of the teacher towards the use of games in the classroom will influence their success or failure.

Why?
1 Children seem to play games less at home than they used to. As

always, the children who need to play them, have the least opportunity.

2 Games can be played purely for pleasure. There is a place for this in the classroom, as a great deal of incidental learning takes place in this area.
3 For the more reluctant pupil, games offer a disguised form of learning, and have an important role to play here.
4 Mathematical ideas can be introduced, reinforced and consolidated through the use of games. They can be used to develop or increase computational skills.
5 One area that is particularly neglected is that of logical thinking and the development of strategies. Nothing can replace the use of games here. They also provide an excellent opportunity for social interaction and development.

When?

Games should be played at anytime that is appropriate and should be incorporated into the class routine as a normal part of the learning process. They should not be played only on Friday afternoons, wet playtimes or when the children have finished their 'work'.

How?

1 The organisation of the classroom will certainly influence the use of games, but there are many games suitable for use with the whole class, groups of children, pairs of children and individual children. So whatever the organisational consideration, there are suitable games available.
2 Games should be easily accessible to the children so that there is an element of choice.
3 Games may be set up as part of an activity corner.

Which?

1 Games may be classified into games of strategy, number games and games to teach a specific idea. Games of strategy put children into problem solving situations and are good for the development of logical thinking.
2 Number games can give valuable computational practice. They can develop speed and accuracy.
3 Teaching a specific idea, for example measurement of length or telling the time, can be incorporated into a game. The game will probably follow, not precede, the teaching point.
4 The teacher should choose which games are suitable for the needs of children in the classroom.

Taking all these points into consideration, remember that the attitudes that the children have about games will largely depend upon the attitude of the teacher. If the teacher considers that games form an integral part of the learning process then the children will appreciate their importance.

A game for the whole group: two-dice bingo

Materials: two dice, outline bingo card with six spaces but no numbers

a) Participants fill in on their cards any six numbers which may arise when throwing two dice and adding together their scores.
(Concept 1: the numbers must fall between 2 and 12, inclusive)

b) Play bingo using the dice.
(Concept 2: reinforcement of number bonds to 12)

c) Look at the winning card. What numbers have come up? Do the numbers chosen have any effect on the fact that this person finished first?
(Concept 3: probability. 7 is the most probable number to occur.)

Discussion

Probability and its classroom application.

Games

Participants look at a variety of games to use with individuals, groups or the whole class. An example of a game for use with a small group is given in Figure 12.1.

Conclusion: what are the criteria for choosing a good game?

Liedtke (1980) identifies eight criteria. He states that:

> It is unlikely that any one game or setting will meet all the suggested criteria, but it is assumed the more criteria met, the better the game.

Figure 12.1 The moon race game

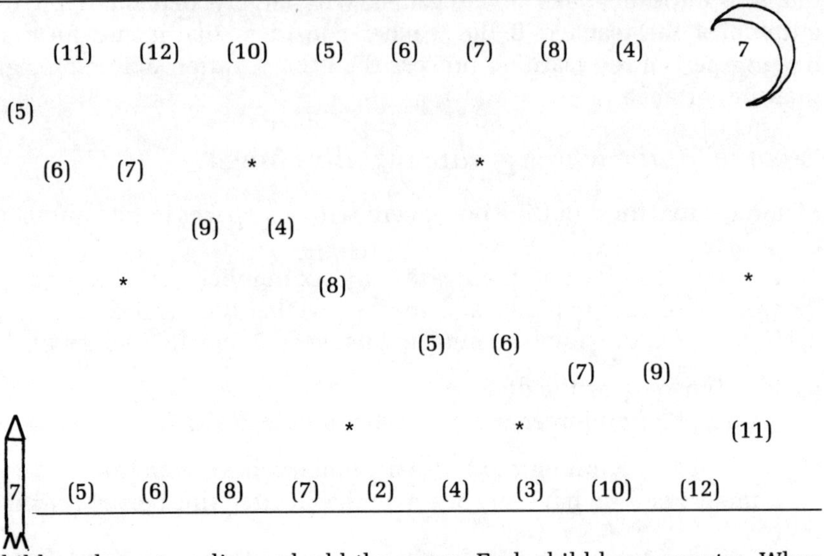

Children throw two dice and add the scores. Each child has a counter. When the scores of the two dice add up to seven, a child may place the counter in the rocket.

Children throw the dice again, add the scores and move along the row of numbers to the one which shows the total of the two dice they have just thrown (eg if a child throws a 5 and a 3 they will move along the row of numbers to number 8).

The first player to land on the moon is the winner.

Liedtke's criteria are as follows:

1 *Simple rules.* Young children consider rules to be very important, but they often forget or break them. Allowing children to modify existing rules or invent new ones can become a useful creative activity.
2 *Quick action.* Lengthy games lead to frustration.
3 *Simple setting.* The game should have few pieces, demand little in terms of preparation time and be easy to set up and store.
4 *Non-distractive.* Children should not be distracted from the intended learning outcomes.
5 *Chance.* Games will have winners, but the emphasis need not be on winning. The final outcome should be a chance outcome.
6 *Learning experience.* Avoid settings where children have to miss turns or drop out. Children should be able to correct themselves whenever a mistake is made.

7 *Adaptable.* The game should be usable in a variety of situations. It should be playable by large or small groups or even individuals. Teacher guidance should be minimal.
8 *Open to new ideas.* The game should enhance a variety of learning situations so that skills and concepts can be reinforced or reviewed in familiar settings.

The use of games for staff development activities works just as well as their classroom use. However, they must not be trivialised. There must be a clear learning experience for teachers as well as classroom applicability and a sense of fun. The INSET budget may well run to paying for training materials to make new games so that the benefits from playing are not reduced by poor-quality materials.

13 Staff development in primary science

13.1 Background

What is different about staff development in primary science, as opposed to development in other core areas such as maths and English or a foundation subject such as history? The main difference lies perhaps in the relative lack of qualifications and experience in this area of the curriculum amongst primary school teachers. This tendency – and the mystique so often associated with science – leads to widespread unease and apprehension amongst staff about the whole business of science and science teaching. In the past this led many teachers largely to ignore the place of science in the primary school curriculum – despite the existence of pockets of excellent practice and the long-standing availability of potentially fruitful resources such as *Nuffield Primary Science* and *Science 5–13*.

The advent of the National Curriculum removes the option of ignoring science in the primary school. Every primary teacher now has a responsibility to provide an education in science in accordance with the statutory provisions. Perhaps for the first time, almost all staff, understandably with varying degrees of enthusiasm, *want* to be 'developed', ie to gain the necessary knowledge and expertise in fostering children's scientific learning to be able to meet the requirements of the National Curriculum. How is this to be achieved?

The strategies available can usefully be divided into two broad and related categories. These are:

1 'Traditional' courses
   a) for individual development;

   b) for subsequent whole-staff, school-based development (the so-called 'cascade' model, see Chapter 16.4).
2 School-based development
   a) from within the school's own expertise and resources (including staff who have undertaken courses with subsequent developments as in b) above);
   b) with the help of outside agents (eg LEA advisers, college or university lecturers, LEA support services).

Clearly, there is, and will continue to be, a place for 'traditional' courses, but school-based consultancy is in growing demand. At the moment this demand outstrips the 'supply' of consultants with expertise in primary science. The nature of the demand also varies. Some schools have simply wanted someone with whom to talk over issues, clarify thinking and discuss their own plans for meeting National Curriculum requirements. Others have asked for a more extensive exploration of the nature of primary science, the requisite scientific concepts, practical work and experiments suitable for classroom use and help with policy guidelines and programmes of work. One of the prime objectives must be to build teachers' confidence and to remove both apprehension and any lingering mystique from primary-school science.

The expressed needs of teachers on 'traditional' courses and those involved in school-based development seem to be very similar, viz:

- to understand the provisions of the National Curriculum in science;
- to develop ideas on how attainment targets are to be addressed, particularly through integrated or thematic approaches to learning and teaching;
- to develop sufficient understanding of the relevant scientific processes and concepts to give confidence in addressing the requirements of the National Curriculum;
- to have help in identifying and evaluating essential resources and forms of organisation;
- to consider assessment in primary science.

In the case of school-based development, it is usually the case that schools also want help in developing some sort of coherent policy document for science teaching in the school. Some schools are much more 'advanced' than others and may request only some fresh ideas and 'fine-tuning' of what goes on. Others, perhaps the majority, may be much nearer to first base. Rarely do they begin from nothing. Needs analysis must therefore be carried out to determine the level of existing expertise. This may be achieved by informal discussion among the whole staff, for example using the Report of the National Curriculum Council's Science Working Party (December 1988) as a starting point.

A necessary follow-up to this is to arrange for staff to undertake some simple scientific investigations for themselves. The view of children's learning in science incorporated in the National Curriculum is one of active development through processes of exploration. It is important, therefore (and fun) for teachers to have similar experiences, which may very well be at odds with their own education in science.

Adult learning is in many ways similar to that of children. Through such activities, teachers are modelling those approaches identified with good practice in primary science teaching. If teachers are to take up the challenges of introducing science to children, they need to experience, understand and internalise these processes themselves.

Teachers may work together in twos or threes and undertake a variety of tasks designed to illustrate a range of scientific concepts in different areas (forces, energy, materials etc) and in ways suitable for different age-groups. The example of 'whirly copters' is used later in this chapter to illustrate this. Practical activities such as these can be used:

- as ice-breakers ('This is not going to be too formal and stuffy');
- to increase confidence and motivation ('science really is quite fun and not too hard');
- to de-mystify science ('I understand that now');
- to illustrate and examine the characteristics and processes of scientific enquiry (observation, identification of variables, measuring, classifying etc);
- to familiarise participants with some relevant scientific concepts;
- to provide teachers with practical ideas of immediate use in classroom situations ('I'll try this with Y4');
- to help teachers see how practical activities can begin to address the National Curriculum attainment targets ('I can see how that might help');
- to illustrate the value of discussion, planning and co-operation in promoting scientific development;
- to illustrate how structure and content of activities can be modified for different ages and abilities of pupils;
- to illustrate the cross-curricular potential of work in science.

It is important that all examples are drawn from scientific investigations and involve scientific concepts and resources suitable for primary school children. An emphasis on skills and processes (compared with prior subject knowledge) usually helps teachers feel more secure with the subject.

Of course, concerns will always remain. What about assessment? This is always problematic and, at the time of writing, largely uncertain. Teachers are rightly concerned about the difficulties of resourcing and organising practical activities within a class grouping of about 30 children. Most teachers are apprehensive about truly open-ended investigations and their ability to capitalise on opportunistic happenings. They tend to fear 'wasting time', or misleading children, or 'not knowing the answers', or deviating from prior planning. For these and other reasons they often feel happier with more structured activities where the range of outcomes is, for them, predictable. In a sense, though, this is to misunderstand the unpredictable and exploratory nature of primary science and indeed of scientific knowledge. Children bring a store of ideas to a new experience. These are linked to further experiences. These links are made and then refined by developing skills such as observing and hypothesising. The focus for the curriculum co-ordinator, therefore, is to encourage teachers in their thinking of how this kind of learning can be promoted. The emphasis is on nurturing the growing powers of explanation in children whilst at the same time developing scientific skills and attitudes.

A variety of commercially-produced primary science books, schemes and packs are available. The range will undoubtedly increase as the National Curriculum is fully implemented in schools. It is important, though, that staff development in science is not simply equated with a broadening experience of an increasing number of published materials. Before any decision is made on resources, teachers should ask and answer a number of fundamental questions. Staffs need to develop a very clear view of what science means to them – not only in terms of content, but also of its overall place within their view of children's learning and related aspects of classroom organisation. Differing materials demand differing responses in terms of class management and may carry strong implications for individual, small group or whole-class arrangements.

Only when the staff have fully explored these considerations can decisions on which resources to purchase be taken. It may well be that published materials provide a framework of useful ideas and advice, but they should not be allowed to dictate or short-circuit the necessarily slow processes of reflection and growth involved in staff development in this or any other curriculum area.

The following guide may be useful to those responsible for setting up school-based staff development programmes in science.

The science co-ordinators 'rule book'

1 Ensure that most ideas, suggestions etc come from the staff.
2 Ensure maximum involvement.
3 Keep sessions bubbling and *active*.
4 Ensure that staff do not rely on you to provide all the answers.
5 Make sure that staff accept responsibility and *ownership* of ideas and materials produced.
6 Don't 'tread on toes' or undermine confidence inadvertently (eg by displaying seemingly vast knowledge and scientific ability, or highlighting weaknesses).
7 Despite all this, don't play down your own knowledge and responsibility.
8 Plan a way of following up after the activities have been tried in class.

13.2 Whirlycopters

The 'Whirlycopters' activity represents an example of a task which can be adapted to a wide range of ages, aptitudes and abilities. It also has some important cross-curricular potential.

A whirlycopter is a paper spinner, easily made, which can be used to investigate the effects of various variables on the quality of 'spin' or flight. The spinners can be:

Increasing task demand

- ready-made;
- made by pupils using a template;
- made by pupils using a diagram and specific instructions;
- made by pupils following a general design brief.

The investigations themselves can vary in several ways:

1 The variable being investigated can vary (eg weight, wing length, construction material – thickness of paper).
2 Extension activities can be included which are more open-ended (eg 'Can you design an even better flyer?' 'What would you change?'

Figures 13.1 and 13.2 illustrate some of these points.

Figure 13.1 Whirlycopters: level one exercise

1 Make some whirlycopters using the template provided and some thick paper. (To complete a whirlycopter bend the wings over and put paper clips on the bottom.)
2 Make a few practice flights with your whirlycopter.
3 Discuss with your partner what you mean by 'best flyer'.
4 Try to find out how much *weight* (paper clips) makes the whirlycopters fly best.
5 Now try:
   - *no* paper clips
   - *one* paper clip
   - *two* paper clips

   and so on.
6 How can you make sure your test is *fair*?
7 Which whirlycopter flew best?
8 Write down what you did and what you found out. (Remember to write down what you decided about a good flyer and how you make sure your test was fair.)
9 Do a drawing of your experiement.

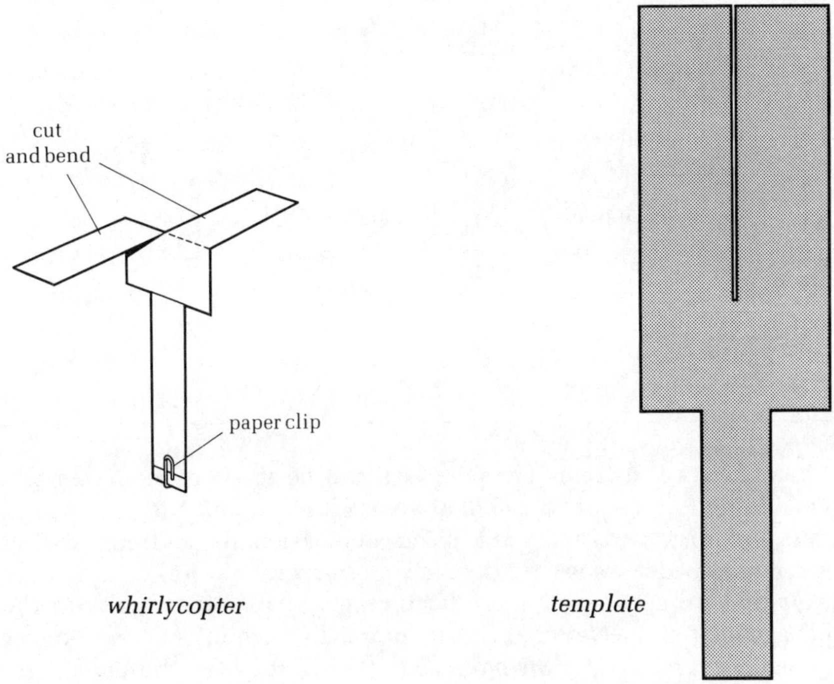

Figure 13.2 Whirlycopters: level two exercise

1 Make some whirlycopters using the design provided.
2 Experiment with the whirlycopters; try to find out how much weight (paper clips) makes the best flyer. (Before starting, discuss with your partner what you mean by the 'best flyer'.)
3 Try:
- *no* paper clips
- *one* paper clip
- *two* paper clips

and so on.

4 How can you make sure that your tests are fair?
5 Write down what you did and what you found out. (Remember to write down what you decided about a good flyer and how you made sure that your test was fair.)
6 Do a drawing to illustrate your experiment.
7 Can you design an even better flyer?
8 What things could you change to try and make an even better flyer? Have a go.

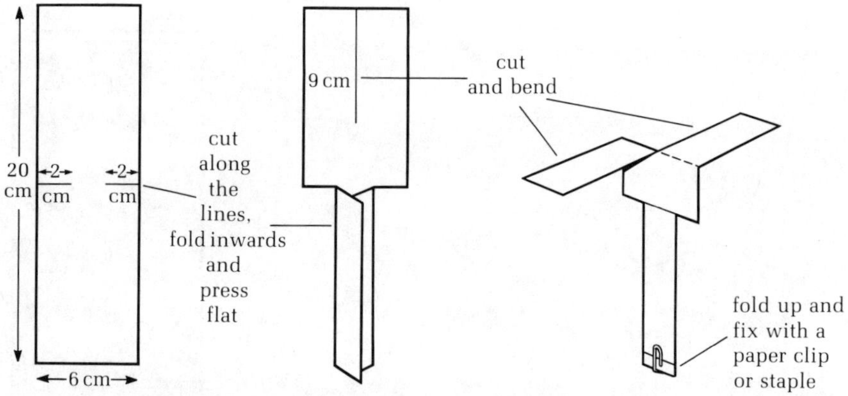

Figure 13.3 illustrates how the task can be made more subtle and demanding for groups to tackle at an adult level, and can give rise to quite complex and extended discussion. Such discussions should encompass wider issues, particularly cross-curricular links. One of the ways that primary schools are beginning to come to terms with the management of the National Curriculum is through integrated, topic or thematic approaches. HMI have consistently reported the benefits to children's learning when they are encouraged to appreciate the significance of work in one area of the curriculum through opportunities to

apply that work in a variety of contexts. Science is no exception.

So 'whirlycopters' involves not only a consideration of scientific processes, but could include, for example, those of mathematics and

Figure 13.3 Whirlycopters: level three

1 Have a look at the design of a whirlycopter shown below.
2 Make one from paper. Try it out. Does it fly?
3 What *variables* might make a difference to how well a whirlycopter flies. Write a list of these.
4 Choose one variable which interests you particularly. Devise a test to see whether that variable does in fact make a difference to how well the whirlycopter flies.
5 Try to discover the value of the variable which makes the whirlycopter fly best.
6 Now choose a different variable. Repeat your investigation.
7 What have you discovered so far? What problems or difficulties have you encountered? What problems do you think would arise if you wanted to find the *best design of all*?

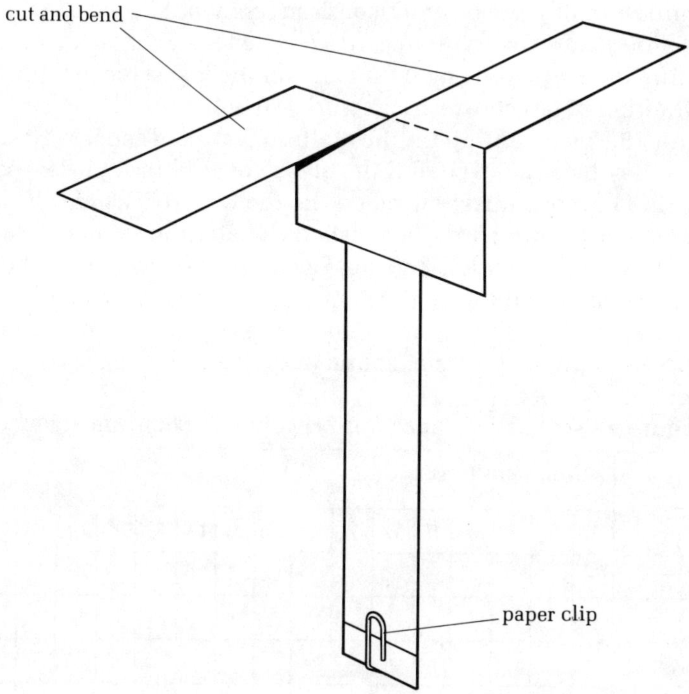

language. In other words, though an activity may be weighted towards the area of science it is important for teachers to understand its potential for learning experiences across the primary curriculum.

It may well be that assessment procedures related to the National Curriculum can only be satisfied – without distorting and fragmenting primary practice – by developing teacher expertise in recognising assessment opportunities for several different curriculum areas present in one rich learning activity.

13.3 Staff development in science: a case study

A large junior school with 350 pupils embarked on a curriculum development project in science. The initiative began with the arrival in school of the document *Science in the National Curriculum* (1989). All members of staff read through the document and a staff meeting was devoted to discussing the practical implications of its content.

A series of steps to action were agreed at the meeting:

1 *Examination of present practice.* Teachers would look at what they were doing already with regard to science. Each teacher would examine the work done by their class on the last science topic, using the attainment targets as a framework. To help with this, a large chart (Figure 13.4) was put up on the staffroom wall. Teachers ticked the topics they had achieved and the areas covered in their last science project. They put question marks in the squares where they were unsure or had only partially satisfied the attainment target, and left blank those areas which had not been covered in class. The chart ended up as a pattern of ticks, question marks and blank spaces, indicating clearly that the areas not being covered were the physical sciences – light, magnetism, sound and electricity.

Figure 13.4 Analysis chart for National Curriculum science

Areas of study (themes)	*Attainment targets*																
	1	2	3	4	5	6	7	8	9	10	11	12	13	14	15	16	17

2 *Where do we go next?* Teachers complained about the 'dry' presentation of information in the books available. It was agreed that practical activities should be organised for staff. Four one-and-a-half hour sessions were planned. The workshops were led by the science co-ordinator and focused on classroom practice. Ten practical activities were set up and teachers were encouraged to try as many as possible. Other support included:
   - individual teachers attending external courses on science in the National Curriculum;
   - advisory science teachers spending time in classrooms working with class teachers;
   - science co-ordinator holding conversations with individual staff to discuss classroom issues.

3 *Where did we get to?* The workshops generated discussion and led to changes in practice. It became clear that some of the 'gaps' on the original chart were now being filled. In fact, interest has been generated to the extent that concern has shifted from whether or not attainment targets are being met to what level they are addressing and how they should be assessed.

13.4 Resources

Useful sources of reference for primary science

Gilbert, C. and Matthews, P. *Look! Primary Science*, London: Addison-Wesley.

Gilbert, C. and Matthews, P. *A first look! Science for 4 to 8 year olds*, Edinburgh: Oliver and Boyd.

School Curriculum Development Committee. *Learning Through Science*, London: Macdonald.

School Curriculum Development Committee. *Science 5–13*, London: Macdonald.

'Free' materials for school science and science education

Most of the bigger companies will send you materials on request, eg: ICI, Cadbury-Schweppes, British Steel, British Rail, British Gas. Government departments can also be generous. A useful source is:

Department of Energy
Education Unit
Blackhouse Road
London SE99 6TT

In particular, it supplies materials on energy in primary science.

With a little effort and imagination and an alert eye, much can be gained for relatively little!

14 Setting up a programme for special needs

14.1 Introduction

The case study that follows is of a large primary school whose staff had identified special needs as part of their INSET requirements for one particular year. The headteacher of the school had delegated the role of staff development co-ordinator to his deputy and, together with the teacher responsible for special needs, had begun to piece together a programme of staff development which would culminate in the drawing up and implementation of a special needs policy for the school. The following programme was established:

1 Staff development sessions – awareness raising and setting the framework for a special needs policy.
2 Working party led by teacher responsible for special needs to draw up a policy and present to staff and governors.
3 Implementation of agreed policy.
4 Monitoring, evaluation and further review as necessary.

The teacher responsible for special needs worked closely with the staff development deputy to plan and organise the programme. A consultant was identified (an advisory teacher) and an initial visit set up. The consultant visited the school some three months prior to the period in which the INSET had been planned and, in the initial meeting with head and deputy, discussed the format of the programme.

Two evening INSET sessions were held, led by the advisory teacher. The first session was presented as a lecture-style format, although in a relatively informal setting, setting the background to special needs. The second session saw teachers asking many questions, discussing certain areas in small groups before reconvening to discuss these as a whole group. In this way teachers responsible for different age-ranges consulted with colleagues, discussed available materials brought along by the consultant and made personal notes on these. At no time did the consultant attempt to recommend any particular test or strategy, choosing instead to try to present many different viewpoints. The consultant saw this as a beneficial two-way process receiving useful first-hand feedback from the teachers.

Following these sessions the school's staff development co-ordinator prepared an evaluation schedule which included this area along with the others covered during the term. The schedule sought answers to three straightforward questions:

1 Did you find the content of these sessions worthwhile?
2 Did you enjoy the presentation of these sessions?
3 Would you like more sessions on this area?

Additionally, teachers were given space to add any other relevant comments that were either concerned with the INSET or that would aid the planning of the future INSET programme.

Teachers were generally pleased with the two sessions and stated a preference for the presentation of the second session (workshop activities). Teachers also expressed a desire to have further sessions on devising individual programmes of learning strategies for children with special needs.

14.2 Setting up the policy

Once the INSET had been concluded the head asked the teacher responsible for special needs to commence work on producing a new school policy document on the area of special needs. The teacher decided to contact a number of people who would be able to advise and offer guidance on current literature and educational debate.

During the next few weeks documents and relevant information were collected, including references to the Education Acts of 1981 and 1988, DES Circular 1/83 and the Warnock Report (1978) and National Curriculum Council Statements such as Circular Number 5. In addition to this, the first draft also considered a suitable and workable system of recording and identifying special needs in the primary school.

Alongside the development of the policy the teacher responsible visited one of the authority's special schools and began to compile a directory containing various local names and organisations which could be contacted and relied upon to provide support and assistance if required. This was considered important if the policy was to be properly followed and adhered to.

At this stage, the second draft of the document, complete with the programme of record-keeping, was presented formally to the staff. Extracts are reproduced in section 14.3 below. At this meeting the staff were asked to consider the whole document but to pay particular attention to the tri-annual assessment of all children from which would follow identification of children with perceived special needs. Teachers were also made aware of the procedures to follow if any child required any programme as a result of being identified as having a special need. These sheets included the Class Teacher's Plan of Action, Parental Consultation and any form of Referral to Outside Agencies.

The staff accepted the document, and this was then introduced and administered for the first time at the beginning of the following term. From staff identifying the special needs policy document as an area of high priority, through the INSET programme to the production of a workable policy with accompanying document took one year. At the time of writing the school is about to embark upon the next stage of monitoring and evaluating the process of implementation in view of the implications of the 1988 Education Reform Act. The policy document published here is therefore seen as 'Mark 1', with amendments to follow as the policy is seen to work in practice.

14.3 Extract from case-study school's policy document – a system for identifying pupils with special education needs

Introduction

The Education Act of 1981 made provision with respect to children with Special Educational Needs. For the purposes of this Act 'a child has *special educational needs* if he has a learning difficulty which calls for special educational provision to be made for him.' (Section 1 (1)). It also states that 'a child has a *learning difficulty* if he has a significantly greater difficulty in learning than the majority of children of his age.' (Section 1 (2a)). Also 'It shall be the duty of the governors, in the case of a county or voluntary school, and of the local education authority by whom the school is maintained, in the case of a maintained nursery school, to secure that the teachers in the school are aware of the importance of identifying and providing for, those registered pupils who have special educational needs.' (Section 2 (5c)).

The Act indicates that a child is not to be taken as having a learning difficulty because the language or form of language used at home is different to that used in school. But there are of course degrees of learning difficulty and the Warnock Report, which laid the foundation for the 1981 Education Act, suggests three levels of learning difficulty. They are:

1 *Mild* learning difficulty, ie those children whose reading requirement differs only slightly from that offered to 'normal' pupils.
2 *Moderate* learning difficulty, ie those children whose reading requirement differs to a visible extent from that offered to 'normal' pupils.
3 *Severe* learning difficulty, ie those children whose reading requirement differs substantially from that offered to 'normal' pupils.

The system

Each registered pupil will have an assessment sheet which will include the following areas of pupil functioning:

Social
Emotional
Behavioural
Physical

and Academic, ie:

Mathematics
Language, Reading/Writing
Science
Other curriculum areas.

There will be a tri-annual assessment of each child, one assessment to be completed at the end of each term on the Continual Assessment form (Referral 1), thus building up as full a picture as possible of the child's strengths and weaknesses over the Academic Year. The Continual Assessment form is designed to comment on what a pupil can do as opposed to what he/she cannot do.

Three other record sheets are available to staff. These are:

1 *Plan of Action* (Referral 2)
To aid the teacher and other professionals involved as to what has been tried, tested, achieved, whether successfully or otherwise over a period of time.
2 *Parental Consultation* (Referral 3)
To give details and dates of all parental contact concerning a child's Special Educational Needs.
3 *Referral to Outside Agencies* (Referral 4)
To give details and dates of all contact with Advisory or school Psychological Services.

These record sheets will help to form an overall assessment of the child's attainment and development, thereby striving towards the school goal of having a multi-professional team approach to determine what a pupil might need in the way of specialist teaching (Appendix B gives examples of each of the referral sheets).

The system can therefore be broken down into three areas:

1 IDENTIFICATION
2 PLAN OF ACTION
3 MONITORING

Monitoring is effected initially through the Referral 1 form. The plan of action(s) is given in the Referral 2 form and monitoring the outcome of any plan of action(s) is reflected in both the Referral 1 and Referral 2 forms.

The sequence of Referral action, when appropriate, is as follows:

1 Class Teacher – To initially identify a pupil's difficulty/need area(s). Documented on *Referral 1*.
2 Coordinator (in the area of curriculum where the Special Need occurs) – To provide expert advice in the area of concern. Documented on *Referral 2*.
3 Head Teacher and Deputy – To support the coordinator with respect to the implementation of the programmes of action identified by the coordinator in conjunction with the Class Teacher. Documented on *Referral 2*.
4 Parents – To be informed of any special programmes developed for their child as well as acting as a source of information on

their child. Documented on *Referral 3*.

5 Referral to Outside Agencies (School Psychological Service) – when appropriate. To gain specialist advice. Documented on *Referral 4*.

6 Statemented/De-statemented – where appropriate, according to the procedures of the 1981 Education Act.

7 Requirements of statements to be implemented in school (eg placement in a small class) and school action to be monitored according to annual review demands of the 1981 Education Act.

Referral 1

CONTINUAL ASSESSMENT

YEAR/TERM______/______

PUPIL'S NAME________________ DATE OF BIRTH________

TEACHER'S NAME_____________ CLASS______________

OBSER-VATIONS	DATE	VERY GOOD	GOOD	ACCEPT-ABLE	POOR OR UN-ACCEPT-ABLE
General					
SOCIAL *Comments*					
EMOTIONAL *Comments*					
BEHAVIOURAL *Comments*					
PHYSICAL *Comments*					
Academic					
MATHEMATICS *Comments*					
LANGUAGE *Comments*					
SCIENCE *Comments*					
OTHER CURRIC. AREAS *Comments*					

Referral 2

PLAN OF ACTION

YEAR/TERM_______/_________

PUPIL'S NAME____________________ DATE OF BIRTH__________

TEACHER'S NAME________________ CLASS____________________

ACTION TAKEN	DATE	DURATION	SUCCESSFUL	UNSUCCESSFUL

Referral 3

PARENTAL CONSULTATIONS

YEAR/TERM_______/_________

PUPIL'S NAME____________________ DATE OF BIRTH__________

TEACHER'S NAME________________ CLASS____________________

DATE	COMMENTS

Referral 4

REFERRAL TO OUTSIDE AGENCIES

YEAR/TERM______/________

PUPIL'S NAME____________________ DATE OF BIRTH_________

TEACHER'S NAME_______________ CLASS___________________

DATE	AGENCY CONTACTED	DETAILS

15 Display in the primary school

The following case study charts a staff development programme concerned with the presentation and display of children's work and the general environmental ethos of the school.

15.1 How the project was initiated

Looking back over the project, it is perhaps true to say that three factors were significant in contributing to the identification of this particular area as appropriate for a staff development programme:

1 The headteacher had visited schools at some distance from her immediate locality whilst on a management course and was both impressed and inspired by what she saw. She described her experiences to her staff and showed them some colour slides she had taken.
2 Staff undertook their whole school needs identification exercise and prioritised display. In the case of this particular school, staff were no doubt influenced in their decision by the headteacher's enthusiasm.
3 At the same time, the school agreed to become involved with a national arts education project. This involved a member of staff, her pupils and an artist engaging together in work both in the classroom and in a local art gallery. It was felt by the headteacher that the considerable commitment given to the project, in terms of resources and time, would reap benefits for the school as a whole, and not only in the personal development of the class teacher involved.

Figure 15.1 Some needs identified

1. DISPLAY – tips/techniques.
   - for quick but effective display;
   - use of fabrics/drapes;
   - choice of background colours/papers/mix 'n match effects.

2. DEVELOPMENT of basic art/craft/design techniques and practical experience.

   eg. further applications of printing as children's skills become more sophisticated.

3. ORGANISATION of art/craft materials for different age-groups.
   - practical storage tips for easy access by children
   - keeping materials tidy and well-organised.

How do nursery/reception classes in other schools organise use of art/craft materials?

4. ASSESSMENT of children's work
   - How do staff select for display/competitions?
   - What criteria should be applied to selection?

5. SCHEME OF WORK FOR ART/CRAFT DESIGN
   - Content
   - materials
   - progression

15.2 The first staff meeting to identify training needs on aspects of display

In this fairly healthy climate, then, the staff met to discuss the area in which they felt they needed most guidance. Responses were summarised as shown in Figure 15.1 by the teacher involved in the arts project.

15.3 Approaching the consultant

At this stage, the head felt it would be advisable to look outside the school for some help. Anticipating the need for external consultants, the local teacher education college had distributed publicity leaflets to all schools in nearby authorities. One of these leaflets caught the head's eye, and she arranged with the college for one of their art education lecturers to pay a visit to the school. In the meantime, she sent him a copy of staff responses to the identification of needs exercise.

15.3.1 The consultant's first visit

It was arranged that the consultant should arrive early, before the school day ended, so that the head could show him around the school and point out particular areas of weakness. He was then introduced to the staff and was able to discuss with them the finer detail of their concerns, allowing him to get a fuller picture of what they required. It was also an opportunity for him to tune in to the general climate of the staffroom: which members of staff were positive and enthusiastic; which were defensive, negative, or nervous at the prospect of INSET. He tried to present a non-threatening front, in the hope of gaining their confidence.

15.3.2 Submitting a proposed staff development programme

The consultant devised the rough draft of a programme which he hoped would accommodate all that the staff had specified. He sent it with a covering letter to the head, and asked if she would discuss it with the staff and let him know whether or not it was what they wanted.

The head replied, saying that the staff had agreed the plans. She requested a list of books and/or resources that she should have in school so that they would be fully prepared for the subsequent INSET sessions. The consultant broke down his rough draft into greater detail, and sent it off with a list of resources (Figures 15.2 and 15.3).

Figure 15.2 Possible programme for INSET consultancy

TERM 1	
*SESSION 1	*Discussion* – Identification of criteria for evaluation of the programme
*SESSION 2	*Display: why and what?* – Discussion followed by slide presentation
*SESSION 3	*Display: how?* – Practical workshop
SESSION 4 SESSION 5	*Visits* to schools to see good practice – with the support of the LEA primary adviser
SESSION 6	*Display: discussion* – Reflections. What have we seen? What can we learn? Where do we go from here?
TERM 2	
*SESSION 7	*Drawing* – Children's developmental stages
*SESSION 8	*Drawing* – Practical session. Drawing materials
SESSION 9 SESSION 10	*Tasks for children* – Drawing from imagination and observation
*SESSION 11	*Monitoring and formative evaluation* – How is the programme going? Do we need to make changes to future sessions? *Drawing* – Reflections on children's work
*SESSION 12	*Painting* – An introduction
*SESSION 13	*Painting* – Practical session: colour mixing
*SESSION 14	*Painting* – Using works of art in conjunction with children's own work, as stimulus and support
SESSION 15 SESSION 16 SESSION 17	*Painting project for children* (?)
TERM 3	
*SESSION 18	*Printing* Monitoring and formative evaluation: are changes needed?
*SESSION 19	*Printing* Practical session – various printing techniques
*SESSION 20	*Printing* Introducing sequence and progression
SESSION 21 SESSION 22 SESSION 23	*Printing* – Implementing activities in school
*SESSION 24	*Assessment of children's work in art* – Should we? Can we?
*SESSION 25	*Evaluation* – What have we done? What did we think of it? What did we learn? Where do we go from here?

* Asterisk denotes sessions to be conducted by consultant. Other sessions to be conducted by curriculum leader.

Figure 15.3 List of materials and books

For display	• guntacker • pinpusher • rotary trimmer • sharp craft knife or Stanley knife • steel ruler • paper and card, eg frieze paper, hessian (paper-backed), corrugated card, sugar paper (black, grey, coloured), white card, coloured Daler board • glue (eg PVA) • paste brushes.
For drawing	• pencils (variety of grades, eg B, 3B, 5B, 7B, 9B) • charcoal • coloured pencils • fixative • pastels (oil) • pastels (soft, eg Greyhound) • markers (black and coloured) • cartridge paper (white) • pastel paper or sugar paper (tinted) • inks • pens (old fashioned variety) • fine brushes.
For painting	• paints in yellow, red, blue, purple, white, brown, black • mixing palettes • water jars • variety of brushes (thick, thin, hog's hair, nylon, etc).
For printing	• printing inks (water-based) • finger paints • rollers • plastic trays or pieces of Formica • Berol 'Pressprint' – polystyrene tiles for printing.
For work with clay	• earthenware clay • rolling pins • clay boards (or pieces of Formica) • knives (old cutlery from home).
Books	Barnes, R., *Teaching Art to Young Children 4–9*, London: Allen and Unwin. Calouste Gulbenkian Foundation, *The Arts in Schools.* Clement, R., *The Art Teacher's Handbook*, London: Hutchinson.

Gentle, K., *Children and Art Teaching*, London: Croom Helm.
Joicey, H. B., *An Eye on the Environment*, London: Bell and Hyman.
Lancaster, J., *Art, Craft and Design in the Primary School*, NSEAD, 7a High Street, Corsham, Wiltshire, SN13 0ES. Tel (0249) 714825.
Morgan, M. (ed.), *Art in the Early Years of Schooling*, Oxford: Basil Blackwell Ltd.
Taylor, R., *Educating for Art*, York: Longman.

It was made clear by the consultant that the programme of work outlined was subject to modification by the teachers involved. It was then scheduled to begin at the start of the new academic year and coincided with the appointment of a new member of staff, to be responsible for aesthetics in the school. The new teacher was also asked to take over the running of the INSET programme, and to liaise with the consultant.

15.4 Running the INSET programme

Session 1

In order to identify the criteria for evaluation, the first session began by staff being asked to say what it was that they expected from the course. Most of the consequent discussion corresponded with the needs that had been identified above. It followed, therefore, that the criteria for evaluation would be derived from the content of the programme of work. This, although it had been tentatively fixed, would probably be amended and revised in the light of formative (on-going) evaluations made during its course. Instead of identifying a definitive list of criteria at the very beginning of the course, it was deemed to be more realistic and manageable to determine the aims/purposes/goals/objectives for each session at the end of the previous one. For example, the aim of the next session would be to identify some of the elements of good display in schools. However, in concluding the first session, it was suggested by one of the teachers that a general aim of the course might be for members of staff to gain confidence in teaching art. This seemed to meet with general approval.

15.5 Formative evaluation

At the end of the first term, the work programme was reviewed and there was a general feeling amongst staff, as a result of visits to other schools, that some modifications should be made. Staff requested a craft, design and technology input, and also asked for some book-making workshops. They felt that drawing could be omitted from the programme as they had benefited significantly from the presence of the professional artist in the school. The class involved had done a great deal of drawing, using a variety of materials. The work they achieved proved to be inspirational for the rest of the staff.

The initial programme of work was subsequently revised as follows:

TERM 2: CDT
TERM 3: Bookmaking
Printing
Painting

Because of the largely practical nature of the INSET sessions, it was possible for the consultant to talk informally to individuals and to pick up reactions to how things were going. This allowed for regular (informal) appraisal and discussion. It also allowed for consultant, staff and headteacher to get to know each other better, to chat over their work, and to have the odd joke. This helped to alleviate the strain that can sometimes be felt when teachers stay on after school for imposed in-service sessions.

The remainder of the programme was implemented as planned. Eventually, the end of the academic year was in sight and it was time to make a summative evaluation of the staff development programme.

15.6 Summative evaluation of the programme

A whole session was given over to this. It began with the consultant asking teachers to consider the following questions and to discuss them in pairs.

1 Have we done all that we set out to do?
2 What have we found most worthwhile?
3 If we had had to leave one thing out, what would it have been? What might have been done differently (if anything)?
4 Where do we go from here?

The resultant discussion and conclusions were summarised by the consultant. Copies of the summary were sent to the school, for approval by the staff.

15.7 Summative evaluation: summary of staff responses

1 Have we done all that we set out to do?

Of the issues identified in the first session it was seen that a number of amendments had been made. Sessions on drawing had been curtailed to accommodate bookmaking, which had been specifically requested. However, there had not been enough time to touch on:

- textiles work;
- three-dimensional work (other than CDT);
- assessment/evaluation of children's art work;
- planning a school policy.

2 What was most worthwhile?

Responses to this question were difficult to generalise. Individual responses were noted, eg:

- display;
- bookmaking, printing, CDT;
- everything;
- bookmaking and display;
- display and visits;
- CDT and colour mixing;
- display and painting.

3 What might have been left out/done differently?

- less time discussing display (two people);
- more time on printing techniques and colour mixing;
- no need for painting and colour mixing;
- could have left out bookmaking (two people);
- would have preferred to have kept to original plan.

It is interesting to note that, in the response to questions 2 and 3, there are diametrically opposing views – what some people found worthwhile other people would have preferred to have omitted.

4 Where do we go from here?

- Occasional INSET days to be given over to practical art, craft and design workshops.
- Should the issue of assessment and evaluation of children's work be tackled? Some disagreement here. Perhaps staff should decide amongst themselves whether they need to pursue this area.
- Main focus to be the preparation of a scheme of work across the age-range and to be integrated with other curriculum areas, a suggestion given added impetus by the implementation of the National Curriculum. The point was made that, while art might well be linked with project/topic work, there was also a good argument for doing 'art for art's sake'.

On the whole, it was concluded that the original aim for the programme, ie for staff to 'gain confidence in promoting children's learning in and through art', had been realised.

15.8 Some observations

The consultant involved in the project has made the following observations:

On reflection, after a lapse of some time, it is possible to identify some good points and some not-so-good points about this project.

(1) First, the good points:

Setting the climate for INSET

It is worth pointing out the considerable amount of preliminary work that was done by all those involved before the staff development programme started to run. There was plenty of opportunity for dialogue between staff, between staff and head, and between the school and myself.

The way was well prepared for the consultancy. I was always made to feel welcome, and I looked forward to my visit.

This is not always the case. I have often been invited to a school by the head to discover that the staff have no idea what to expect. Little wonder that I am sometimes confronted at the end of the school day by hostile, suspicious, tired teachers. This is not the most fruitful atmosphere in which to conduct INSET.

Good relationships

I got on very well from the outset with both the head and the curriculum leader. A feeling of mutual respect and liking was established. This seemed to transmit itself to the other members of staff and workshop sessions became happy, light-hearted affairs where any conflict was recognised, discussed and (usually) ended with a joke.

(2) The not-so-good points:

Lack of time

I was unhappy about the fact that only one hour was given to the INSET sessions. This was really not long enough for practical work, where materials and equipment would need to be distributed at the beginning and cleared away at the end. I felt that this tended to give teachers a very superficial taste of whatever was being done. A suggestion that the hour be extended to an hour-and-a-half was met with resistance, so sessions had to stay as they were.

This lack of time also precluded the opportunity to reflect on what had been done and to discuss it in a formal situation, in order to arrive at some kind of philosophical rationale for what we were doing, however simplistic.

Teachers seemed to think that discussions were a waste of time when they could be actively engaged in 'doing' something. Indeed, this attitude is sometimes reflected in the classroom where there is a lot of 'doing' but not so much thinking or talking with children about 'why'.

This general tendency towards superficiality is perhaps a feature of school-based in-service, where the emphasis is on short-term training, *rather than on* education. *I find it a little worrying.*

On the whole, though, I think that this has been quite a successful project.

15.9 Conclusion

In analysing this case study, one thing above all shines through, and that is the crucial role of the headteacher. She played her part well, in initiating the work, facilitating development and handling people diplomatically. Her sympathetic support was the key factor in making the staff development programme effective. Whether or not the impetus is maintained will depend very much on her continued support and enthusiasm.

PART FOUR

STAFF DEVELOPMENT: THE WIDER ISSUES

In developing our ideas on school-focused staff development a number of wider issues have emerged. The necessity for staff development to be related to individual teacher needs has been highlighted, but all too often requests for teachers to attend courses to obtain further qualifications (M.A., M.Ed., etc) are seen as 'selfish' (ie having little use for the *school*). This raises questions of in-service training and professional development which we shall consider in the next chapter. The use of external consultants is addressed in Chapter 17, and the particular challenges for managing staff development in small primary schools are looked at in detail in Chapter 18.

Chapter 19 examines the increasingly important linkage of staff development and teacher appraisal, and this is followed by a case study of a primary school headteacher's attempt to reflect on her own position and that of her staff through a programme of teacher self-evaluation. The concluding chapter assesses some of the implications for the management of change in primary schools.

16 Training and learning

16.1 In-service training and professional development

In Chapter 1 we presented our definitions of the terms in-service training, staff development and professional development. Although the latter expression is used less frequently, the first two are used almost interchangeably.

As we have seen, some schools have a deputy head as the designated staff development co-ordinator with the responsibility of planning and administering a programme of activities for staff. The co-ordinator's job may be to spend the school's allotted INSET budget and to ensure that the time allocated to each teacher for INSET activities is used up. If this task is carried out purely in an administrative fashion it may be argued that the deputy head's role is one of 'INSET manager' rather than staff development co-ordinator. The concept of staff development extends beyond attendance at in-service activities. It is based on the notion that the quality of a school relates directly to the qualities of its teachers. Holly's (1985) 'thinking' or 'problem-solving school' only emerges where teachers demonstrate such qualities. Staff development is, therefore, all about encouraging individual teacher growth and developing this as an institutional resource. This seems logical and sensible until the head or deputy in the primary school begins to think of ways of 'encouraging individual teacher growth'. Professional 'growth' or development is not tangible. It is not measurable like physical growth. It is not even the same as assessing intellectual development since the acquisition of knowledge and the generation of new ideas are only two aspects of the multi-faceted role of the teacher. To illustrate how wide the interpretation of a teacher's role can be,

Suffolk Education Department (1985) identified four concepts of teaching:

1 Teaching as labour – a checklist approach to teaching. The teacher's role is to carry out pre-specified activities.
2 Teaching as a craft – the acceptance that not everyone can teach effectively. Teaching requires certain skills as well as the physical ability to do the job.
3 Teaching as a professional activity – there is a theoretical body of knowledge to be acquired in addition to possessing practical skills. 'The professional is required to exercise judgement as to when one . . . or more of the range of skills should be applied.'
4 Teaching as an art – teaching is a highly personal activity. It cannot be standardised. 'The teacher makes use not only of a body of professional knowledge and skill but also of personal resources which are . . . uniquely expressed according to the teacher's personality and the interactions between him and individual pupils or whole classes.'

Suffolk's report ('Those Having Torches') was written in the context of appraisal. We consider this further in Chapter 19. The conclusions reached on teacher effectiveness have relevance here, however, since they throw some light on how we should interpret 'individual teacher growth' in the context of staff development. The report suggests that:

> To make, or help to make, a teacher more effective in the job [we] must take account of the complexity of the task of teaching; [we] must take account of the fact that there is . . . a spectrum of teacher competence; that much of what a teacher does and achieves cannot be 'measured' and that some of his work . . . does not bear immediate fruit.

How, then, can such a complex analysis of teaching help the staff development co-ordinator in encouraging individual teacher growth? It is useful to work on three principles. First, that staff development is adult education (andragogy) and must 'start from where the learner is'. It means that teacher development must begin in the classroom (or, increasingly in the case of non-teaching heads in larger primary schools, from their roles as managers and administrators rather than teachers). Individual teacher growth must therefore be dependent on critical examination by the individual of classroom or managerial practice, with the aim of improving that practice.

Second, that staff development programmes should be planned to reflect this complexity of role. They should include activities which develop *skills* (classroom management, use of resources, teaching styles), *knowledge* (subject content and expertise), *concepts* (approaches to pupil-centred learning, curriculum planning) and *attitudes* (relationships with pupils, parents, governors and a personal commitment to continuing education and self-evaluation).

Third, teacher development is not something achieved in isolation but through the sharing of ideas and discussion with colleagues on the staff of the school and with teachers from other schools.

In trying to make practical sense of this complex task, the staff development co-ordinator will consider three further issues. First, that there is considerable evidence to suggest that teachers need to look outside their classrooms and schools if they are going to meet their longer-term needs. Second, that teachers need to build on the self-evaluation of classroom or management practice, and third, that programmes of staff development should respond to the needs identified by teachers.

In reality, however, the ideals of education do not match the practicalities. Teachers may certainly benefit from looking outside their own schools, but with the decline in secondment and the increase in school-based activity, this is becoming more difficult to arrange. The result is that teachers may become too introspective. The dangers of 'groupthink' (discussed in more detail later in this chapter) become real. The shortage of suitable supply teachers restricts daytime mobility of teachers. The excessive demand for teachers who are also effective trainers often leaves schools with little opportunity of providing their staff with 'free time' in which to research and reflect on what is happening in other schools. The increase in formal after-school activities ('INSET detentions') may also tie staff to the school. The proposed arrangements for a new style of teacher training in which graduates are trained in a school rather than in a College of Education may only enhance the 'narrow-mindedness' of a future teaching force unless training programmes include the facility to observe good practice in more than one school. The staff development co-ordinator has this new dimension to tackle in the coming years. The programme of induction is likely to require a more meaningful and structured approach as licensed teachers are appointed to the staff of a school.

The second issue, that self-evaluation forms the foundation for effective teacher education, relates to the notion of 'evaluation for development'. This means asking teachers to become:

- more critical about their own practice;
- more open in sharing their experiences;

- more active in making decisions;
- more committed to implementing plans.

It remains to be seen how teachers in general will react to appraisal. Will they become more defensive about their own practice? How will they react to merit payments? Or to governing bodies with the powers to 'hire and fire'? Teachers who see their roles in a 'professional' context may well continue to be self critical in their analysis, but there will be many who will keep tight-lipped and take a formal, approved approach to teaching to avoid the risk factor associated with the implementation of new ideas.

The third issue, that staff development programmes should reflect needs identified by teachers, has been overturned in the tidal wave of reform that swept education in the late 1980s. It is interesting to read books on education written in the 1970s or even the early 1980s. Theories of change advise against imposition of ideas from external sources. Staff development programmes, they say, should be nurtured from complex needs-analysis exercises so that they truly reflect staff requirements. We hold this view ourselves and the arguments presented in this book reflect this. However, by 1989 the results of such complex exercises could often be predicted: teachers identified a need for training in National Curriculum science, mathematics, language, assessment and record-keeping. Heads identified a need for training in curriculum planning, local management of schools, appraising staff, education law and the relationship of heads with governing bodies. The identification of national priority areas and the allocation of specific grants to each; the changes brought about by the need to meet National Curriculum requirements; the knowledge that attainment targets will establish standards for pupils and their schools; and the announcements regarding cascade training provision to meet teacher's needs in core and foundation subject areas all served to push the individually identified needs of teachers on to lower priority status.

Hence the swing from in-service teacher *education* to in-service *training*. Short-term goals are met most successfully by specific training. Training programmes which fit with precise objectives are easier to evaluate ('at the end of this course, teachers will be able to . . .'). Short, sharp training sessions are more cost-effective. They give teachers a higher degree of immediate satisfaction. They solve current problems. They offer 'tips for teachers'. They will also, if offered without the balance of more reflective activities, produce a teaching force which is 'trained' to perform to specified criteria set by those outside the school with an interest, often political, in education.

The plea from the consultant running the programme on display

(Chapter 15 of this book) reflects this dual dimension:

> Teachers seemed to think that discussions were a waste of time when they could be actively engaged in 'doing' something. Indeed, this attitude is sometimes reflected in the classroom where there is a lot of 'doing' but not so much thinking or talking with children about 'why'.

On the other hand, one can only sympathise with teachers who need immediate solutions to externally imposed initiatives. A recent course on managing staff development produced the response: 'We need a lifebelt not swimming lessons!'

We need a lifebelt, not swimming lessons.

The staff development co-ordinator's role, in this context, is one of maintaining the credibility of teaching as a profession by maintaining the integrity of teachers as educated rather than trained people. It is therefore the responsibility of the staff development co-ordinator to balance individual and whole-school programmes so that training sessions are supplemented with more reflective approaches to classroom practice and management.

16.2 Teachers as learners

Throughout this book we have referred to the fact that teachers attending INSET activities are little different from the pupils in their own classes. They have different abilities, experience and interests. They are motivated by different things and will perceive the benefits to be gained from the activity in different ways but their learning processes are substantially similar. If the increase in school-based INSET has done little else, it has helped to give all teachers the feeling of being learners. As a result, empathy with pupils is increased.

In any group of teachers on an INSET activity there will inevitably be those who show little interest in what is going on ('what use is this to me?', 'early retirement looms'); those who retreat into their shells and say very little; those who seek attention by constantly asking questions or picking up on contentious points and those who are 'discipline problems' ('INSET conscripts', 'this wouldn't work with Y3'). There are also, thankfully, the majority who strive to gain something of practical use from each activity and who share ideas with the activity leader.

Teachers are sometimes bad learners.

Southworth (1984) says that 'Teachers regard much of their job as telling and in time their own capacities to learn become blunted. Teachers become bad learners partly also because the process of teaching does not acknowledge a "learner role".' In 1975, Stenhouse argued that the reasons why curriculum developers were not getting through to the average class teacher was not because of *resistance* to change but because of *barriers* to change. He identified these as:

- lack of clarity about new ideas;
- teachers lacking skills and knowledge required to implement change;
- lack of resources and equipment;
- incompatible organisational arrangements (for example, rigid time-tabling).

Freeman (1988) analysed barriers to teacher learning as they related to the delivery of effective INSET. She noted that school-based INSET involves a high degree of social control. Choice of topic, venue and nature of the activity is frequently made by the head or deputy, often without consulting or involving staff. The obligatory nature of contractual school-based activities may set up barriers to learning. The degree to which the activity meets personal, as opposed to institutional, needs is also an important factor in establishing individual motivation amongst staff.

Cunningham and Davies (1985) highlight the importance of appropriate delivery of INSET. They stereotype presenters into three categories, the extremes of which are:

- *the expert* – teachers are there to be told what to do; information is there to be passed on; the presenter is the fount of all knowledge on the topic in question. In general, teachers are becoming less patient with this approach. They are on their home ground during school-based sessions and the traditional 'politeness' shown by practitioner audiences to professional academics has almost disappeared. Freeman comments that:

  > this style of approach can be risky for the deliverer in that the

receivers may feel uninvolved and therefore more critical, and able to reject the message. More importantly the extreme expert treats the teachers as children, without responsibility for their own learning, and without respect for their cumulative experience, expertise and knowledge.

At the other extreme is

- *the consumer model* – the approach adopted here is similar to that of student-centred learning. Participants on INSET have responsibility for their own learning, and content and method are negotiated. The provider is seen as a guide or facilitator rather than expert.

The reaction of teachers to each approach varies with the perception of the individual. Many find the 'expert' approach intimidating and threatening. Feelings of hostility may be generated and questioning of the provider may become aggressive and even embarrassing to the head or staff development co-ordinator who had made the invitation. On the other hand, teachers are often frustrated by sessions which are totally process-oriented and which, through interminable discussion and debate, try to tap what is known already by them. They argue: 'Why re-invent the wheel? If you have experience you should pass it on in the most efficient and effective way possible. Time is too precious to be spent philosophising!' Many teachers prefer activity-based approaches to learning which have some outcome of direct use in the classroom. This may not necessarily be a 'tips for teachers' approach although there is a danger of activities becoming overpractical and product-oriented.

Perhaps the most efficient and effective INSET sessions are those which enable teachers to reflect through discussion while working on activities which will have, for them, practical outcomes which meet their own perceived needs.

Groups of teachers have a global identity but individual needs.

The dichotomy of approach to INSET presentation is real. It presents providers of INSET (increasingly known as 'trainers') with the dilemma of identifying expectations of a group of teachers who have a global identity yet individual needs. The evaluation of the activity will reflect the dominant perception of learning and what has been gained. Inglis (1985) distinguishes between 'soft knowledge' and 'hard knowledge'. Some characteristics of each are:

Soft knowledge: subjective, evaluative, intuitive, personal, imaginative, of the heart, artistic, moral.

Hard knowledge: objective, factual, calculable, public, rational, of the head, scientific, political.

Teachers often go into INSET activities with preconceived ideas about the potential value of the activity. 'Training' sessions tend towards the preference for hard knowledge. In-service *education* focuses more on the processes associated with soft knowledge. There will of course be unintended outcomes for participants, but the skill of the provider is to meet the need for hard knowledge without losing the educational benefits that result from learning associated with soft knowledge.

16.3 How do adults learn?

An understanding of andragogical factors is therefore important to the INSET provider. Teachers acting in the role of trainers need to understand how adults learn. Weindling, Reid and Davis (1983) comment that:

> a higher proportion of adults than formerly thought may be operating at what Piaget calls the concrete operational stage rather than the formal operational stage of intellectual development. This suggests that . . . abstract talk sessions alone are not sufficient to change behaviour.

They summarise the findings of Wood and Thompson on adult learning:

1 Adults need realistic, job-related goals for a learning programme to be effective.
2 Adult learners need to see the results of their efforts and have accurate feedback about progress.
3 Learning a new skill or concept may produce anxiety and fear of external judgement.
4 Adults will resent learning situations which they see as an attack on their competence.
5 Adults prefer to learn in an informal learning situation where social interaction can take place.

Stuart (1988), a training development consultant writing in a journal of industrial management training, adds the following conditions which, in his opinion, need to be present to enable adults to learn effectively:

1 Adults become ready to learn when they recognise a deficiency in their own performance level and accept that they need to take action to remedy that deficiency.
2 Adults want learning to be problem-based leading to the solution of particular problems facing the individual.
3 Adults want to be involved as an equal participant in planning, carrying out and evaluating the learning.
4 Adults want to be treated as adults, enjoying mutual respect with the trainer.
5 Adults bring with them to the learning situation their unique
   - motives for wanting to learn;
   - previous learning history (good and bad experiences);
   - self-confidence and self-image;
   - learning style and pace of learning.

A clear understanding of how to create effective learning situations for professional adult colleagues would seem an essential requirement for the increasing number of teacher trainers operating at higher education, local authority and school levels.

16.4 Teachers as trainers

The development of the National Curriculum programme has relied heavily on the cascade method of disseminating knowledge, concepts and skills. The idea behind cascade, simply, is that an 'expert' runs INSET for a group of teachers who return to their schools and 'cascade' the information/ideas/skills gained to their colleagues. At best, it involves teachers in the process of training and gives them credibility as curriculum leaders within their schools. At worst, it fails at each stage as the message becomes more and more distorted or diluted as distance from the source increases. Nevertheless, cascade is seen as the most economic way of reaching the large number of primary schools and teachers in a local authority. The logistics of 'training' all primary teachers in the knowledge and skills required to meet National Curriculum requirements are complex in terms of manpower, time and, in rural areas, distance. Cascade is seen as the only solution in the short term. But if it is to be more effective than the much-criticised INSET for GCSE in secondary schools, which also used the cascade method, training teams and individual teachers/curriculum leaders in schools need to be aware of the training skills required to produce effective INSET.

The problems facing teachers as trainers are clear:

1 Many teachers feel uneasy when addressing colleagues.
2 The relationships between teacher and pupil which mark effective classroom practice may not exist between teacher and peer group.
3 Conflict and 'hidden agendas' detract from the seemingly simple task of conveying skills or ideas to others on the staff.
4 Many teachers resent being put in the position of 'experts' after attending one or possibly two INSET sessions.
5 For some teachers, the knowledge that they have to go back to school and 'perform' for their colleagues interferes with the learning experiences which they should be gaining on the main INSET activity. Aims and reasons for participating become confused.
6 If the initial INSET activity is poor, the quality of the cascade is unlikely to be much better.
7 Levels of stress increase if the school-based activity fails.

There are, of course, many advantages to cascade apart from those of time, cost and manpower:

1 Many colleagues will have gone through the experience of cascading and will be sympathetic to the 'teacher-provider'.
2 The teacher-provider will know the idiosyncracies of staff and be able to adjust the learning experience more effectively.
3 The teacher-provider is working on home ground.
4 The teacher-provider's self-esteem is raised.
5 Teachers are likely to get more from an INSET activity if, at a later date, they have to run a similar activity in their own schools.
6 The pool of skilled trainers is increased.
7 Teacher-providers may be required to service more than one school (or schools may combine for particular INSET activities). This increases school liaison and teacher interaction.

For cascade to be successful a number of conditions are generally necessary:

1 The climate must be right. This is the responsibility of the head-teacher.
2 Teacher-providers must be given full resource and moral support for their INSET activities.
3 The initial INSET activity (the 'source' activity) should include aims

and objectives to develop training skills as well as to pass on information and ideas (the provider must address *how* to cascade as well as *what*).

4 Teacher-providers should focus on the process of learning rather than content to minimise the risk of being labelled 'expert'. The notion of 'curriculum leader' or 'facilitator' does not have to convey the impression of total expertise.
5 Sessions should operate on the basis that all teachers taking part (including the teacher-provider) are learners.
6 Ideas should be shared as openly as possible. The feeling of 'we're all in this together' should pervade.
7 Learning and sharing of ideas should continue long after the formal INSET activity.

An understanding of the factors which affect adult learning is important if the design of the INSET activity or programme is to be effective. Oldroyd (1985) summarises the level of impact of different types of INSET activity. His summary is reproduced as Figure 16.1 below. Although it is interesting for INSET to be designed predominantly at level 6 (application) because of the high level of impact, it would be wrong to ignore levels 1 and 2 in the process of continuing teacher education. School-based staff development programmes should operate at all levels. Levels 1 and 2 will often be used to reinforce levels

Figure 16.1 Level of impact of different types of INSET activity (from Oldroyd, 1985)

Level of impact	*INSET activity*	*Type of learning*	*Source of learning*
Low ↓	1 **Description** What? 2 **Explanation** Why?	Knowledge for understanding	*Received* from 'experts' and/or colleagues
	3 **Demonstration** How? 4 **Action planning** What? When? Where? Who?	Knowledge for action	
High	5 **Practice** off-the-job with feedback 6 **Application** on-the-job with feedback	Skills for action	*Generated* by participants with experts and/or colleagues

5 and 6 rather than precede them, as teachers begin to question *why* they are carrying out particular actions. Joyce and Showers (1980) made a similar analysis (see Chapter 21, Figure 21.1).

16.5 'Groupthink'

Organisations are made up of individuals and groups. In most large organisations, including secondary schools, task groups or teams generally operate more effectively than individuals. Group activities bring together a variety of interests, enable more effective division of labour and provide learning experiences for group members. In primary schools, functional groups are often too small to operate effectively. Nursery, reception and infant teachers may well regard themselves as a team, separate from their junior colleagues. However, often the number of teachers in, for example, a small junior school means that the whole staff will operate as a single 'group'. Where this is the case there is a danger of what Janis (1982) called groupthink. Progress becomes limited because:

1. Members of the group come to think alike.
2. Complacency sets in if staff turnover is low.
3. Discussions frequently become tangential to the main point and drift into social conversation.
4. One member of the group (not necessarily the headteacher!) may hold a dominant position and unduly influence decisions.
5. The group comes to believe in its own invulnerability ('They can't change us if we all stick together') and morality ('We are doing this for the benefit of the pupils').
6. The group begins to think uncritically ('We've discussed this before. We don't need to go over it again').

They can't change us if we stick together.

Groupthink is a barrier to learning. If it is to be avoided in primary schools there needs to be a clear move away from the conservative approach of 'we're alright as we are' to a more radical analysis of teacher expertise and potential. It may require:

- rotation of curriculum responsibility to provide fresh viewpoints;
- setting up specific tasks for individuals to achieve (with measurable outcomes and clear time limits);

- sharing leadership roles across the group;
- using outsiders (consultants or LEA representatives) to inject different perspectives or facilitate school review.

The coming of the new 'era' in education in the late 1980s may have brought with it many problems in meeting the challenge of the revolution in education. It also brought with it the need for teachers to think critically about their practice and to examine ways of accommodating curriculum and management initiatives for the benefit of themselves and their pupils. If the in-service education and training activities associated with these changes are to be effective, and the INSET is to transfer to positive classroom outcomes, staff development co-ordinators in primary schools must understand the characteristics of teachers as learners. They must also balance formal INSET training activities and continuing professional education to ensure that maximum effectiveness is gained from the process.

17 Using consultants

It is likely that, at some point in the process of staff development, a school will look outside for advice, support, guidance or reassurance. This might occur at the beginning of the process when staff feel that they are too near the problem and would like a more detached, objective view of things from a disinterested party. Alternatively, a particular kind of expertise might be required later on in the process to provide input in a specific area. This chapter examines the issue of outside agents as consultants in the staff development process and aims to answer some of the questions a school might wish to ask in relation to consultancy.

17.1 What is consultancy?

The term 'consultant' is borrowed from industry and at its simplest describes

> the use by an organisation of an external expert in order to enhance its efficiency
>
> (Lewis, 1985)

In the context of the primary school, Eraut's (1977) definition is more explicit:

> A consultant is any external agent from within the education system who involves himself in discussing the education problems of a class . . . or school with a view to improving the quality of teaching and learning.

Hoyle (1971) was uneasy about the term 'consultant' because he felt it smacked of some omniscient being who has the answer to all problems. He preferred the term 'change agent'. Sefton Davies (1982) agreed that the term 'consultant' is an 'unfortunate label', but nevertheless it is one that has become generally accepted. However, he emphasised that the consultant–client relationship should be based on 'a mutual wish to cooperate in the resolution of problems' – not on the superior knowledge of the expert.

17.2 Who are the consultants?

It is probably true to say that the main source of consultants is from the LEA, local institutes of education or university education departments. They have varying characteristics and limitations as Figure 17.1 below illustrates.

Figure 17.1 The consultants: advantages and disadvantages

Consultant	*Advantages*	*Disadvantages*
Advisers	• Usually, were good practitioners in the classroom • Have an overview of the situation in the authority • In possession of information about current trends and situation • In a position of influence	• New demands being made on them mean increasingly inspectorial role, so less likely to be available
Advisory teachers	• Appointed because they were good practitioners • Well versed in the subject area • Knowledgeable about current trends, etc • Used to working in the classroom with teachers *and* children	• Not enough to go around • May be subject specialist with little primary-school experience • Sometimes misused (as supernumerary instead of in advisory role)
Other teachers	• Good practitioners – high credibility • Specialised knowledge of children, school, existing practice	• Skills in the classroom not necessarily the same as those required to conduct INSET with peers

	• Practical skill in the organisation of the learning process	• Difficult for teachers to be released to other schools on a regular basis
College/ university lecturers	• Can usually offer substantial body of specialised theoretical knowledge in a wide range of educational situations • In response to government requirements, many lecturers now have 'recent and relevant' experience in the classroom	• 'Credibility gap' between schools and colleges • 'Ivory tower' syndrome: many teachers have memories of highly authoritarian tutors from their own college days

Other agencies within the education system who may be called upon as consultants are:

- Teachers' Centre leaders
- Resource Centre leaders and officers
- Education Officers in museums and galleries
- Field study/urban study centre wardens.

Now that there is an open market for INSET providers, a number of people are currently setting up as consultants in education. These may be former advisers who have taken early retirement, or practitioners of one kind or another who in the past have subsidised their own personal work with part-time teaching (eg in art colleges, extra-mural departments and so on). It is worth keeping an eye out for any local registers of such initiatives, or any relevant publicity leaflets.

Many primary schools are beginning to think creatively about INSET consultancy support. People from the local community have frequently been used as a classroom resource (for example, police officers to talk on road safety). They may also be used to give a broader dimension to in-service education. 'Seminar-type' sessions might be held for teachers on use of the local library (county librarian), drug and solvent abuse (local health officer), social problems (Education Welfare Officer or Social Services), aggression and disruption (schools' psychological service). Representatives from local industry may be happy to entertain small numbers of teachers in their workplaces if there is an interest in forging links between school and industry (this may even extend to sponsorship if the school and the firm feel that such a link is appropriate). Projects based on the manufacturing process are enhanced by initial contact between the employer and teachers. An example of such a consultancy is given at the end of the chapter.

Another source of consultancy is the expanding educational resource 'industry'. Representatives of firms selling educational materials and equipment are often pleased to address teachers if they see potential sales in local schools. Teachers may use such sessions to enhance their knowledge and understanding of new developments in educational technology or resource availability. Examples include:

1 Three primary schools combining and inviting a representative from a computer firm to demonstrate educational software (games, programmes, etc) and hardware (printers, scanners, etc).
2 Representatives from a publishing company explaining and displaying assessment 'packages' to teachers from a secondary and feeder primary schools.
3 Representatives from a firm producing art and design materials giving advice to staff on what materials to use and how to use them.

It should be noted that although some firms will be pleased to send representatives to a school, the size of most primary schools makes it uneconomic for a longer commitment to be made. On the other hand, if schools combine to form a larger 'interest group'/'market', and if some form of dissemination/publicity is agreed, firms may give longer term advice on the use of their products in the classroom. It may be possible in these circumstances to develop a true consultancy situation rather than a one-off sales talk.

Developments within the National Curriculum framework have implications for the use of secondary school 'subject experts' as consultants in primary schools. The consequences of this recommendation are discussed more fully in Chapter 10.3.

17.3 What is the role of the consultant?

Schmuck (1973) identifies three roles for the consultant. They are:

- consultative assistant
- content consultation
- process consultation.

The first two roles can be said to focus on specific problems or aspects of an organisation, whereas the third, process consultation, covers the organisation as a whole. Subsequent commentators (for example, Bell, 1985; Hopkins and Vickers, 1986) prefer the simpler distinction between *task* consultancy and *process* consultancy. The differences between these categories are described in Figure 17.2.

Figure 17.2 The distinction between task and process consultancy

Task consultancy	*Process consultancy*
Helping a school to identify specific training needs. (Sefton Davies, 1982)	Helping a school to understand its own practice. (Bell, 1985; Murgatroyd and Reynolds, 1984)
Helping a school to improve certain aspects of the curriculum (eg maths) – ie a set task. (Bell, 1985; Hopkins and Vickers, 1986)	Helping a school to become more receptive to change, to identify change processes appropriate to its needs. (Hopkins and Vickers, 1986; Murgatroyd and Reynolds, 1984)
Providing skills training. (Bell, 1985)	Educating professionals. (Bell, 1985)
Helping a school with *specific* problems. (Gray, 1987)	Helping a school with more *generalised*, less obvious problems. (Gray, 1987)
Dealing with *part* of the innovation. (Hopkins and Vickers, 1986)	Dealing with the innovation *itself*. (Hopkins and Vickers, 1986)
Assisting a specific group to develop work beyond its current state. (Murgatroyd and Reynolds, 1984)	Engaging in the promotion of 'organisational health'. (Murgatroyd and Reynolds, 1984)

The task-based consultancy is usually considered to be easier and more straightforward to negotiate, implement and evaluate than the process consultancy. Both Sefton Davies (1982) and Lewis (1985) hold that, more often than not, success in a task-based consultancy, where specific problems are addressed, can open up the way for an examination of the deeper issues. Lewis suggests that schools should, in the first instance, identify concrete every-day problems that have a more realistic chance of being resolved than the general, broadly-based concerns. These less obvious problems may well emerge naturally in the process of attending to the more superficial detail.

Within the remit of the two categories of consultancy described here – task and process – there are a number of widely disparate subordinate roles that a consultant may be required to take. Jung (1977), for example, has identified nineteen; they include: catalyst, stimulator, adviser, manager, facilitator, trouble-shooter, scapegoat, instructor, counsellor, critical friend, change agent and enabler. Jones (1986) adds: interventionist, confronter, data collector, designer and evaluator.

This list not only illustrates the diversity of the consultant's role, but it also emphasises its complex and delicate nature. Indeed, the consultant may well take on the mantle of several of these parts (Jung has suggested over a hundred different combinations). It is therefore crucial that all those to be involved in the INSET activity are made aware of what exactly the role or roles are to be. Client and consultant need to be open and forthright with each other and build together a climate of common acceptance and mutual regard.

Without this, INSET organisers may find that participants refuse to co-operate. If they are made to feel unsure of themselves, threatened or overwhelmed by new ideas and unfamiliar jargon, they may become aggressive or withdrawn. As Doran (1981) says, fear of failure is the most paralysing and constricting of emotions. It hinders open-mindedness and receptivity to new ideas.

The choice of consultant, therefore, is of paramount importance. The time-consuming work of establishing an appropriate climate for INSET and encouraging staff to feel that they are wholly involved in the staff development programme can be undone in one fell swoop by the wrong choice of personnel. However 'expert' he or she may be in a certain field, the consultant must also be in possession of other qualities and characteristics, in particular:

- an understanding of the theories of change;
- a willingness to establish an equal balance of power in the relationship with the client;
- a sensitivity to feelings and emotions.

We shall now take each of these in turn:

Understanding the theories of change

The consultant who comes to a situation with prepared answers, solutions or packages is more likely to be met with a wall of resistance, where teachers will back off and become defensive. On the other hand, the consultant who understands how change may be effected will give teachers time to assimilate new ideas, and build upon those they already have. He/she may also offer support and 'aftercare' back in the classroom.

An equal balance of power

Gray (1987) highlights a possible power and authority gap between teachers and providers – although it is fair to say that this is not always of the consultant's making. It is sometimes imposed by the clients themselves. This is because many primary school teachers lack confidence when confronted by the subject specialist or so-called 'expert'. Perhaps the first task of the consultant in establishing a relationship with the client is to encourage teachers to recognise their own abilities and expertise, and to build up confidence and self-esteem. The primary school teacher's own particular brand of expertise often complements the consultant's own narrow specialism, so that together the partnership can begin to address the problem in hand.

Sensitivity to feelings and emotions

None of this can be done effectively unless consultants have an understanding of common humanity – what makes people 'tick'. They need to be sensitive to inter-personal relationships amongst staff and other school personnel, and be receptive to the psychological and political life of the school. Gray (1987) points out that one of the most important functions of an effective consultant is to be concerned

> with the complexity of human dynamics in organisations and with helping people . . . to work out what is going on in the organisation and to find out how to do things better.

Schmuck *et al.* (1975) give an indication of the kind of qualities providers need in their analysis of what is required in order for the consultancy process to develop successfully. They suggest six basic requirements:

- that the consultant and client develop clear communication;
- that trust can be built and understanding increased by opening close personal communications. This enables the consultant to deal with hidden agendas and feelings;
- that more people should be involved in the decision-making by encouraging information-sharing;
- that the consultant should create an open problem-solving climate by helping teachers to identify and confront problems in the first place and subsequently to proceed in collaboration to a workable solution;
- that teachers be helped to analyse and improve procedures for

carrying out their tasks and increase the effectiveness of the group;
- that the consultant provides participants with opportunities that allow conflict to emerge.

What becomes apparent in this consideration of the role of the consultant is that it is a very demanding one. Headteachers and INSET organisers would be well advised to choose with care.

17.4 Choosing a consultant – some do's and don't's

Do

- ask around for advice about consultants: enquire of colleagues in other schools for personal recommendations;
- consult the staff before you invite anyone – ask them if they know of any alternatives;
- make sure you, the staff and the consultant are left in no doubt as to the nature of the consultancy, and the proposed content of the session(s);
- ask how the INSET activity is to be evaluated: make sure you and the staff collaborate with the consultant when the evaluation is made;
- be sure to meet the consultant at least once, beforehand, to discuss these things;
- find out what equipment/materials will be needed;
- ensure that the proposed venue for INSET is appropriate to the consultant's needs (ie venue to be used will depend on whether session to consist of discussion/formal presentation/workshop);
- put the provider in the picture about your reasons for the INSET: is it the result of democratic discussions, or is it something the headteacher wants done?
- ask for any preliminary reading, if appropriate;
- try to make yourself available to greet the consultant, especially on his or her first visit;
- ensure that you have enough funds in your INSET budget to cover the consultants' fees/expenses;
- involve the consultant in planning follow-up activities or 'aftercare' when the INSET comes to an end.

Don't

- just ask the first person who is available;
- assume that someone who is 'expert' in a particular field is neces-

sarily the best person to conduct INSET with your staff;
- forget to put the consultant in the picture about any members of staff who may be defensive/aggressive about the particular subject area being covered;
- forget to make the consultant feel welcome; introduce staff, offer a cup of tea, etc;
- treat the consultant as a suspicious interloper;
- expect the consultant to achieve the impossible (eg 'Display in the Primary School' in one hour).

17.5 What's involved in setting up a consultancy?

Once a school has identified a consultant who appears to have all the required attributes, the next stage is to consider the kind of procedure that must be undertaken to ensure that the consultancy will be successful.

According to Eraut (1978), the consultant's part in the INSET activity has three phases: planning the activity, creating the opportunity for teachers to undertake INSET and 'aftercare'. These three phases reflect the structure of the whole staff-development process itself. Eraut's point is that those external agents who are asked to contribute to the INSET activity should be involved not only in the activity itself but also in the planning and follow-up. This, of course, relates to the ideal world: reality may be a different matter. One thing is certain: the quality of communication between INSET provider, INSET organiser, headteacher and school staff before, during and after the INSET activity is of utmost importance if Eraut's phases are to be translated to the everyday world of the school. Murgatroyd and Reynolds (1984) break down Eraut's three stages further into the following steps:

- initial contact between school and consultant;
- establishment of a contract to work;
- consultant accepted and understood by staff;
- diagnosis – consultant reaches a conclusion about the nature of the problem;
- active intervention following a development plan – workshops dealing with the diagnosed problem;
- level of involvement of consultant reduced and eventually terminated.

In the next section these steps are interpreted to produce a practical guide for a headteacher or INSET co-ordinator.

17.6 Setting up the consultancy: a practical guide

1 The consultancy should be *fully* discussed by the head/INSET co-ordinator in collaboration with the *whole staff* before any external agents are invited into the school.
2 After ensuring that there is agreement, and that it has been arrived at democratically, the head/INSET co-ordinator contacts the consultant (probably by telephone).
3 The consultant follows up this contact with a visit *as soon as possible*. He or she should be made aware of staff 'needs', probably by the head/INSET co-ordinator in the first instance.
4 The consultant and head/INSET co-ordinator meet with staff to share views, problems, fears, and to collaborate on the planning of the INSET.
5 The consultant draws up a plan of action (the 'contract'), interpreting staff responses and being sensitive to the feelings they have expressed. The plan may be written, although this is not always necessary. It depends on the degree of formality appropriate to the situation and the nature of the people involved. The important thing is that details of the plan should be made clear to all concerned.
6 The draft programme is presented to the staff by the consultant (either personally or through the head/INSET co-ordinator). Comments/amendments are welcomed. Final decisions are made on a number of points. These are summarised in Figure 17.3.

Figure 17.3 Drafting an INSET programme: setting the parameters

INSET Programme

1 Aims and objectives?
2 Number of sessions?
3 Timing and length of sessions?
4 Venue? (needs to be comfortable and appropriate)
5 Resources needed?
6 Follow-up?

7 INSET programme begins. Evaluation criteria need to be established at the outset. Formative evaluations need to be made by all during the course of ensuing sessions, and INSET modified accordingly, if necessary.
8 Summative evaluation of INSET should be undertaken on a collaborative basis: consultant, INSET co-ordinator and teachers to be equally involved.

9 Follow-up/aftercare, to assess the longer-term benefits/effects of INSET on teachers and children. Also to provide support, encouragement, reassurance and counselling for the teacher and feedback for the consultant.
10 Further evaluations in collaboration with staff, as appropriate.
11 Finally, responsibility is devolved to the teachers. The consultant 'lets go'.

An example of how a consultancy might be organised is given below:

1 AGREEMENT
by whole staff
↓
2 CONTACT
with consultant
↓
3 NEGOTIATION
with whole staff
↓
4 PLANNING
collaborative
↓
5 'CONTRACT'
clear to all
↓
6 ACTION
INSET runs
↓
7 FORMATIVE EVALUATION
collaborative
↓
8 MODIFICATION
if necessary
↓
9 SUMMATIVE EVALUATION
↓
10 FOLLOW-UP
in the classroom
↓
11 COUNSELLING
if appropriate
↓

12 FURTHER EVALUATIONS
as necessary/together
↓
13 DEVOLUTION
to the teachers

17.7 Consultants from the community: an example in practice

The local newspaper

1 One or more teachers decided to use the local newspaper as a cross-curricular theme for study in the junior school.
2 The staff development co-ordinator brought together teachers to discuss ways in which:
- the topic could be used across the curriculum;
- the topic could be used at different levels from Y3 to Y6.

3 One-hour INSET session.
Theme: using the local newspaper as a resource.
Activity: brainstorm as many ways as possible to utilise the newspaper in pupils' work.
Some responses:
- reporter to talk to class/school on 'A day in the life of a reporter' (*listening skills*);
- children draw cartoons for cartoon page (*graphicacy*);
- children design a 'logo' for their own school newspaper (*design*);
- children use word processors to compile a monthly newsheet (*CAL*);
- children write about school and local news or stories (*literacy*);
- children simulate a sports report (watch an extract of sport on video and 'telephone' a description of the event to another pupil who writes up a report of the incident) (*oracy*);
- photography (take a photograph of the headteacher or another pupil for inclusion in the newspaper) (*recording; use of evidence*);
- calculate the cost of the newspaper (simplified: cost of paper divided by number of possible sales). Is it better to keep the cost down or try to make a profit?
- visit to the newspaper offices to observe
  a) compilation of news stories;
  b) production of the newspaper.
- project on 'how a newspaper is made', finding out:
  – Where does the paper come from?
  – How does it get to the offices?

   – How many people work on the production of the newspaper?
   – What do they do?
   – How many different sections are there in a newspaper (sport, local news, national news, editorial, small ads, block advertisements, entertainment, letters page, etc)?
   – What time of day does printing finish?
   – What happens to the paper when it leaves the printers?
   – How does it get to newsagents?
   – How many paperboys/girls are needed to deliver to homes?
   – What proportion of newspapers are sold 'over the counter'?
 - make a display of how a newspaper is produced;
 - invite parents to an evening when pupils describe how they set about their newspaper project.

4 The editor of the local newspaper was invited to become a 'consultant' for this initiative. He set up opportunities for his staff to talk to teachers in the school and for teachers to visit the newspaper offices. Y6 pupils were invited to tour the printing works, and the school was allowed to print a page of news for one edition of the paper. A representative of the newspaper attended the parents' open evening.

The project was a learning experience for staff and pupils. The use of representatives from the newspaper as 'consultants' throughout the process gave the project greater credibility, gave reporters a clearer insight into primary education and provided useful publicity for the newspaper and for the school.

18 Staff development in the small primary school

18.1 What is a small primary school?

Complete consensus on a definition of when a primary school may be unequivocally defined as 'small' is hard to find. In some cases, roll number is used as the criterion and the term applied to schools, for example, containing less than 130 pupils (West Glamorgan, 1985). The Education Reform Act (1988) requires that primary schools with a roll of more than 200 pupils must have delegated budget control by April 1993. Schools below 200 pupils on this definition are therefore small.

Other sources use organisational features to define 'small', for example the necessity to group children in classes containing more than one age-group (Aston, 1981). In a sense, the term is a relative one. The figure of 130 given above, though considered small in some areas of England and Wales, would be thought large in others. In 1985, for example, 49 of the 119 primary schools in Powys (Mid Wales) and 143 of the 337 primary schools in Dyfed (South West Wales) had below 50 pupils on roll (NUT, 1985). The typical primary school in England and Wales contains fewer than 200 pupils.

Smallness, anyway, is a dynamic concept. A school may be dubbed 'small' because its roll number is at a specific point and rising, or, conversely, because its roll number was once large and is diminishing. Both situations require quite different, but very necessary, staff development strategies.

For the purposes of this chapter the small school is one with two or three members of staff, a head with very considerable class teaching duties and minimal ancillary or secretarial assistance. Although arbitrary, such a description allows consideration of staff development in a context very different from that of the large primary school. It also enables discussion of alternative strategies in an environment which does not include a variety of subject-specific curriculum consultants or even, perhaps, a deputy headteacher. It is highly unlikely that a very small school will have an incentive allowance available to staff, as size determines their allocation. Thus, it is extremely difficult to acknowledge particular expertise or experience in financial and, de facto, status terms.

Small schools exist in a variety of settings. The tendency, however, is for such schools to be found in predominantly rural areas. Of the 2150 primary schools in England and Wales with fewer than 50 pupils on roll in 1985, only 70 were in metropolitan districts (NUT, 1985 in Wallace and Butterworth, 1987). The schools can probably be grouped into four broad categories: village, rural, semi-rural and urban. Generalisations are difficult to make and should be treated cautiously. Schools which are apparently similar in size or environment can reveal important differences in aspects of practice and organisational structures.

Since the majority of such schools are located in rural areas, this chapter looks primarily at the small school in this context. Some of the suggested challenges for successful staff development may apply to schools in other settings; others, such as geographical remoteness from teachers' centres or resource centres, may not. For example, one small school, known to the authors, is located in a suburban context. It has a staff of three assistant teachers and headteacher and has convenient access to a teachers' centre some eight miles distant and fruitful contact with the teacher education department of an institute of higher education located three miles away.

18.2 Challenges for professional development in the small rural school

The particular challenges for the small school in developing educational opportunities for pupils have been documented at some length (and with differing emphases) over a number of decades. The Hadow Report (1931) was concerned that the small number of pupils in such schools meant that instruction could not easily be matched to the needs of differing ability groups. Put crudely, it meant that streaming was not viable and each class would therefore contain a wide spectrum of aptitudes, so creating difficulties in teaching and learning.

The catalogue of alleged difficulties currently cited in discussing small schools can be traced to the Gittins and Plowden Reports of 1967. Bell and Sigsworth (1987) list the following educational disadvantages of small schools:

1 Teachers in small rural schools may be professionally isolated, having little contact with teaching colleagues in other schools and limited access to resource centres, teachers' centres and in-service provision.
2 Teachers in small rural schools have the problem of providing appropriate learning opportunities for the wide age-range of pupils in mixed-age classes.
3 It is very difficult to provide an adequate range of learning opportunities across the breadth of the curriculum given a small number of staff.
4 A very limited peer group does not provide adequate stimulation and competition for children.
5 Small schools are very costly to maintain and make disproportionate demands on scarce resources.

(Bell and Sigsworth, 1987)

Recent research by Roberts (1988) investigating organisation in a sample of schools in Wales identified similar perceptions of the challenges facing small schools amongst their headteachers.

Currently, the rise of the concept of curriculum-led staffing in the thinking of central government has demanded a reappraisal of the traditional generalist role of the primary teacher. Instead, there is a need, expressed for example through the criteria laid down for teacher education courses in the 1980s, for all teachers to have particular expertise, linked to a specific curriculum area. By this means, it is planned that staff in primary schools will have specialist curriculum knowledge available to them from their teaching colleagues acting as consultants or co-ordinators. It is likely that the delivery of the National Curriculum, conceptualised as it is within a subject specific register, may accelerate this reappraisal. This has led to:

1 Prescription of those areas which are to make up the curriculum of the primary school.
2 A redefinition of the primary teacher as one possessing a particular curriculum specialism.
3 The notion that a primary school ought to be staffed so that each area of the curriculum may be informed by a specialist curriculum consultant or co-ordinator.
4 The suggestion that the minimum size of a primary school ought to

be determined by the ability to meet this criteria.

(Bell and Sigsworth, 1987)

The contemporary challenge, then, is that of providing a broad curriculum from within limited staff expertise (a challenge based on a particular view of the primary curriculum and pedagogy). It is not surprising, therefore, that, in one sense, staff development in the small school has become synonymous with extending a limited range of curricular skills and knowledge; a pragmatic reaction to a traditional challenge, given fresh impetus by the current political climate. There are strong counter arguments. The reader is referred to Bell and Sigsworth (1987), for example, for a detailed alternative perspective on the qualities of the small rural school.

Aside from views on the efficacy of particular sizes and viability interpreted in terms of curriculum coverage, there is a further issue which ought to be recognised before the background to the context for staff development is complete. There appears to be an assumption that the large urban primary school is the appropriate model and provides an acceptable framework of discussion for primary schooling in general. For example, the debate concerning systems for the appraisal of teachers has simply failed to address the issue in the particular context of the small rural school (TES, 1986).

The small school, too often, is perceived as a 'fringe' issue in national debate on educational provision, despite the fact that in 1984, there were 20,001 primary schools in England of which 12,391 fell into a 'below 200' category (DES, 1984). This 'large urban' tendency has been reflected in both the location and focus of traditional INSET provision. Small rural schools have responded in various ways, often by adapting ideas gained on courses to their own particular two or three teacher school needs. Thus, before the 1987 changes in funding arrangements for INSET there was already in place a tradition of school-focused INSET, or at least a pragmatic eclecticism within the small school, born out of necessity. It is not that teachers within small rural schools generally shunned courses provided in the traditional manner. On the contrary, they did attend, often at personal inconvenience. Rather, the doubt existed that such provision really met their specific needs (Bell and Sigsworth, 1987).

So, staff development in the small school probably owes less to elaborate theorising and more to pragmatic adaptation to circumstances. Faced with problems of accessibility to sources of INSET provision, the schools themselves, often with the help of local authority advisers, began to explore ways of improving teaching and learning (Bell and Sigsworth, 1987).

The remainder of this chapter describes some of the developments from within this proactive movement and suggests ways in which such processes may be initiated and sustained.

18.3 Making full use of available potential

It may be useful to consider at this point the potential for growth which may lie untapped within a school itself. Like charity, staff development begins 'at home'.

One of the persistent challenges to the small school is that of providing breadth in learning opportunities for pupils, given limited staff expertise. Sadly, there is some evidence that available expertise is not fully exploited.

The same could also be said of some larger schools, of course. In a report on Welsh primary schools HMI commented:

> On the whole ... insufficient use is made of class teachers' specialisms and interests. In one small primary school, teachers' initial training provides a good coverage of the curriculum, including science, but there is a failure to exploit potential through developing schemes of work or inviting contributions to school-based training. The well qualified science teacher already chairs a science panel at a local teachers' centre, but the school does not capitalise on this. In general, insufficient use is made in small schools of the potential for leadership embodied in the interests and expertise in class teachers. As small schools face particular difficulties in providing a broad, balanced curriculum, failure fully to exploit expertise among staff is particularly detrimental to the achievement of the school's aims.
>
> (HMI (Wales) 1985, p. 14)

An important first task, then, is to identify and use existing human resources. One small, three-teacher school, for example, attempting to develop its science work, as a first step identified the relevant personal interests of the staff. These were found to include spinning, metalwork and music. A science programme was begun, matching starting points for children's work in published materials to staff strengths. A teacher's personal interest in weaving led to dyeing, hence to the production of dyes from various sources by the children and finally to identification and classification of flora within the local environment. This then led to work on colour and light, the teacher gaining confidence and satisfaction alongside the child because what may have been perceived as a daunting area proved not to be so. A strength was encouraged to grow from a strength.

The framework below (from Whitaker, 1983) gives suggestions for the main headings that could be used in compiling a professional profile. This would perhaps be a useful exercise to undertake early on in a new, small-school headship:

Figure 18.1 Framework for constructing a staff profile

- Qualifications and training
- Background and experience
- Current teaching role
- Particular responsibilities
- Range of experience within the school
- INSET record
- Professional reading and study
- Enthusiasms, interests and expertise
- Career aspirations.

(adapted from Whitaker, 1983)

The headings are intended to provide a general structure and may be subdivided to accommodate more detail as required.

18.4 Organisational change as a means of stimulating staff development

In an account of her early days as headteacher of a small Cambridgeshire school, Lin Whyte (1987) outlines a strategy for bringing staff together, recognising their potential and beginning a staff development programme through organisational change within the school itself. The context is familiar enough: a small village school staffed by a headteacher with a 95 per cent teaching commitment, one full-time infant teacher and one part-time teacher. The school had a rigid organisational structure, one teacher being responsible for a class containing children across a four-year age span. In removing this organisational rigidity and creating a more flexible and co-operative teaching approach, she hoped to:

- provide a greater variety of learning opportunities for the children;
- encourage the professional growth of staff by enabling them to work as a team across the entire primary (4–11) age-range.

She structured a programme of staff development, timed to take place over two and a half years which would prepare staff for the reorganisation.

Initially, informal discussions on non-threatening (to teachers) aspects of school life were used to create an appropriate climate for change. These led to more general considerations of joint topic work and school aims.

Only after a tentative twelve months was this kind of 'learning together' sufficiently established for any kind of formal INSET programme to be implemented. Whyte makes the crucially important point that:

> to encourage and sustain professional development in a small school, support was necessary, both from within the group and from outside the school.

Her project then moved on to consider the teaching of aspects of the curriculum and began to involve outside contributors, parents and the community.

Whyte's article illustrates the need for adequate preparation for change and respect for individuals and relationships. The teachers in her school recognised and accepted their own limitations and decided that their own enthusiasm and mutual support would take them a long way before involving external agencies.

18.5 Co-operative ventures

The 1978 HMI Survey, like the Plowden Report of a decade earlier, indicated some of the challenges faced by small schools in their efforts to provide a suitably broad range of educational experiences for their pupils. In the wake of the survey, the Essex educational inspectorate (1980) published a review of the then-existing practices to be found in the county's small primary schools.

In the spirit which underpins much of the staff development in small schools these were informal, grass-roots activities, generated and sustained by mutual interest. A sample, given below, may form a useful starting point for discussion for those seeking opportunities to begin co-operative ventures. Headteachers of large primary schools may also find such initiatives of value in promoting staff development.

1 A wide variety of informal contacts had been established through activities such as chess and swimming.

2 Sports coaching was sometimes undertaken by visiting teachers on an exchange basis.
3 In music, joint rehearsals, performances and concerts had been held. Interested children, spread across one area, had come together to form a recorder consort.
4 Contacts had been formed with other schools in a different environment through pen friendships and exchange of taped messages.
5 Children with particular expertise (such as screen-printing, pottery or bookmaking) visited other schools to pass on their skills to groups of children.
6 Teachers *visited* each other's schools, these occasions being of greatest value when the receiving classes were carefully selected to match the professional needs of the guest teacher.

18.6 Clustering

Perhaps one of the best-known strategies, increasingly adopted by small schools in an attempt to maximise learning opportunities for their pupils, is that of coming together on a more formal basis, known as 'clustering' or 'federation'. (Sometimes the terms are used interchangeably, but generally speaking clustering implies a loose voluntary system of collaboration of autonomous schools. Federation suggests a more formal linking, perhaps where one group of schools is the responsibility of a single headteacher.) In this section, the term clustering is used throughout, indicating a voluntary grouping of schools each retaining individual autonomy.

Clusters are not a new phenomenon. The Plowden Report (DES, 1967, para 484) describes the 'close relationships . . . developed by groups of small schools', 'staff interchange', and children visiting other schools for 'team games, music making and country dancing'. The Report sees such developments as a means of combating professional isolation and extending learning opportunities for children. The role and importance of the local authorities' advisory services in promoting and fostering these initiatives is also recognised.

Typically, clusters appear to have their origins in pragmatism, neighbouring schools voluntarily coming together to satisfy a mutual need through sharing expertise or resources. Survival and continuity, though, eventually seem to require a more formal structure.

This section raises some general issues which have emerged from the differing experiences of cluster groupings and considers the future of clusters in the light of recent central government initiatives.

18.6.1 *Why cluster?*

Cluster groupings report some benefits which seem to be common to all, and others which are quite specific, dependent upon local circumstances. For example, the Powys Project (Welsh Office, 1987) provided the opportunity for a cluster to employ supply teaching assistance. This in turn generated debate about the best use of such staff. Not all clusters are able to do this. Incidentally, the Education Reform Act (1988) may provide increased opportunities of this kind depending upon local arrangements for budget delegation.

Some of the more general claims made for clustering are that:

1. Such collaboration overcomes limitations in providing a broad curriculum because of increased staff numbers. (However, it would be a mistake to assume that simply creating a large number of available staff will of itself broaden curricular expertise. It may conceivably serve only to duplicate a narrow range of interests!)
2. Clustering increases the available range of resources (of all kinds).
3. It provides more opportunities for professional contacts.
4. It increases peer-group contacts for children.

18.6.2 *A framework for considering clustering arrangements*

The clustering principle has been interpreted in many different ways. Figure 18.2 poses some questions associated with clustering. It is interesting to note that, with little or no history of support for small schools, separate local authorities identified common strategies consisting of two elements, a) a number of schools would be grouped together in a distinctive arrangement, b) support for these schools would be provided via the cluster (Bell, 1988).

Clusters differ in size, may be constituted formally, through the local authority, or linked voluntarily. They may be located in a single secondary-school catchment area, with access to some secondary-school facilities or they may not. Sometimes support teachers are appointed. Sometimes extra financial help is provided by the local authority. Bluntly, the variations are endless (Bell, 1988). Reasons are not hard to find. The final form taken by a cluster is the result of many considerations.

An analysis of several existing arrangements raises a number of questions. Some examples – not asked in any order of priority or in isolation – are given below. Clearly, any organisational change impinges

Figure 18.2 Clusters: decisions to be taken

1 How will decisions be made within the cluster? (How will governing bodies of individual schools be involved?)

2 How much autonomy will be granted to the cluster by the local authority?

3 Following the 1988 Education Reform Act, to what extent may the local authority delegate budget management?

4 Will it be possible to obtain additional support for teachers? If so, what will be the role of extra personnel?

5 Could the cluster continue if external support from the LEA was withdrawn and budget control given to the schools at a later date?

upon multifarious aspects of school life, a point worth considering in itself.

Who is to lead the cluster?

There are a number of important issues involved here and various answers may be possible. What does seem to emerge is that, from a typically pragmatic voluntary scheme, more formal support mechanisms are needed if such arrangements are to flourish. The Plowden Report (DES, 1967) recommended that local authorities use their advisory services in this way. Similarly, HMI Wales (Welsh Office, 1984) commented that co-operation would be 'significantly assisted by the establishment and implementation of appropriate policies on the part of local education authorities' (p. 19). The nature of local authority involvement should therefore be considered at the earliest stage.

Some existing clusters have identified the need for a cluster co-ordinator currently employed by the local authority to sustain their work. Simply, the task of supporting an initiative is likely to become over-burdensome on any one member of a cluster, such as a teaching head. Financial aid may best be used not on material resources but on providing such assistance. In this context the implications of the 1988 Education Act, not as yet fully clear with regard to small schools, may be further complicated by the fact that schools in different areas could have differing experiences of budget delegation.

The advantage of leaders being drawn from the 'inside' of clusters, such as teachers or heads, is that they would possess a detailed knowledge of the local situation and its needs. On the other hand, 'outsiders' such as advisers may well be in a better position to give support as the structure becomes established and more formal.

It is worth noting that the House of Commons Select Committee Report (1986) recommends that

> each cluster of small schools should have a named member of staff who is responsible for coordinating the training needs of teachers in all the schools and advising on how those needs might best be met.
>
> (in Wallace and Butterworth, 1987, p. 14)

Can the cluster be sustained?
At some stage – probably in supporting what began as an informal arrangement – external support, at present usually provided by the local authority, will be required. For example, at a very basic level, one of the most commonly identified 'non-curricular' resources required to enhance the work of clusters is transport. So one authority allows a small school to use its minibus for a part of the day when it is not required for other duties.

What will be the extent and geographical location of the cluster?
There may be some advantages in schools which feed the same secondary school coming together, perhaps enhancing curriculum continuity. In Wales, schools teaching through the medium of Welsh could also be grouped advantageously. As for size, the Powys project (1987) seems to suggest that an optimum lies in a membership of between five and nine schools. Eleven is considered too large, though it is interesting to note that the figure of fifteen has been proposed for moderation of assessment procedures associated with the National Curriculum.

How may the cluster develop?
Identify clearly the ways in which member schools may co-operate. Consider the pace of development envisaged within the cluster. It is reasonable to articulate expectations for the end of the first term or first year. Set realistic expectations to avoid disillusionment.

What sources of expertise are available?
Identify and use sources of expertise. These may be advisers, parents or lecturers. Traditional centres of support for teachers (teachers' centres, resource centres) are a considerable asset and where they exist (generally there is underprovision in rural areas) can make an important contribution. It may be worth considering the possibilities of teacher exchange. However, there are problems in this: perhaps producing an unnecessary fragmentation of children's curricular experiences. For example, particular and defined times have to be allocated to

accommodate a visiting teacher 'specialist'. One head of a small village school, anticipating these difficulties, used teacher exchange as a means of sharing expertise amongst staff rather than making use of a 'specialist' teacher for allocated times in the classroom.

How will the community be involved?
The small rural school is usually (but not always) a part of a close-knit community. The support of the community for a co-operative venture is important.

What are the management implications?
For the headteachers there is opportunity for development in management skills through dealing with a larger, more varied group of colleagues. In every cluster grouping, headteachers are involved. For success, heads must collaborate with professional colleagues. Perhaps a reconceptualisation of individual school autonomy and the unique powers of the headteacher within the tradition of primary education is required. Headteachers, then, may legitimately influence the operation of a neighbouring school. Headteachers have to learn to cope with a demanding form of collaboration and all its implications. Similarly, advisers, advisory teachers and other support staff may be expected to work in a new way. It may well be that a staff development need identified early in the life of a cluster is that of reorientation of these professionals to a new role (Wallace and Butterworth, 1987).

18.6.3 Clustering: the future?

In 1984, through the Education Support Grant scheme, local authorities were invited to bid for funding to support projects aimed at improving curriculum provision in rural primary schools. As Bell (1988) notes, this should not be mistaken as a belated recognition of the qualities of small schools. Rather, it was an acknowledgement of the fact that such schools would always be with us, long after any rationalisation programme. The projects were funded for a maximum of five years. Bell goes on to suggest that an interesting side effect of this initiative was to stimulate those authorities who had been unsuccessful in their bids to central government to support their own rural schools from within their own resources.

Established clusters, on one view, form convenient points of delivery of the new INSET (Welsh Office, 1987). Administratively, large expensive resources are more easily targetted to what appear to be convenient reference points. But herein lies a dilemma (Bell, 1988). The difficulty with such a view is that it is assumed that the cluster can function quite smoothly, independently of any activity by teachers. It is, frankly, a device for the delivery of external support. Development, then, does not grow from teacher initiatives. Rather, development is seen to be properly initiated by external agencies. This approach, of course, mirrors the discredited curriculum development movement of the 1960s, which assumed that strong central initiatives would enhance practice, with scant regard for teacher 'ownership' of such developments.

The dilemma is accentuated by the National Curriculum's Task Group on Assessment and Testing recommendations (TGAT, 1988). The necessity for results to be moderated across schools will require the formation of regional moderation groups. The report suggests that 'Groups of schools are established in such a way that each group forms a reasonably compact and stable geographical unit' (Appendix H, para 4). Groups will have the responsibility of comparing the spread of results from standard assessment tasks alongside the results from teachers' assessment in order to decide whether:

- differences can be explained by differences in criteria used by particular teachers . . .;
- there are some local factors . . . which can justify rescaling the national assessment results;
- there seems to be something amiss with the overall results on the national tests rather than with school assessments.

(TGAT digest report, p. 13)

It is unclear how schools or local authorities will meet the recommendations of the Task Group. At best, moderation groups will give a new dimension to regional inter-school collaboration. At worst, the need to meet National Curriculum requirements will result in assessment issues overshadowing general education concerns.

Typically, clustering began in a voluntary way, a means of enhancing professional development through collaboration. Some would argue that if such development is to flourish it must allow risk taking and even some resource wastage.

> If the purpose really is to enable a larger group of teachers than ever a single small school can muster to share their expertise and take collective responsibilities for ensuring the quality of their schools, they must be accorded considerable freedom to exercise their own judgement . . .
>
> (Bell, 1988, p. 187)

The realities of local authority responses to central requirements in implementing the National Curriculum and revised INSET funding arrangements may make this a difficult point of view to sustain.

More likely, perhaps, is that 'clustering' will, broadly speaking, take two forms:

1 schools coming together voluntarily to increase their INSET opportunities (described elsewhere);
2 the establishment of more formal clusters by a local authority, perhaps for purposes of curriculum continuity.

Examples of both types of arrangement are given below.

Figure 18.3 An analysis of the development of a co-operative teaching project in Cornwall (from Ohlson, 1983)

The challenge:	How to increase available expertise

↓

The resources:	Three headteachers with specialisms in music, environmental studies, science

↓

The plan:	Three headteachers in three-way exchange on two afternoons per week

↓

The problem: (1)	• Travelling time uneconomic • Heads felt that they were absent from their own schools for too long

↓

The solutions: (1)	• Use two mornings each week (9.00 AM–10.30 AM) • Visiting headteachers travelled directly to receiving school from home, taught their own 'specialism' and moved on to their own school at morning break leaving follow-up work to be continued

↓

The problem: (2)	• 'Specialist' work was self-contained • 'Specialist' work was difficult to maintain

↓

The solutions: (2)	'Specialisms' subsumed into topic work – each headteacher responsible for a component

The benefits:	• Spread of specialist expertise • Headteachers visited each others schools discussed expectations, standards, behaviour

External support – Schools Council Cornwall LEA

18.7 Co-operative teaching: an example

The following is an account of a co-operative teaching venture in Cornwall based on a report by Ohlson (1983). It illustrates the problems involved in attempting to share expertise and exchange staff within a group of small rural schools. Figure 18.3 gives an outline of the project. More detailed accounts may be found in Bell and Sigsworth (1987) and Schools Council (Wales) (1983).

The setting
Three small schools were involved (roll numbers in 1980 were 52, 28 and 44 respectively). The schools serve an area of Cornwall which borders Devon, a short distance from the Tamar. The population is scattered and pupils travel to school mainly by bus. Only a tiny number are within walking distance. Travelling time from one school to another is about fifteen minutes.

The origins
At a local meeting held in 1980 to consider the implications of the HMI Primary School Survey (DES 1978), the problem for small schools in providing a broad curriculum from limited staff expertise was raised. Three small school headteachers who had attended the meeting, reasoned that co-operation may be a way of meeting their difficulties, feeling, as they did, stretched too thinly in too many directions. The philosophical niceties of what 'specialism' may mean were overwhelmed by the feeling of relief that someone else may be responsible for a part of the curriculum in each school, thus easing the load.

The plan
Each of the three headteachers had a specialism: music, environmental studies and science. Each agreed to be responsible for planning and teaching his own 'area'. This helped to 'free' some time in school by

easing the preparation load. That is, each head did not now have to plan and prepare for the other two curriculum areas.

The working of the venture

Ohlson (1983) makes the point that in establishing co-operative working, the personalities of the individuals involved are at least as important as the expertise they can offer. The three heads enjoyed an amicable relationship and were not unduly worried about a headteacher colleague teaching in their 'own' school. Initially, the venture was low-key – quite secretive, in fact, so that it could flourish (or not) without undue external pressure.

The first exchange took place in 1980 involving the three headteachers and their respective junior classes. In the beginning, discussions were held so that each knew what the other was doing, but each took full responsibility for all the work in their own separate subject area.

The benefits

The heads discovered more about their own schools and how expectations differed. Each learnt about the other's way of working. Discussions were friendly and reassuring. Ohlson remarks that too much discussion in larger formal groupings earlier in the venture may have inhibited the growth of co-operation. Too many theoretical meetings without a basis in shared experience may simply serve to dampen enthusiasm.

A change in plans

By 1981, the headteachers felt that changes were necessary. Each felt the sessions (two-and-a-half hours) away from their own school were too long, and travelling time needed to be cut down. Therefore it was decided to use two mornings each week (9.00 AM–10.30 AM). The heads drove directly from home to their receiving school, then moved on during the morning break to their own school. Follow-up work was left to be completed. This proved to be unexpectedly beneficial, because it necessitated weekly planning meetings. The separate 'subjects' became subsumed into topic work.

Postscript and conclusions

Ohlson offers the following conclusions:

1 Clusters cannot be prescribed. Relationships are important and need to be based on mutually recognised needs.
2 All co-operatives face inevitable change; LEA support is needed. (This venture was eventually supported by Cornwall LEA and the then Schools' Council).

3 Expertise is best exchanged when it can fit into a topic-based framework.
4 It may be useful for each school to build up a particular resource bank to support one particular curriculum area.

18.8 Case study: Clustering arrangements for continuity between primary and secondary phases in Northamptonshire

The following is an account of clustering arrangements within the county of Northamptonshire, designed to support and promote curriculum continuity between the primary and secondary phases of schooling based on a report by a county inspector involved in the programme (Spencer, 1988).

There is a substantial research literature on problems of transfer, pupil and teacher attitudes and effects on pupil progress (eg ILEA, 1988). This example has, as its specific focus, curriculum continuity and progression rather than mechanisms for effecting smooth transfer. The trend in recent publications has been to consider the curriculum across age ranges from 5 to 16 instead of in separate primary and secondary phases. The advent of the National Curriculum in its turn poses serious questions of continuity for schools.

Other counties (eg Suffolk) have also established pyramid clusters based on 'feeder' relationships to secondary schools.

Background

Between 1983 and 1984, the local authority began to recognise the need to establish county guidelines for continuity and liaison. A necessary first step in formulating such a policy was to gather details of existing practices. This information, together with the observations of HMI on the county's transfer strategies in 1984, suggested the need for more consistent and systematic procedures. One response has been the development of clusters of schools established on a cross-phase basis.

The organisation of the clusters

Northamptonshire is predominantly rural. About 173 of the county's 382 schools of various kinds are involved in cross-phase liaison activities. These schools are arranged into nine rural and five urban clusters of between 13 and 30 establishments across the county's two-tier (primary–secondary) or three-tier (primary–secondary–tertiary or lower–middle–upper) provision.

Each cluster has a steering and planning group comprising the headteacher of each member primary school, headteacher of the lower school (in the three-tier lower–middle–upper structure found in Northampton itself), head of teacher's centre, advisory teachers, assistant education officer and a general inspector. From each grouping, a representative primary–secondary co-ordinator reports to a county co-ordinating group on the working of the cluster.

Each group has addressed three main areas of concern:

- transfer and induction strategies;
- curriculum continuity;
- record-keeping.

Not surprisingly, given the uneven pattern of existing liaison arrangements, the clusters began from very different starting points. The initial periods of activity were marked by lengthy meetings to begin to establish common ground and uniformity of approaches (see Figure 18.4).

Figure 18.4 Summary of phases in establishing curriculum continuity (adapted from Spencer, 1988) (one-year cycle)

Chronology of procedures for one cluster

Day conference (using a staff development day)
↓
Primary/secondary headteachers' meeting
↓
Primary-phase conference
↓
Inter-school visits (primary–secondary, secondary–primary) and reflections
↓
Secondary-phase departments'/primary headteachers' meeting
↓
Meeting of staff involved
↓
Dissemination of emerging ideas to all staff of all schools involved
↓
Implementation, monitoring and evaluation of programme
↓
Reports to governing bodies

The role of the local authority in sustaining and promoting co-operative ventures, in particular that of the county's inspectorates has already been highlighted. The involvement of the general inspector is central to the strategy adopted by Northamptonshire in:

- establishing a clear framework within which clustering ventures can work;
- initiating new clusters;
- providing an objective assessment of the operation and success of co-operative ventures;
- identifying and resourcing in-service needs arising from the working of the clusters.

Conclusions

Spencer's report of the Northamptonshire project (1988) suggests that the most significant steps forward in continuity have been made in science and mathematics.

> As a result of sustained activity working groups in many areas of the county have reached agreement on sequences for concepts, skills and content which have led to planned changes in school curriculum, teaching styles and organisation.
>
> (Spencer, 1988, p. 41)

Considerations in establishing a curriculum continuity programme

The following points were identified from within the experiences of the Northamptonshire project for consideration by those considering a similar venture:

1 A clear, but flexible statement of policy (from the LEA) is required to provide a framework for activities.
2 Such a venture is a long-term, complex and costly affair. Resources have to be made available to facilitate opportunities for many people to meet, and for appropriate in-service provision.
3 Headteachers in both primary and secondary phases have to give due priority to curriculum continuity. This may involve, of course, a partial surrender of autonomy. A planned programme bringing together all staff involved with a clear focus and agreed criteria in order to gauge progress is essential.
4 Participating schools should agree on a curriculum area where problems of continuity and mismatch are pronounced. Establishing

continuity is a lengthy business. A programme lasting for one year devoted to one particular aspect of the curriculum is required for progress and development.

5 Each grouping should have a co-ordinator with a flexible secondment of twenty to thirty days to ensure consistency between member schools.

6 An LEA inspector or adviser should be appointed with clear (and preferably no other) responsibilities other than those for such liaison programmes.

It may well be that contemporary urgency in establishing such initiatives will be provided by the imperatives of the National Curriculum. Given the requirement for teachers to be involved in monitoring and assessment procedures, and their moderation within a particular geographical area, it may well be that such groupings provide the most appropriate structures.

A summary of one cluster programme of development in curriculum continuity is given in Figure 18.5. It is based on the working of one cluster consisting of one comprehensive school and eleven feeder primary schools.

Figure 18.5 Summary of one cluster's programme of development in curriculum continuity (adapted from Spencer, 1988)

1 Headteachers meeting with inspector to identify needs of cluster.
2 Primary headteachers, allowance holders and relevant secondary heads of department meeting with adviser/inspector for identified curriculum area to plan liaison programme.
3 Year 6 teachers from primary schools visit secondary schools.
4 Meeting of primary headteachers to establish consistency.
5 All secondary teachers who teach early secondary years visit primary schools.
6 Primary headteachers and allowance holders meet to prepare common agreed document for secondary colleagues.
7 Secondary department staff meet to prepare common agreed document for primary colleagues.
8 All involved staff meet to exchange and discuss documents (staff development day).
9 All involved staff meet with inspector to evaluate progress.
10 Progress reports and documents circulated to all staff in all schools involved.

19 Staff development and appraisal

19.1 Moving towards appraisal

The issue of teacher appraisal has ceased to be the 'skeleton in the cupboard' of education. Regardless of any contractual obligation to become involved in appraisal procedure, most teachers would agree that they have a professional obligation to evaluate the work that they are doing. The reasons for introducing clear, unambiguous appraisal systems for teachers and heads have been made in detail elsewhere (Suffolk, 1985; Gane, 1986; Day, Whitaker and Wren, 1987; Wragg, 1987). They include:

- a professional responsibility to improve performance for the benefit of pupils;
- a management responsibility to improve effectiveness for the benefit of colleagues and the school as a whole;
- the need for more objective judgement of an individual teacher's/ head's effectiveness;
- the need to identify and disseminate examples of good practice;
- the need to identify barriers to effectiveness so that they may be made explicit and acted upon;
- the need to define clearly the expectations of each individual within the organisation of the school;
- the need to formalise a situation of professional analysis which might not occur without some contractual obligation;
- the need to give clear terms of reference for those to whom teachers and heads are accountable;

- the need to ensure that individual teachers are giving 'value for money'.

Obviously, the arguments used to support the introduction of teacher appraisal will vary, depending on the perspective of the individual. Most teachers would decry the final item on the above list. However, with heads and governing bodies becoming increasingly responsible for staffing under the arrangements for the local management of schools, the 'opportunity cost' of a teacher will inevitably be discussed. Governing bodies will have to decide whether the expenditure on a *person* is likely to be of more value to pupils than the large amount of resource support which a teacher's salary might purchase.

Discussions about the reasons *why* appraisal will be introduced have taken a back seat to the debate on *how* appraisal systems will operate and *what* will be appraised. Examples from industry and commerce have been sought out and commended by many in education as a sound base on which to build.

The dangers of using industrial models are apparent, however. The term 'personnel management' has given way in industry to the expression 'human resource management'. It may be playing with words, but the perception of teachers as a human resource (as opposed to physical resources (buildings) or technological resources (computers)) may indicate a particular management viewpoint which finds it easy to talk about teachers in terms of value for money. The parallel with manufacturing industry is also difficult to make when the aims of the organisation (profit motive as opposed to educational values) and product (manufactured goods as opposed to well balanced individuals) are considered.

Secondary schools and further education colleges have found it easier to come to terms with the industrial model of appraisal than primary schools. Their size (over fifty and often over one hundred staff) makes a more formal management structure acceptable and necessary; working to objectives set by examination syllabuses, with public examination results being an important performance indicator, gives them arguably a much more product-orientated approach than primary schools should seek to achieve. Certainly, the industrial aim of manufacturing a product with 'zero defects' might be a worthwhile, if unachievable, educational aim!

Can we achieve zero defects in education?

The introduction of arrangements for the local management of schools (LMS) and open enrolment has brought the hard world of the small business organisation closer to that of the primary school. Can the need to maximise pupil numbers be seen in commercial terms as a profit motive? Certainly, the aggressive marketing strategies adopted by some primary heads to publicise their schools closely resemble public relations exercises used by commercial organisations to market their 'images'.

An objectives-led National Curriculum also makes the gap between the primary school and the small service industry much smaller. Primary heads may see themselves in the position of a partner in a firm of solicitors, for example. They lead a small team of professionals working in an area where interpersonal relationships are very important. Their aims would be similar: to compete and survive in an open market while serving their clients in the most effective way possible, to the benefit of those clients and of themselves. The senior partner in such a firm would have some responsibility for appraising staff. It may operate through a formal, annual appraisal system with set criteria. In many partnerships, however, measures of efficiency and effectiveness are implicit, and time spent on bureaucratic procedures to determine quality of performance is often regarded as costly.

The primary head is not in the position of a partner of a small firm, nor are the governing bodies equivalent to senior partners. They are all accountable to higher authorities and, for this reason, bureaucratic systems of appraisal are inevitable. It is most important, therefore, that the professional perspective of appraisal is not lost in the bureaucracy that is likely to be present in teacher–superior relationships.

19.2 What to appraise

The National Development Centre for School Management Training in the National Steering Group's report on appraisal pilot schemes (1988) posed questions about the appraisal process. These questions included, under the heading 'What should be appraised?', the following possible indicators:

- the effectiveness of the teacher's work in the classroom and general contribution to the operation of the school?
- all or only some aspects of the job?
- personal qualities?
- performance?
- potential?
- measures of targets achieved?

The first of these questions is arguably the most pertinent. There is a need to determine the effectiveness of the teacher's work in the classroom and *with pupils* in the widest sense. The definition of 'effective teaching' is not one which is easy to arrive at or agree on. Traditionalists and progressives will have their own ideas about what makes an effective teacher and how the learning process can best operate. Some teachers would fight hard to retain their closed-door, formal style of teaching. It may be highly didactic, lack cross-curricular application and be old fashioned but, they argue, it gets results in the three Rs. They will argue, in our view mistakenly, that the National Curriculum, with its accompanying subject-based attainment targets, supports this perspective. Others argue strongly for a child-centred approach incorporating carefully structured group work, investigational opportunities, cross-curriculum learning and activity-based approaches. They will point out that the attainment targets of each subject area have sufficient in common to be able to be met through integrated work which builds on the enjoyment pupils get from learning. There never will be a consensus on the best way to be effective as a teacher.

Kyriacou (1986) devised a framework for thinking about effective teaching. He divided the factors which affect teaching into three groups of variables:

Context variables including teacher characteristics (age, experience, personality); pupil characteristics (age, ability, social class); class characteristics (size, range of ability); school characteristics (size, building, ethos) and characteristics of the occasion (time of day, weather, time of year).

Process variables being the three-way interaction of teacher perceptions and behaviour, pupil perceptions and behaviour and characteristics of the learning activities.

Product variables including short- or long-term objectives and cognitive or affective educational outcomes.

Wragg (1987) suggests that the criteria by which teachers should be judged fall under three headings:

> *The behaviour and experiences of pupils* (whether what they are doing is worthwhile, whether they appear to be absorbed in their task or are misbehaving, the extent to which the task matches the pupils' ability and previous experiences).
>
> *The behaviour of the teacher* (professional skills such as the

ability to explain new concepts, ask appropriate questions, manage the badly behaved, prepare lessons, organise a classroom, assess and monitor progress).

Outcomes of teaching (what pupils appear to have learned, including the knowledge, skills, attitudes and values they acquire as a direct or indirect result of whatever the teacher has done).

In 1988 an interim report was published outlining the progress of appraisal schemes in six LEAs (National Steering Group, 1988). The importance of teachers having a clear understanding of their roles and responsibilities was a central theme in all six reports. The need for clear job descriptions is therefore seen as important for all teachers holding a management role. Isaacs (1987) offered possible job descriptions for primary heads, deputies and curriculum leaders. They included:

The Headteacher
The headteacher should be responsible:

- i) for the overall administration of the school in accordance with LEA procedures and policies and in relation to local needs.
- ii) for the general direction of the school in terms of curriculum policy after consultation with LEA, colleagues and governors.
- iii) for the management of resources in terms of equipment and personnel and ensuring their effective deployment . . .
- vi) for the planned personal and professional development of colleagues . . .
- vii) with colleagues, for reviewing and evaluating the direction of the school.
- viii) for keeping professionally up to date by attendance at courses and reading appropriate literature.
- ix) with colleagues, for the quality of children's learning.

The Deputy Head
The deputy head should be responsible:

- i) for having a working knowledge of the school's administrative procedures . . .
- ii) for planning, with the head, the general curriculum policy of the school . . . to ensure continuity and progression in children's learning.
- iii) for assisting the head in the management of resources . . .

iv) for a class for a major part of the time but to be entitled to negotiated release in order to perform the tasks outlined above . . .

vii) for taking charge of the school in the absence of the head.

viii) with colleagues, for the quality of children's learning.

The Curriculum Leader (called the 'Post Holder' in Isaacs' outline)
The [curriculum leader] should be responsible:

i) for leading the work in the appropriate curriculum area by promoting debate and discussion amongst colleagues.

ii) for preparing a scheme of work . . .

iii) for liaising with the head, deputy head and other [curriculum leaders] to ensure the curriculum of the school is seen as a unified whole, that sufficient attention is paid to continuity and progression, that work is appropriately matched to children's abilities . . .

There is some debate as to how detailed a job description should be. One school of thought is that the role should be defined clearly and precisely and, as members of staff change, new occupants should take on the job description already defined. A second school of thought is that it is the *person* in post not the job detail that is important. The job description should be moulded to fit the present incumbent and, if necessary, responsibilities redefined as staffing changes. The description should be developmental and should reflect what can be reasonably expected of a person at this particular moment in time, with his/her experience, and the nature of the task in hand. As such, it will require modifications and additions as the role develops. An example of a more detailed job description is given below. The responsibility is that of deputy head (staff development co-ordinator).

Job Description for Deputy Head (Staff Development)

i) *General*

a) to accept full responsibility for all aspects of staff development

b) to be the formal link between the school and all outside agencies concerned with providing in-service activities

ii) *Student teachers*

a) to liaise closely with the higher education institution over all students on teaching practice

b) to advise staff concerning working arrangements with students

c) to introduce students to the school and organise a professional programme for them
d) to monitor the progress of students and prepare final reports

iii) *Induction*
a) to organise an introduction to the school in July for all new staff
b) to draw up a comprehensive programme of induction
c) to ensure that all curriculum leaders are fully briefed on their supportive roles in induction
d) to observe the lessons of new teachers and provide support and advice

iv) *Staff development programme*
a) to draw up, monitor and evaluate an annual programme of staff development based on the identified needs of staff
b) to co-ordinate all school-based and out-of-school INSET activities
c) to take overall responsibility for the organisation of INSET days
d) to manage the INSET budget
e) to advise staff concerning their own development
f) to maintain an efficient record system of individual staff development activities
g) to evaluate the effects of the staff development programme on pupils' learning
h) to produce termly reports on staff development activities for presentation to the governing body, advisory service and other interested parties

v) *Staff professional resource area*
a) to maintain a resource area of professional publications (DES, HMI, LEA reports, books and journals), computer software, publishers' catalogues, etc
b) to oversee the uses of the school's electronic mail system (TTNS) and ensure that staff are trained in its use
c) to receive suggestions from staff regarding additional materials for the staff resource area

As the definition of management or teaching responsibility becomes more precise, so there is an inclination to move into the realm of objectives-led performance appraisal and the use of 'performance indicators' to assess the effectiveness of a programme, or even of staff. Although there are many in industry and commerce who would argue that 'management by objectives' is no longer a useful model to follow (it produced managers who were blinkered, failed to examine the process as long as the product was being achieved and who 'slackened off' when the stated objective had been reached), there are many who are strongly advocating its use in education. The debate about objectives-led management and objectives-led curricula will not be rehearsed here. MacDonald-Ross (1973), Stenhouse (1975) and Eisner (1985) provide interesting analyses of the role of objectives in education. What does need to be stated briefly is the move towards evaluation of teaching and management by the use of performance indicators. The Further Education Unit (1987) listed a number of performance indicators which may be used to evaluate staff development programmes. They included:

- staff attitudes to programme activities;
- unit costs for staff training;
- preparedness/reluctance of staff to undergo further development in the same area;
- increased personal confidence;
- changes in curriculum/classroom practice;
- demands for new facilities/equipment/resources.

A performance indicator for a primary-school staff development activity on computer-assisted learning would be increased use of the computer by a particular class and a wider use of software. Indicators for a course on display would be in evidence in a teacher's classroom and in the corridors around the school. Short-term indicators for a course on staff development would be a well designed and evaluated programme for staff and a carefully managed budget.

Staff appraisal systems will use many criteria to judge effectiveness of individuals. It will be the responsibility of the headteacher to determine the criteria for appraisal within the context of any particular school; it will be the responsibility of the staff development co-ordinator to follow up the appraisal process with suitable individual-oriented staff development programmes.

19.3 The link between staff development and appraisal

The ACAS agreement of 1986 defined appraisal as

> a continuous and systematic process intended to help individual teachers with their professional development and career planning, and to help ensure that the in-service training and deploy-

ment of teachers matches the complementary needs of individual teachers and the schools.

Appraisal is not the same as staff development though they are obviously closely interrelated. Staff development will be needed to support the appraisal process, both in preparing teachers for the appraisal system itself and by providing appropriate follow-up to meet the needs identified in the appraisal exercise. Gane (1986) stated that:

> To support a phased introduction of appraisal nationally, considerable INSET preparation will be needed for the roles of appraisee and appraiser. The resource implications are of massive proportions. INSET should include:
> a) Awareness raising for:
> - all teachers, possibly based within one or a group of schools . . .
> - heads . . .
> - officers and advisers
> - governors
>
> b) Training for appraisers in:
> - lesson observation
> - interviewing skills
> - analysis of context and task
> - gender issues
> - ethnicity issues . . .
> - recording
>
> c) Training for appraisees in:
> - negotiating and contracting skills
> - self-evaluation
> - procedures and process.

Classroom observation and interview are seen as the two main ways of conducting teacher appraisal. Both need to be considered carefully if the process is to be effective and meaningful. More detail on these and other research methods may be found in Hopkins (1985). The result of appraisal will normally be an action plan on the part of both appraiser and appraisee. The staff development programme will be used to enhance this target-setting process. The nature and extent of formal and informal follow-up will be crucial to the credibility of any appraisal scheme. Gane (1986) listed some general points regarding follow-up to appraisal:

- be wary of the assumption that an outcome of an appraisal

interview will be in terms of specific 'training'

- to achieve credibility ... the appraiser must be in a position to deliver the 'contract' agreed at the interview

- INSET resources for follow-up must be controlled by a manager who has decision-making powers ... and is seen as a credible facilitator

- the appraiser must be able to match individual wants or needs with what is available by matching an overview of the school with the individual's perception.

The processes of appraisal and staff development become almost indivisible in this context. If responsibility for the two processes is divided (with, for instance, the head taking responsibility for the appraisal interview but delegating lesson observation and management of staff development follow-up to a deputy) communication must be of the highest order to ensure that what is 'contracted' in the appraisal process is delivered or supported by the staff development process. The onus will inevitably be on the headteacher to create a climate in which the complementary systems work *for* the teachers. Teachers must co-operate if appraisal is to operate on a professional level. Fundamentally, self-appraisal or self-evaluation should set the basis for all appraisal schemes. We consider an example of teacher self-evaluation in the next chapter.

20 Needs identification through teacher self-evaluation

A junior school sited in a predominantly working-class urban area provides the setting for this case study. The school building is new and affords a pleasant working environment for the ten members of staff and their pupils. Mrs Gates, the headteacher, has been in post since the opening of the new school two years ago, and this is her first headship. She has firm ideas about the nature of education and the way in which children learn. Children should become actively engaged in the learning process and this is best achieved by providing them with opportunities to speculate on their first-hand experiences (by formulating and testing hypotheses) within a structured framework devised by the teacher.

If teachers adopt this view then it follows that their own learning and development must be guided by the same procedures. They should examine classroom experiences and reflect on their importance. Teacher self-evaluation thus becomes not just a method of gauging performance but an integral part of the educational enterprise. The quality of pupil learning becomes inextricably intertwined with the process of teacher development. And it is in this that the role of the headteacher becomes vital. For, just as the headteacher is reliant on the teachers involving the children in the educative process, it is the headteacher's responsibility to engage the teachers in the same process. Furthermore, these principles do not only apply to pupil and teacher learning but also to headteachers who also learn by evaluating their own actions and reflecting on this. It may be a cliché but it is still worth stating that all persons involved in the education process are both teachers and learners.

Mrs Gates became increasingly concerned as it became clear that these principles were not shared by her staff. She was also failing to communicate them effectively. The experiences of many staff meetings revealed that this lack of communication was because the teachers perceived the role of the head as one of authority and this differing perception was clearly creating a barrier. Mrs Gates voiced her concerns about this problem in the following way:

> *Why can't I communicate with the teachers on my staff in a meaningful way when I could communicate with colleagues when I was a class teacher?*
>
> *Why don't the staff contribute to discussions in meetings? Why do they seem to accept everything I say as if it were received 'truth' and then not do anything about it? Why do teachers act on insights gained from other members of staff?*
>
> *What is it about being a headteacher that seems to prevent me from being an educator?*

In reflecting on these questions, Mrs Gates reached two conclusions:

1 The headteacher has to begin where the teacher is, just as the teacher has to interact with the child to gain insights into his or her conceptual understanding;
2 The headteacher/educator has to make his or her philosophy explicit in the means by which teachers are engaged in the process of professional development.

How was this to be achieved? There are no blue-prints for action in situations such as this; it is for the headteacher to initiate the process, monitor what is happening and on the basis of this make the necessary changes. The headteacher thus learns through self-evaluation of her own actions in the same way as the teachers and the children.

20.1 Bold beginnings: an attempt to involve teachers in the process of education

Telling teachers doesn't get you anywhere (Headteacher)

Mrs Gates decided to begin by involving teachers directly in self-evaluation in as non-threatening a way as possible, in the hope that they would themselves come to understand the purpose and the benefits of the process. A start was made by talking to the staff about teacher self-evaluation and stressing that its essential purpose is to enable teachers to improve their practice in a way which placed *them* in control. Some of the techniques for conducting evaluation were then presented and discussed and the staff were asked if they would try some of these out. It was emphasised that they should not do anything with which they might personally feel uncomfortable. The reaction of the staff to all of this was uncertainty (what is the point of this?) and suspicion (what is the head really up to?) but nevertheless they agreed to try.

Mrs Gates then gave each teacher a diary form (Figure 20.1) and a reflection sheet (Figure 20.2) and requested that these be filled in by the following week. All staff completed this exercise.

Figure 20.1 Suggested diary form

(Please feel free to alter)

Write down the two most significant events in each session:

Break

Lunch

Break

This sheet is the personal property of the writer and *no-one* has right of access.

Figure 20.2 Reflection sheet 1

Please bring the diary forms and this sheet to the next meeting, but I will not read them unless you wish me to. Neither should you feel obliged to discuss the contents.

1 Why did you choose these events and not any others?

2 Does this choice of events indicate to you what *you* really believe is important in how children learn?

3 Does any of your data indicate to you that you should make changes to maximise learning? What and how?

4 Make the change(s) (one at a time?) and monitor what happens. If you wish, ask for advice and/or support in making the change. You are a responsible professional. (PS Other professional views can be helpful.)

5 Has this exercise helped you in thinking about how people learn? If yes, in what way?

6 Is the exercise worth repeating? Why?

The next meeting was organised into two discussion groups from both of which Mrs Gates excluded herself. One group consisted of scale post-holders, the other of scale 1 teachers, the reason for this being that discussion would be likely to be freer in situations in which hierarchy does not intrude. Both groups then addressed the following questions:

Please discuss:

Diaries:

1 Has this exercise helped you in thinking about what *the children* do in your classroom?
2 Has this exercise helped you in thinking about what *you* do in the classroom?
3 Is it worth repeating?
4 Why?
5 Would you alter the exercise in any way?
6 Is there any help you need now in your classroom teaching?

The two groups then came together and reported their earlier discussions on the value of diary-keeping, though no teacher commented on the contents of their personal diary. The consensus was that diaries were worth keeping and that although they are designed to focus on what the children were learning, they also had the effect of leading teachers to consider what they themselves were doing.

At the same meeting the issue of the place and purpose of curriculum guidelines in schools was discussed. Mrs Gates, in reflecting on the use of curriculum policy statements as a means of staff development, had reached the conclusion that written materials often became an authoritarian voice and that their value lay in the staff discussion stage prior to being written up. If this was the case, then would not the minuting and circulating of the proceedings of staff meetings provide a way of maximising the benefits of this discussion stage? It would be focusing on those elements of the process most conducive to staff development.

Staff were asked to consider the suggestion that 'the value of curriculum documents lies in their ability to generate staff discussion and exchange of ideas, rather than in the documents themselves. The discussion of such documents in staff meetings should be minuted. These minutes will form the basis of day-to-day action plans based upon general statements of policy.'

There was a strong feeling in favour of minuting staff meetings. So, after this meeting and every subsequent meeting, Mrs Gates wrote up the minutes and circulated them so that everyone had a copy. The minutes were then filed and retained to constitute proof of attempts at staff development.

Before the next meeting the teachers' classroom research was taken a stage further as they used the observation sheet (Figure 20.3) to document the activities of one child and the second reflection sheet (Figure 20.4) to consider the importance or relevance of the activity.

Discussion of the observations and the sharing of experiences was subsequently conducted in two groups, one of lower and one of upper junior teachers, on the basis that it seemed expedient to initiate discussion of professional issues as a team. In both groups, agreement was reached that this was a technique which could be useful for researching into the learning of children with particular problems. One teacher proffered the view that self-evaluation increased guilt feelings. This was something Mrs Gates was acutely aware of in her own experience and it provided an opportunity to discuss the view that self-evaluation should not induce feelings of guilt or failure as something has always been learned in the process and this must be seen as a positive development.

Now that the staff had become familiar with the purpose and used some of the methods for self-evaluation, Mrs Gates felt that the time had come for making explicit the personal values that inform evaluation. Education is not a value-free enterprise so that in making decisions about their practice teachers are constantly engaged in

Figure 20.3 Observation sheet

Find 10 minutes when you can observe rather than interact with the children. Choose one child.

1 What is the child supposed to be doing?
2 Record on the sheet what he/she is really doing.

Minute	*Observation*	*Any relevant comments*
1		
2		
3		
4		
5		
6		
7		
8		
9		
10		

Study the data:

1 Should *you* have done something differently?
2 What change(s) can you make?

Figure 20.4 Reflection sheet 2

A If you did not fill in the observation sheet was it because:
   1 You viewed it as a kind of a test and were afraid you'd complete it incorrectly? (If so, I apologise that I have been doing my job badly.) Any implications for the learning of the children in your class?
   2 You couldn't find the time? Any implications for classroom management?

B If you did fill it in:
   1 Was it a useful means of gathering information about the learning in your classroom?
   2 Were any difficulties encountered?

If you wish, yourself, to carry on with the idea please feel free to modify it to suit your own needs.

Please bring the observation sheet and this sheet to the next meeting, but no one will read them and you should not feel obliged to discuss the contents.

Figure 20.5 Extract from *About Our Schools* by Sir Alec Clegg

There are, I believe, certain qualities which exist in any first-class teacher, whether he teaches formally or informally. The following are some of these qualities:

He believes that love is a better spur to learning than fear . . .

He believes that the sort of person a child becomes is often more important than what he knows.

He is hesitant about accepting a syllabus of learning . . . devised by a person who has no knowledge of the background of the children in his class.

He tries to ensure that every child has an experience of success . . .

He knows the lamentable effect on children of incessant failure.

He knows the limitations of trying to measure what a child has learned . . .

He knows and acts on the fact that delight in the performance of a skill is essential to the real mastery of it.

He gives responsibility not only to children who can discharge it but also to children whose development needs this experience.

He knows how to encourage older children to help the young and the strong to help the frail.

He uses knowledge as material for the mind to work on, and not as a lump of matter to be forced into a container.

He knows that it is part of his job to cultivate initiative, sensitivity and confidence as well as to impart facts.

He knows that there are times when he will be more effective if he works with a group of colleagues than if he works singly . . .

He knows that knowledge is doubling every decade or so and that the bit of it that he uses to stimulate his children today may be very different from the bits he used five years ago, and the bit he will use five years hence . . .

He knows also that a number of his pupils will have come from homes with very little support and resource and that somehow this will have to be made up to them . . .

Figure 20.6 Reflection sheet 3

Please read carefully this extract from *About Our Schools* by Sir Alec Clegg. Read it *before* considering the following?

1 Which value statement has struck you most forcibly?

2 Why is this?

3 Do you agree with it?

4 Why, or why not?

5 If you agree: does your classroom really match up to it? (Honest). Think and look tomorrow. If you wish to write a response please do so. You can share it if you wish, or keep it personal.

6 If you don't agree with that particular value statement choose one that you do and work on point 5.

7 Please write a *short* response to the extract. (Please take note, *short*.) You may be asked to share this response with the whole group.

List five things that you think a teacher should be or do that enable children to learn.

Re-write them in order of priority.

Choose one from the corporate list that *you* believe is *very* important.

During the week collect evidence that you really do act on what you believe. If you are brave enough, maybe you could jot down instances that show you that you do not always act on what you believe. (There are wide gaps between most people's beliefs and actions. We do not always do what we think we do.) You will be asked to share the positive. It would be useful if you would share the negative, but that is your choice.

making value judgements. An extract from *About Our Schools* by Sir Alec Clegg (1980, Figure 20.5) was issued to all staff along with Reflection sheet 3 (Figure 20.6) to form a basis for discussion.

In the meeting which followed, the three values in Clegg's work teachers wanted to focus on for discussion purposes were:

1 He believes that love is a better spur to learning than fear.

2 He tries to ensure that every child has an experience of success.
3 He knows it is part of his job to cultivate initiative, sensitivity and confidence as well as to impart facts.

The teachers' views about the nature of control in the classroom, love in the teaching relationship and fear as an inhibitor of learning surfaced in the discussion and resulted in a fruitful sharing of ideas and concerns in an open and honest debate.

As a result of the discussions and self-evaluation experiences of the previous term, the staff identified the following as matters arising for future school-based INSET:

1 What are possible 'educational' activities with which to occupy a class so that the teacher can interact for some length of time with a group of children?
2 How can you keep records for discovery work?
3 Observational work. What is the value of the discussion? If the teacher doesn't heavily direct the discussion, will they observe?
4 How do you organise computer simulations?
5 How should we respond to children's work? What messages are we giving the children when we mark their work?

Mrs Gates observed that these perceived 'needs' bore no relation to the needs identified on the INSET forms filled in during the previous year. Instead, they show a move from concern with practical matters to those arising from values which draw attention to the quality of interaction between teacher and child/children. In the previous year, this aspect of teaching had not been considered, as the staff had been at that time conceptually stuck into the conventional classifications of knowledge, eg science, art and craft, mathematics.

20.2 Headteacher's self-evaluation

Throughout the various attempts to involve her staff in the process of self-evaluation, Mrs Gates was active in monitoring the impact of her own suggestions and actions. A particular focus for her self-evaluation was the conduct of meetings, as it is in this context that the 'authority' of the headteacher often acts to stifle the emergence of staff views and the sharing of experiences which must be essential elements in staff development. A conscious effort was therefore made by Mrs Gates to ask 'open' questions that would encourage participation and to refrain from trying to control discussion. After one meeting Mrs Gates reflected that:

> *I am learning to keep quieter, but still talk too much and am inhibiting cross-group comments. Discussion is very much from an individual to myself. I always comment rather than give the initiative back to someone else.*

After another meeting Mrs Gates observed that:

> I am *learning to keep quieter in discussion. All teachers are joining in the discussion: some are sharing insights gained from reflection. I need to offset the negative feelings of guilt and fear by drawing attention to our successes over the last two years.*

But important also is the fact that Mrs Gates' own professional growth was enhanced as a result of all her efforts. Her previous feelings of uncertainty about how to be both headteacher and educator diminished as she came through self-evaluation to assume more control over the impact of her own activities by learning how to modify her practices in order to obtain the results she desired.

> *In terms of my own personal development I have learnt much about myself and have gained valuable insights into teachers' thinking. My own situation is no longer threatening as I understand it better. I have reminded myself of what I believe education is and have applied it to my present role . . . I have much to learn both about group dynamics and adult education. Self-evaluation is a powerful personal motivator for learning, as well as an educational necessity.*

In addition, self-evaluation can

> *remove the threat of external evaluation because you can 'prove' you are learning and improving your practice. The external evaluator can tell you very little that you do not know already.*

20.3 Comment

What can we learn from this case study about how to involve teachers in self-evaluation?

1 Involving staff in the process from the outset is important because teachers can come to appreciate the purpose by experiencing, to some degree, the benefits.
2 Perception of 'authority' can be modified and teachers can become active partners in the process of staff development, provided the headteacher monitors how his or her own activities can contribute to this.
3 It offers a way of identifying 'needs' which arise directly from teachers' analysis of the nature of the teaching task and the values which are embodied in the process.
4 It can encourage teachers to focus on the way in which the teaching relationship can facilitate learning and can de-emphasise the stress that is often placed on content and subject areas in other types of needs identification. While both are important the latter tend to be much more easily identified than the former.

21 Conclusion: managing change

It was not the number of changes or even the nature of change in the late 1980s that proved problematic for teachers. It was, arguably, the speed of that change. Teachers embroiled in the busy day-to-day running of a classroom found it difficult to keep abreast of all the current developments. Change is a worrisome, threatening phenomenon. The most human and legitimate reaction to it is resistance. However, resistance is not an option that we are at liberty to choose: the Education Reform Act and the National Curriculum are with us.

It is crucial that professionals in education acquaint themselves with the process of change and examine how it might be effected successfully in the primary school. We have already considered the importance of establishing a suitable climate before introducing change (Chapter 4). It is fitting that we conclude the book with a brief examination of how staff development programmes can act as the 'lubricant' which enables change to be introduced with the minimum of conflict. This, then, is the focus for our chapter.

21.1 How change occurs

In the past, the major function of those who sought to initiate educational change (eg the Schools Council) was to research, develop and disseminate. The putting into practice of the innovation was up to the schools themselves. The experience of the now defunct Schools Council in all its projects showed that implementation was in fact the most problematical element of all in the change process. As Fullan (1979) has pointed out, the main focus tended to be on curriculum materials, and not enough attention was paid to factors such as the social system of the individual school concerned. The relationships between teachers, the effectiveness of leadership in the school, available resources and external support were things that were rarely considered or accommodated. This led to what Fullan (1979) called 'tissue rejection'. The innovation would be dropped or be adapted out of all recognition to its original purpose. We would be wise to learn from these mistakes

> We must guard against 'tissue rejection'.

in implementing the National Curriculum and to examine the conditions that need to be met to ensure the successful take-up of an innovation. The main difference between the initiatives of the Schools Council and the National Curriculum, of course, is in the strength of the political pressure underpinning the change. For this reason the nature of these innovations cannot be directly paralleled.

It appears that there is no single recognisable strategy or panacea that can be applied in order for change to occur successfully. It is possible, however, to identify a number of factors which must be considered in establishing a favourable climate for the adoption of change. These have been identified in Chapter 4 (section 4.3). Of these, the quality of leadership and ability of the head to build a 'team' of staff are perhaps the most important in establishing effective change.

21.2 Leadership and change

If the headteacher does not understand the dynamics of the change process, then individual teachers within the school can often feel a sense of confusion or a lack of direction. Within their own classrooms, good teachers are continually engaged in curriculum change and development through a process of practice, reflection and renewal. Moreover, Bolam (1982) argues that teachers are the 'most effective vehicle and focus for improving the educational process'. However, while they should (and do) share the burden of curriculum change, there is a limit to their influence in terms of whole-school strategies: that really has to be the province of the headteacher.

It is not enough that heads provide a general endorsement to change: specific support is needed that is active, direct and interactive.

There is no doubt that the head's role is crucial in either facilitating or blocking change; and this role is becoming increasingly powerful as more and more responsibilities are being devolved to heads. There are obvious implications here for the prudent selection of headteachers with the appropriate leadership qualities. An excellent classroom practitioner does not necessarily have the skills required for successful headship. Different qualities are required.

According to Whitaker (1983), heads would need to score highly on two dimensions that are central to leadership. They are:

- concern for task and
- concern for people.

Reid *et al.* (1987) break down these categories further and identify the tasks of management in the following way:

- to lead by example, so that the head shares with staff the tensions and stresses of being involved in change;
- to set the climate for change;
- to promote amongst staff a view of themselves as learners; amenable to problem-solving; creative thinkers;
- to work continually at achieving a fusion of personal (individual teacher) and institutional (whole school) initiatives;
- to be supportive at all stages of the change and implementation process;
- to maintain this support by providing the framework for development (setting deadlines; employing a systematic, structured approach);
- to establish internal co-ordination for the development work. The head, as overseer, will be more aware of possible links than those who may be too near the 'chalk face' to see the whole picture.
- to challenge embedded ideas without invoking unbridled conflict.

This last point throws up an old argument of Stenhouse (1975): that a major task of management is to manage conflict within the school. Instead of pretending it doesn't exist, Stenhouse holds, heads should recognise squarely what is happening and accommodate it. It is important that staff are encouraged to question their assumptions, to listen to others, and to be prepared to modify their attitudes. Leadership that allows for this is strong and confident.

21.3 Organising effective INSET

The link between staff development activities in the school and the change process is vital to reduce or eliminate natural staff anxieties emanating from proposed new innovations. Therefore, careful consideration needs to be given at all times to the way staff development activities are planned and carried out.

Joyce and Showers (1980) have undertaken considerable research in the field of in-service education, and maintain that, in order to be effective, it should include as many of the elements as possible which are shown in Figure 21.1. The relative importance of the elements of theory and classroom application have already been discussed (Chapter 16). It is for heads, staff development co-ordinators, 'providers' and staff to determine the most effective combination.

Figure 21.1 Elements and processes in in-service education (derived from Joyce and Showers, 1980)

ELEMENT		*PROCESS*
Theory	Not powerful on its own, but important in conjunction with other factors.	Raising awareness
Demonstration	Rowntree (1974) reasons that teachers, like all learners, need to be shown rather than merely told what to do. Joyce and Showers (1984) refer to this as 'transfer of training'. It helps teachers to make what Rudduck (1981) refers to as the 'imaginative leap' that is required to translate what is learned on an INSET course into classroom practice.	Knowledge
Practice	This means practice under simulated conditions. Joyce and Showers suggest that this is a most effective way for teachers to become both competent and confident in a variety of classroom techniques.	
Feedback	The crucial importance of regular and consistent feedback is emphasised throughout the literature on INSET (eg Rudduck, 1981; Joyce and Showers, 1984). It ensures that any problems encountered during implementation can be identified and discussed, so that teachers are helped to maintain any changes that occur.	Practice
Classroom application	Teachers require support and encouragement when they transfer their skills to the classroom.	

In the literature, people who initiate change inside schools or other educational insitutions are often known as 'change agents'. Who are these people? What is their basic function? Change agents can be the teachers themselves, as well as headteachers, administrative and support agents. Indeed, Bolam (1982) puts great emphasis on the part that teachers play in improving the educational process, and Fullan (1982) warns schools against relying too heavily on external resource support, for fear that the effort will not be continued after the support has been withdrawn. You will recall that Chapter 17 examined more specifically the ways in which consultants may be employed and described the procedures that should be adopted for successful consultancy.

External consultants, if wisely used, can help considerably in the change process. They can bring theory, analysis, research and practical support to the process. What is more, they can provide the school with additional resources, and help staff to identify any organisational strains.

21.4 Change and professional development

In planning a programme of staff development to support teachers in meeting demand for educational change, heads or staff development co-ordinators might follow Fullan's (1987) guidelines. He suggests that there are three broad stages: a) initiation; b) implementation; c) institutionalisation, which have the following characteristics:

a) *Initiation phase*

1 The change should be linked to an agenda of political or high-profile development.
2 A clear model should exist for the change.
3 A strong advocate is needed.
4 Commitment needs to be established through early, active initiation.

b) *Implementation phase*

1 Players need to be 'orchestrated'. Those involved should approach the change as a team, rather than as individuals.
2 There needs to be a good mix of pressure and support.
3 Early 'rewards' should be evident.
4 Ongoing INSET is necessary if commitment is to be maintained.

c) *Institutionalisation phase*

1 The innovation should become embedded in everyday practice.
2 If it is a management initiative it should be clearly linked to classroom outcomes.

3 It should not conflict with other priorities.
4 It should not be dropped as a topic for staff development once decisions to implement have been taken.

The National Curriculum is a prime example of an innovation. Its most significant feature, of course, is that all schools in the state system are obliged to implement it: they have no choice in the matter. However, whilst the National Curriculum is a constant element in the system, schools, teachers and children are not. Moreover, the quality of leadership and INSET in each school will vary, so that the way in which the National Curriculum is disseminated and implemented will also vary. Although we have referred to it as an innovation, in truth it is not entirely novel. In fact, much of it is familiar to teachers because it corresponds, more or less, with the teaching and learning activities that were already in operation in a large number of classes prior to its adoption (albeit inconsistently).

In introducing the National Curriculum to their staff, headteachers would be wise to begin with what is familiar. That is one of the fundamental principles of how people learn. If this is not properly managed, it will give rise to anxiety and insecurity amongst staff, which in turn can lead to resentment and mildly paranoid feelings of persecution. Headteachers and curriculum leaders will need to induce in teachers a feeling of commitment to, and 'ownership' of, the National Curriculum.

We must start from where the learner is.

Traditionally, in England and Wales, governments and local education authorities have not intervened in curriculum matters, at least since the end of the Second World War. Therefore we simply do not have the experience, in this context, to make valid estimates of the efficacy of strong central initiatives. Experiences elsewhere suggest that political will can go some way towards imposing change. It would be churlish to suggest that all recent government initiatives have been totally without benefit. Primary schools are beginning to examine their curricular provision, resources and teaching strategies – perhaps in a way and on a scale that they would not otherwise have done.

Where, then, does that leave the sensitive approaches which have been advocated throughout this book? What place has staff development if teachers see the future of education as simply laying out legally enforceable programmes of study? It is well to remember, and to keep reminding ourselves, that the National Curriculum is not the whole curriculum. Other areas of experience are important to children's development – for example, personal and social education.

> The National Curriculum is not the whole curriculum.

It could be argued, moreover, that the reality of the National Curriculum lies in the learning activities which children experience in the primary classroom. The organisation of these experiences will remain a matter for the professional judgement of teachers. Like any other published scheme, document or policy, the National Curriculum will be as alive, creative and imaginative as the primary teachers who implement it. It is in this gap between the hardware and the thousand sensitive, magical moments of classroom learning that staff development finds its home.

Staff development programmes will enable changes to be carried through to the benefit of teachers and pupils, but *professional* development programmes must exist alongside school-based *staff* development programmes. It is essential that the dimension is one of continuing *education* to reflect on the changes that are taking place and not ongoing *training* designed to provide short-term classroom answers to externally imposed change. Achieving this balance with limited time and resource availability is perhaps the greatest challenge for the staff development co-ordinator in the primary school.

Resources

Resource materials for the staff development co-ordinator

Further information on in-service education, training and staff development may be found in the following publications. Many relate to secondary or further education phases, some refer to industrial practice. All give some indication of the ways in which *people* can make a school or organisation more effective. Asterisks denote particular relevance for primary school co-ordinators.

Bennett, R. (1981), *Managing Personnel and Performance*, London: Business Books Ltd.

*Bolam, R. (ed.) (1982), *School-Focussed In-Service Training*, London: Heinemann Educational Books.

**British Journal of In-Service Education*. Various editions. This is an excellent journal with a great deal of practical advice for in-service co-ordinators.

Burke, P. J. (1987), *Teacher Development: Induction, Renewal and Redirection*, Lewes: The Falmer Press.

Carrol, S. and Nuttall, S. (1989) *The Staff Development Manual* volumes 3 and 4, Lancaster: Framework Press.

Easterby-Smith, M. (1986), *Evaluation of Management Education, Training and Development*, Aldershot: Gower.

Further Education Unit (1987), *Planning Staff Development: A Guide for Managers*, London: Further Education Unit.

Further Education Unit/Pickup (1987), *Staff Development Programme*, Project Report, York: Longman (for the Further Education Unit).

Hall, V. and Oldroyd, D. (undated), *Managing INSET in Local Educa-*

tion Authorities – applying conclusions from TRIST, Bristol: NDCSMT.

HMI (1989), *The Implementation of the Local Education Authority Training Grant Scheme (LEATGS): Report on first year of the scheme 1987–1988*, London: DES.

Holly, P., James, T. and Young, J. (1987), *Delta Project: the Experience of TRIST*, London: Manpower Services Commission TVEI Unit.

*Holly, P. and Southworth, G. (1989) *The Developing School*, Lewes: The Falmer Press.

Hopkins, D. (ed.) (1986), *Inservice Training and Educational Development: An International Survey*, London: Croom Helm.

Hunt, J. W. (1979), *Managing People at Work*, Maidenhead: McGraw-Hill.

Jones, K., O'Sullivan, F. and Reid, K. (1987), 'The Challenge of the "new INSET"', *Educational Review*, Vol. 39, No. 3.

National Curriculum Council (1989), *The National Curriculum: Developing INSET Activities*, York: National Curriculum Council.

Oldroyd, D. and Hall, V. (undated), *Managing Professional Development and INSET: a Handbook for Schools and Colleges*, Bristol: NDCSMT. This is an excellent publication full of practical suggestions for managing staff development. At the time of writing it is out of print, but copies were sent to every secondary school and local education authority in England and Wales in 1988. (Contact your LEA INSET co-ordinator for information.)

O'Sullivan, F., Jones, K. and Reid, K. (1988), *Staff Development in Secondary Schools*, London: Hodder and Stoughton.

Rae, L. (1983), *The Skills of Training*, Aldershot: Gower.

Reid, K., Hopkins, D. and Holly, P. (1987) *Towards the Effective School*, Oxford: Basil Blackwell.

*Rodger, I. A. and Richardson, J. A. S. (1985), *Self-Evaluation for Primary Schools*, London: Hodder and Stoughton.

*School Management Training Publications and materials produced by the National Development Centre for School Management Training, 35 Berkely Square, Bristol, BS8 1JA.

Winders, P. and Greig, H. (1987), *Making Best Use of INSET in Lancashire*, Lancashire County Council: Education Resources Unit.

Bibliography

Ashton, P. M. E., Henderson, E. S., Merritt, J. E. and Mortimer, D. J. (1983), *Teacher Education in the Classroom: Initial and In-Service*, Beckenham: Croom Helm.

Aston University (1981), *The Social Effects of Rural Primary School Organisation in England*, Birmingham: University of Aston.

Avon, County of (1980), Unpublished report of the Working Party on In-School Education, Conferences of Primary Head Teachers 1979 and 1980.

Bell, A. (1988), 'The Federation: A support system for rural primary schools', *Cambridge Journal of Education*, 18, 2, pp. 179–189.

Bell, A. and Sigsworth, K. (1987), *The Small Rural Primary School: A Matter of Quality*, Lewes: Falmer Press.

Bell, G. H. (1985), 'INSET: Five Types of Collaboration and Consultancy', *School Organisation*, 5, 3, 247–56.

Bell, J. (1987), *Doing your Research Project*, Milton Keynes: Open University Press.

Blake, W. (1790), *The Marriage of Heaven and Hell: Proverbs of Hell.*

Bolam, R. (ed.), (1982), *School-Focused In-Service Training*, London: Educational Books Ltd.

Clegg, A. (1980), *About Our Schools*, Oxford: Basil Blackwell.

Cooper, R. (1986), *Managing INSET: Learning from TRIST*, Unpublished paper delivered to the Welsh Collaborative Project Conference on 'Core Teams for School/College focused INSET', Llandrindod Wells, Powys.

Cunningham, C. and Davies, H. (1985), *Working with Parents*, Milton Keynes: Open University Press.

Day, C., Whitaker, P. and Wren, D. (1987), *Appraisal and Professional Development in the Primary School*, Milton Keynes: Open University Press.

Department of Education and Science (1967), *Primary Education in Wales: A Report of the Central Advisory Council for Education (Wales)* (Gittins Report), London: HMSO.

Department of Education and Science (1967), *Children and their Primary Schools* (Plowden Report), London: HMSO.

Department of Education and Science (1972), *Teacher Education and Training* (James Report), London: HMSO.

Department of Education and Science (1978), *Primary Education in England: A Survey by HM Inspectors of Schools*, London: HMSO.

Department of Education and Science (1978), *Special Educational Needs* (Warnock Report), Cmnd 7212, London: HMSO.

Department of Education and Science (1983) Circular 1/83 *Assessments and Statements of Special Educational Needs*, London: HMSO.

Department of Education and Science (1984), Statistics of Education, Schools: January 1984, Darlington: Department of Education and Science.

Department of Education and Science (1985), *Better Schools*, Cmnd 9469, London: HMSO.

Department of Education and Science (1986), *Local Education Authority Training Grants Scheme*, Circular 6/86, London: HMSO.

Doran, H. *et al.* (1981), 'Scotland: School-based consultancy in an Orkney Primary School', in Donoughue, C. *Inservice: the Teacher and the School*, London: Kogan Page Ltd.

Easen, P. (1985), *Making School-centred INSET Work*, Beckenham: Open University/Croom Helm.

Education Act (1981), London: HMSO.

Education Reform Act (1988), Chapter 40, London: HMSO.

Edwards, R. and Bennett, D. (1985), *Schools in Action*, Welsh Office Research Project, Cardiff: Welsh Office.

Eisner, E. W. (1985), *The Art of Educational Evaluation*, Lewes: The Falmer Press.

Eraut, M. (1978), 'Some perspectives on consultancy in in-service education', *British Journal of Inservice Education*, 4, 1/2, 95–9.

Eraut, M., Pennycuick, D. and Radnor, H. (1988), *Local Evaluation of INSET: a meta-evaluation of TRIST evaluations*, TRIST/Manpower Services Commission, University of Sussex.

Essex County Council (1980), *Cooperation between Small Primary Schools*, Chelmsford: Essex County Council.

Frazer, B. J. and Fisher, D. L. (1984), *Assessment of Classroom Psychosocial Environment: Workshop Manual*, Bentley: Western Australia Institute of Technology.

Freeman, A. (1988), 'Effective Learning: Implications for INSET', *Educational Child Psychology*, 5, 4.

Fullan, M. (1979), 'School-based In-service: How to Create an Hospitable Environment for New Ideas', in Wideen, M., Hopkins, D. and Pye, I. (eds), *In-Service: A Means of Progress in Tough Times*, Simon Fraser University. Proceedings of a Conference held May 1979.

Fullan, M. (1982), *The Meaning of Educational Change*, Toronto: O.I.S.E. Press.

Fullan, M. (1987), 'The Management of Educational Change' in *Curriculum at the Crossroads*, London: Schools Curriculum Development Committee.

Further Education Unit (1987), *Planning Staff Development: A Guide for Managers*, London: Further Education Unit.

Gane, V. (1986), *Appraisal for Staff Development: Implications for Teacher Education*, Bristol: National Development Centre for School Management Training.

Graham, D. (1988), Initial Advice on Training for the National Curriculum and its Assessment, Unpublished response to Secretary of State for Education, London: National Curriculum Council.

Gray, H. L. (1987), *Organization Development (OD) and the Primary School.*

Hadow Report (1931), *Report of the Consultative Committee on the Primary School*, London: HMSO.

Hewton, E. (1988), *School-focused Staff Development Guidelines for Policy Makers*, Lewes: The Falmer Press.

HMI (1988), *The New Teacher in School*, London: HMSO.

Holly, P. J. (1985), 'The Developing School', CIE/TRIST Working Paper, Cambridge: Cambridge Institute of Education.

Holly, P. J., James, T. and Young, J. (1987), *Delta Project: the Experience of TRIST*, London: Manpower Services Commission/TVEI Unit.

Hopkins, D. (1985), *A Teacher's Guide to Classroom Research*, Milton Keynes: Open University Press.

Hopkins, D. and Vickers, C. (1986), 'Process consultation in school self evaluation', *Cambridge Journal of Education*, 16, 2, 116–25.

Hoyle, E. (1971), 'The role of the change agent in educational innovation', in Walton, J. (ed.), *Curriculum Organization and Design*, London: Ward Lock Educational, pp. 68–75.

ILEA (1982), *Keeping the School Under Review – The Primary School*, London: ILEA.

ILEA (1988), *Secondary Transfer Project*, Bulletin 17: Improving Secondary Transfer, London: ILEA (Research and Statistics Branch).

Inglis, F. (1985), *The Management of Ignorance: A Political Theory of the Curriculum*, Oxford: Basil Blackwell.

Isaacs, J. (1987), *Management Development for Senior Staff in Primary Schools*, Bristol: National Development Centre for School Management Training.

Janis, I. L. (1982) *Groupthink*, Boston: Houghton-Mifflin.

Jones, A. (1986), 'The Role of the Management Trainer', in Mumford, A. *Handbook of Management Development*, Gower Press, 374–89.

Medley, D. H. (1979), 'The Effectiveness of Teachers', in Peterson, P. and Walberg, H. (eds), *Research on Training: Concepts, Findings and Implications*, Berkeley: McCutcheon Publishing.

Jones, K. O'Sullivan, F. and Reid, K. (1987), 'The Challenge of the "new INSET"', *Educational Review*, 39, 3, 191–202.

Joyce, B. and Showers, B. (1980), 'Improving In-service Training: the Messages of Research', *Educational Leadership*, February 1980, pp. 379–85.

Joyce, B. and Showers, B. (1984), 'Transfer of Training: the Contribution of Coaching', in Hopkins, D. and Wideen, M. (eds), *Alternative Perspectives on School Improvement*, Lewes: The Falmer Press, pp. 77–85.

Jung, C. C. (1977), *Organizational Development in Education*, Oregon: North-West Regional Educational Laboratory.

Kyriacou, C. (1986), *Effective Teaching in Schools*, London: Basil Blackwell.

Lewis, H. D. (1985), 'Consultancy, the Tutor and INSET', *British Journal of Inservice Education*, 12, 1, 48–52.

Liedtke, W. (1980), 'Games for the Primary Grades', *Arithmetic Teacher*, December 1980.

MacDonald-Ross, M. (1973), 'Behavioural Objectives: a critical review', in Golby, M., Greenwald, J. and West, R. (1975), *Curriculum Design*, London: Croom Helm.

Morant, R. W. (1981), *In-Service Education within the School*, London: George Allen and Unwin.

Moyles, J. (1988) *Self-Evaluation: A Primary Teacher's Guide*, Windsor: NFER/Nelson.

Murgatroyd, S. and Reynolds, D. (1984), 'The Creative Consultant: The Potential Use of Consultancy as a Method of Teacher Education', *School Organization*, 4, 4, 321–35.

National Curriculum Council (1988a), *Consultation Report: Mathematics*, York: National Curriculum Council.

National Curriculum Council (1988b), *Curriculum Continuity*, Information Pack 1, York: National Curriculum Council.

National Curriculum Council (1989), Circular Number 5 *Implementing the National Curriculum – Participation by Pupils with Special Educational Needs*, York: National Curriculum Council.

National Curriculum Working Group Report (1989) *English for Ages 5–11*, London: DES/Welsh Office.

National Development Centre for School Management Training (1987), *INSET Needs Analysis Pack*, Bristol: National Development Centre for School Management Training.

National Steering Group (1988), 'Consortium of School Teacher Appraisal Pilot Schemes Progress on Appraisal: an interim report', Bristol: National Development Centre for School Management Training.

National Union of Teachers (1985), 'The Small Primary School', *Primary Education Review*, 24.

Ohlson, P. (1983), 'A Cooperative Teaching Venture in Cornwall' in Schools Council Committee for Wales (*op. cit.*).

Oldroyd, D. (1985), 'The Management of School-Based Staff Development at Priory School', *British Journal of In-Service Education*, 11, 2.

O'Sullivan, F., Jones, K. and Reid, K. (1988), *Staff Development in Secondary Schools*, Sevenoaks: Hodder and Stoughton.

Pollard, A. and Tann, S. (1987). *Reflective Teaching in the Primary School*, London: Cassell Educational.

Reid, K., Bullock, R. and Howarth, S. (1988), *An Introduction to Primary School Organisation*, London: Hodder and Stoughton.

Reid, K., Hopkins, D. and Holly, P. (eds) (1987) *Towards the Effective School*, Oxford: Basil Blackwell.

Roberts, J. L. (1988), An in-depth investigation into some of the problems associated with management and organisation of schooling in small primary schools. Unpublished M.Ed. dissertation, Swansea: West Glamorgan Institute of Higher Education.

Rowntree, D. (1974), *Educational Technology in Curriculum Development*, London: Harper and Row Ltd.

Rudduck, J. (1981), *Making the Most of the Short In-Service Course*, Schools Council Working Paper 71, London: Methuen Educational.

Schmuck, R. A. (1973), *Consultation in Organisation Development*, Report of a research programme at the University of Oregon, USA, Paper prepared for E321, The Open University, Milton Keynes: Open University.

Schmuck, R., Murray, D., Smith, M., Schwartz, M. and Runkel, M. (1975), Consultation for Innovative Schools: D.D. for Multi unit Structures. Eugene Ore: Centre for Policy and Management.

Schools Council Committee for Wales (1983), *Small Schools in Concert*, Cardiff: Schools Council Committee for Wales.

Sefton-Davies, R. W. (1982), 'Providing INSET Consultancies for Schools', in Bolam, R., *School-Focussed In-Service Training*, Heinemann Organization in Schools Series, London: Heinemann Educational Books, pp. 189–98.

Skilbeck, M. (1973), 'Strategies of Curriculum Change', in Walton, J. (ed.), *Curriculum Organisation and Design*, London: Ward Lock Educational Limited, pp. 27–37.

Southworth, G. W. (1984), 'Development of staff in Primary Schools', *British Journal of In-Service Education*, 10, 3, 6–15.

Spencer, R. (1988b), 'Continuity, Liaison and Progression: The Northamptonshire approach' in National Curriculum Council (*op. cit.*).

Stenhouse, L. (1975), *An Introduction to Curriculum Research and Development*, London: Heinemann Educational Books.

Stuart, R. (1988), 'Increasing Adult Learning', *Journal of European Industrial Training*, 12, 2.

Suffolk Education Department (1985), *Those Having Torches...*, Ipswich: Suffolk Local Education Authority.

TGAT (1988), *Report of the National Curriculum Task Group on Assessment and Testing*, London: DES/Welsh Office.

Times Educational Supplement (1986), 'Following the Suffolk Signposts', 5 December 1986.

Times Educational Supplement (1988), *Survey Highlights Primary Staff Gaps*, London: The Times Newspapers.

Walker, R. (1985), *Doing Research: A Handbook for Teachers*, London: Methuen & Co Ltd.

Wallace, M. and Butterworth, B. (1987), *Management Development in Small Primary Schools*, Bristol: National Development Centre; Cheltenham: College of St Paul and St Mary.

Weindling, D., Reid, M. and Davis, P. (1983), *Teachers' Centres: A Focus for In-Service Education?*, London: Schools Council Working Paper 74.

Welsh Office (1984), *Curriculum and Organisation of Primary Schools in Wales*, Cardiff: HMSO.

Welsh Office (1985), *Leadership in Primary Schools*, HMI (Wales) Occasional Paper, June 1985, Cardiff: Welsh Office.

Welsh Office (1987), *Helping Groups of Primary Schools*, Report of a Welsh Office Research Project: Groups of small rural primary schools in Powys 1985–1986, Cardiff: Welsh Office.

West Glamorgan County Council (1985), *Resourcing the Small School*, A Report by the Primary Curriculum Working Group Sub-group 5, Swansea: West Glamorgan County Council.

West Midlands Advisory Council for Further Education and Training (1988), *Staff Development Policy in Further Education*, London: Department of Employment, The Training Agency.

Whitaker, P. (1983), *The Primary Head*, London: Heinemann.

Whyte, L. (1987), 'Preparing for innovation in a small school', *Primary Teaching Studies*, 2, (2), pp. 170–8.

Wragg, E. C. (1987), *Teacher Appraisal: A Practical Guide*, Basingstoke: Macmillan Education.

Index